GUIDE TO PREMIER HOTELS IN GREAT BRITAIN
56TH EDITION
1995

TREGLOS HOTEL, CONSTANTINE BAY, CORNWALL.

SIGNPOST LIMITED
FOUNTAIN COURT, STEELHOUSE LANE, BIRMINGHAM B4 6DT
TELEPHONE 021-236 5979, FAX 021-200 1159

Compiled by: Edwina Rhead
Gail Carney-Smith

NATIONAL PHONE DAY
16th APRIL 1995

All area telephone codes will change. We have amended each code accordingly. However, readers may encounter difficulty with some numbers that have changed considerably. If so, please contact directory enquiries.

ISBN 0 901249 25 4
© 1995 Signpost Limited

Printed by Ebenezer Baylis & Son Ltd (Printers & Binders)
London Road, Worcester WR5 2JH

Trade Distribution by W Foulsham & Co Ltd
The Publishing House
Bennetts Close
Cippenham
Berkshire SL1 5AP
Telephone 01753 526769
Fax 01753 535003

Signpost is published in the USA
under the title *Premier Hotels of Great Britain*.

CONTENTS

ENGLAND

Regional Areas	Counties	Pages
The West Country (yellow)	Cornwall	1– 13
	Devon	14– 36
	Dorset	37– 45
	Somerset	46– 49
	Wiltshire	50– 52
London and the South (peach)	London	62
	Berkshire	63
	Hampshire	64– 68
	Hertfordshire	69– 71
	Kent	72
	Oxfordshire	73– 74
	Surrey	75
	East Sussex	76– 78
	West Sussex	79
East Anglia and the East Midlands (bright green)	Derbyshire	86– 88
	Lincolnshire	89
	Norfolk	90– 91
	Nottinghamshire	92– 93
	Suffolk	94– 95
The Heart of England (purple)	Gloucestershire	101–107
	Hereford & Worcester	108
	Shropshire	109–112
	Warwickshire	113–116
The North West (mid green)	Cheshire	123–124
	Cumbria	125–154
	Lancashire	155–157
	Greater Manchester	158
Yorkshire and the North East (orange)	County Durham	167–168
	Humberside	169
	Northumberland	170
	Yorkshire	171–187

WALES

	Counties	Pages
(pink)	Clwyd	193
	Gwynedd	194–197
	Dyfed	198
	Powys	199–200

SCOTLAND

	Counties	Pages
Southern Scotland (dark blue)	Borders	204–205
	Dumfries & Galloway	206–211
Central Scotland (light blue)	Central	215–219
	Strathclyde	220–224
	Tayside	225–227
The Highlands & Scottish Islands (eggshell)	Grampian	232–234
	Highland	235–246

CHANNEL ISLANDS

	Counties	Pages
(dark green)	Guernsey	250
	Jersey	252–253

Counties and Regions

England

The West Country
pages 1–56

London and the South
pages 57–81

East Anglia and the East Midlands
pages 82–96

The Heart of England
pages 97–118

The North West
pages 119–161

Yorkshire and the North East
pages 162–189

Wales

Wales
pages 190–201

Scotland

Southern Scotland
pages 202–212

Central Scotland
pages 213–229

The Highlands and Islands
pages 230–248

Channel Islands

Channel Islands
pages 249–254

WESTERN ISLES

HIGHLAND

GRAMPIAN

SCOTLAND

TAYSIDE

CENTRAL   FIFE

STRATHCLYDE   LOTHIAN

BORDERS

DUMFRIES
AND GALLOWAY

NORTHUMBERLAND

TYNE & WEAR

CUMBRIA   DURHAM   CLEVELAND

ISLE
OF MAN

NORTH YORKSHIRE

LANCASHIRE   WEST
YORKSHIRE   HUMBERSIDE

GREATER
MANCHESTER   SOUTH
YORKSHIRE

MERSEYSIDE

CHESHIRE   DERBYSHIRE

CLWYD   NOTTS.   LINCOLNSHIRE

GWYNEDD   ENGLAND

STAFFS.

SHROPSHIRE   LEICESTERSHIRE   NORFOLK

POWYS   WEST
MIDLANDS

WALES   WARKS.   NORTHANTS   CAMBRIDGESHIRE   SUFFOLK

HEREFORD
AND
WORCESTER   BEDS.

DYFED   ESSEX

BUCKS.

GLOUCESTERSHIRE   HERTS.

WEST
GLAM.   MID
GLAM.   GWENT   OXFORDSHIRE

SOUTH
GLAM.   AVON   GREATER
LONDON

BERKSHIRE   KENT

WILTSHIRE   SURREY

CHANNEL
ISLANDS   HAMPSHIRE   WEST
SUSSEX   EAST
SUSSEX

SOMERSET

ISLE
OF
WIGHT

DEVON   DORSET

CORNWALL

Scale 1:4 800 000

© GEOprojects (UK) Ltd
© Crown Copyright

FOREWORD

Welcome to the 56th edition of *Signpost*.

This year we have re-designed part of the layout of *Signpost*. Each regional area has been colour coded for quick reference, so that "at a glance" you can immediately recognise which region you are looking for. **You must refer to the Regional Map on page v to see which colours are used for each area.** Also within these sections now, are the bargain breaks for the relevant hotels to that area. This we feel is more practical, as it is easier and quicker for you to see any special rates available. As well as featuring a 'Diary of Events' at the beginning of each region, we have added a 'Selection of Local Attractions'. However, we do recommend that if you require any further information on these sections, to contact the individual tourist boards, whose addresses you will find within these pages.

Signpost *Chairman, Christopher Carney-Smith (left) photographed outside Grants Hotel, Harrogate, Yorkshire, with Proprietors Peter and Pam Grant.*

Right: Simon and Alexandra Winton, Owners of Dalmunzie House Hotel, Spittal O'Glenshee, Tayside pictured with Signpost *Inspector Gillian Sheldon (centre).*

Below: Signpost *Inspector David McMurtie (right) pictured at The Manor House, Oban, Strathclyde, with the Managers Patrick and Margaret Freytag, also managers of Killiechronan House, Isle of Mull.*

Left: Signpost *Inspector Sue Long and John Butterworth, Managing Director of F.J.B. Hotels, photographed outside The Haven Hotel, Sandbanks, Dorset.*

Below: Duncan Williams, General Manager of the Manor House Hotel, Moreton-in-Marsh, Glos., with Signpost *Director Gill Carney-Smith.*

Signpost *Inspector John Stenning (right), pictured in the grounds of Whatley Manor, Nr. Malmesbury, Wiltshire with Proprietor, Peter Kendall.*

By the pool at Tides Reach Hotel, Salcombe, Devon is John Edwards, General Manager and Signpost *Inspector Olof White (left).*

Left: Annie Randolph-Dyer (right), Signpost *Inspector, at On the Park Hotel and Restaurant, Cheltenham, Glos., with the Owners Darryl and Lesley-Anne Gregory.*

Below: Peter and Bridget Kindred, Proprietors of the Tyddyn Llan Country House Hotel and Restaurant, Llandrillo, Clwyd, in their garden with Signpost Inspector, Tricia Doyle, (right).

How to use Signpost

1. All hotels are listed in two separate indices:

    (a) On pages 284–290 in county order within their regional areas (as indicated on the map on page v).

    (b) On pages 291–295 under the names of the nearest town or village.

2. The book is divided into sections containing hotels in England, Wales, Scotland and the Islands. Each country is divided into regional areas and the nearest town or village to each hotel appears alphabetically. For example, in The West Country, Treglos Hotel, Constantine Bay, CORNWALL, is on page 1 and Blunsdon House, near Swindon, WILTSHIRE is on page 52, the last page of that regional section.

3. The type of licence each hotel has is indicated by:
F	—Full
R	—Restaurant
R and R	—Restaurant and Residential

THE WEST COUNTRY
SELECTED LOCAL ATTRACTIONS

■ Historic Houses, Gardens & Parks

AVON
Clevedon Court, Clevedon
Sally Lunn's House, Bath

CORNWALL
Cotehele House, St. Dominick, Saltash
Glendurgan Garden, Mawnan Smith, Falmouth
Kit Hill Country Park, Callington
Lanhydrock House, Bodmin
Mount Edgcumbe House & Park, Torpoint
Trebah Garden, Mawnan Smith, Falmouth
Trelissick Garden, Truro
Trengwainton Garden, Penzance
Trerice, Newquay

DEVON
Arlington Court, Barnstaple
Bicton Park & Gardens, East Budleigh
Overbecks Museum & Garden, Salcombe
Rosemoor Garden – Royal Horticultural
  Society's Garden, Great Torrington
Saltram House, Plympton
Ugbrooke House & Park, Newton Abbot

DORSET
Athelhampton House & Gardens, Puddletown,
  Dorchester
Forde Abbey & Gardens, Chard
Hardy's Cottage Garden, Higher Bockampton,
  Dorchester
Kingston Lacey House, Nr. Wimborne

SOMERSET
Barrington Court Gardens, Barrington,
  Ilminster
Clapton Court Gardens
Fyne Court, Broomfield, Bridgwater
Hestercombe Gardens, Fitzpaine, Taunton
Lytes Cary Manor, Charlton Mackrell,
  Somerton
Montacute House
Tintinhull House Garden, Nr. Yeovil

WILTSHIRE
Avebury Manor
Corsham Court
Dyrham Park, Dryham, Chippenham
Great Chalfield Manor, Melksham
Hazelbury Manor Gardens, Box, Corsham
Iford Manor Gardens, Bradford-on-Avon
Lackham Gardens & Agricultural Museum,
  Lacock, Chippenham
Lacock Abbey
Mompesson House, Salisbury
Stourhead House & Gardens, Stourton,
  Nr. Mere
Westwood Manor

■ Walks & Nature Trails

AVON
The Cotswold Way, first part from Bath to
  Chipping Campden
West Mendip Way, starts at Uphill following the
  crest of the Mendip Hills

CORNWALL
The Camel Trail, runs along the River Camel
  from Padstow to Poley's Bridge
The North Cornwall Heritage Coast

DEVON
Dartmoor National Park Guided Walks
The Tarka Trail

DORSET
Brit Valley Walk
The Dorset Coast Path
Hardy's Dorset Walk

SOMERSET
Exmoor National Park Country Walks
West Somerset Mineral Railway, from Watchet
  to Washford

WILTSHIRE
Discover the Villages Trail
The Imber Range Perimeter Path

■ Historical Sites & Museums

AVON
Bristol City Museum & Art Gallery
Harveys Wine Museum, Bristol
Museum of Costumes, Bath
Pump Room, Bath
Roman Baths Museum, Bath

CORNWALL
Launceston Castle
Restormel Castle, Lothwithiel
St. Catherine's Castle, Fowey
St. Mawes Castle
St. Michael's Mount, Marazion
Tintagel Castle

DEVON
Buckfast Abbey, Buckfastleigh
Buckland Abbey, Yelverton
Castle Drogo, Drewsteignton, Exeter
Compton Castle, Marldon, Paignton
Dartmouth Castle
Okehampton Castle
Powderham Castle, Kenton, Nr. Exeter
Royal Albert Memorial Museum, Exeter
Watermouth Castle, Berrynarbor, Ilfracombe

DORSET
Corfe Castle
Dorset County Museum, Dorchester
Maiden Castle, Dorchester
Portland Castle
Sherborne Castle

SOMERSET
Cleeve Abbey, Washford, Watchet
Dunster Castle
Glastonbury Abbey
Nunney Castle
Taunton Cider Mill
Wells Cathedral

WILTSHIRE

Avebury Stone Circles, Nr. Marlborough
Great Western Railway Museum, Swindon
Longleat House, Warminster
Museum & Art Gallery, Swindon
Old Wardour Castle, Tisbury, Salisbury
Salisbury Cathedral
Stonehenge, Amesbury, Salisbury

Entertainment Venues

AVON

Bristol Zoological Gardens

CORNWALL

Cornish Seal Sanctuary, Gweek, Helston
Flambards Victoria Village Theme Park, Helston
Land's End, Penzance
Newquay Zoo
Paradise Park, Hayle
World in Miniature, Truro

DEVON

City Museum & Art Gallery, Plymouth
Combe Martin Wildlife & Dinosaur Park

DEVON (continued)

Dartmoor Wild Life Park & West Country
  Falconry Centre, Sparkwell, Plymouth
Kents Cavern Showcaves, Torquay
Paignton & Dartmouth Steam Railway, Paignton
Paignton Zoological & Botanical Gardens
Plymouth Dome
Plymouth Gin Distillery
Riviera Centre, Torquay
Torquay Museum

DORSET

Brownsea Island, Poole
Lyme Regis Marine Aquarium
Weymouth Sea Life Park, Lodmoor Country Park,
  Weymouth

SOMERSET

Cheddar Showcaves, Cheddar Gorge
Haynes Motor Museum, Sparkford, Yeovil
The Tropical Bird Gardens, Rode
West Somerset Railway, Minehead
Wookey Hole Caves & Papermill

WILTSHIRE

Lions of Longleat Safari Park, Warminster

THE WEST COUNTRY
DIARY OF EVENTS 1995

April 1 to
May 31
: **CORNWALL GARDENS FESTIVAL**
Various Gardens, Truro, Cornwall.

April 28 to
May 1
: **THE GREAT CORNWALL BALLOON FESTIVAL**
Newquay, Cornwall. Hot air balloon festival.

May 1
: **OLD CUSTOM: 'OBBY 'OSS CELEBRATIONS**
In town, Padstow, Cornwall.
Traditional May-Day Custom.

May 4–7
: **BADMINTON HORSE TRIALS**
Badminton House, Badminton, Avon.

May 8
: **VICTORY IN EUROPE EXTRAVAGANZA**
Various venues, Plymouth, Devon.

*May 10–14
: **BENSON & HEDGES INTERNATIONAL OPEN GOLF TOURNAMENT**
St. Mellion Golf & Country Club, Cornwall.

May 13–28
: **BOURNEMOUTH INTERNATIONAL FESTIVAL**
Bournemouth International Centre, Exeter Road, Bournemouth, Dorset.

May 18–20   DEVON COUNTY SHOW – 100TH SHOW
             Westpoint Showground, Clyst St. Mary, Devon.

May 22–27   FESTIVAL OF ARTS & CULTURE: MYSTERY ON THE
             ENGLISH RIVIERA FESTIVAL
             Various venues in Torbay, Torquay, Devon.
             A celebration of mystery and crime fiction, including "murder
             weekends", book signings and much more.

May 31 to   ROYAL BATH AND WEST OF ENGLAND SHOW
June 3   The Royal Bath & West Showground, Shepton Mallet,
             Somerset. (West Country's Premier Agricultural Show.)

June 8–10   ROYAL CORNWALL SHOW
             Royal Cornwall Showground, Wadebridge, Cornwall.

June 11   BRISTOL TO BOURNEMOUTH VINTAGE VEHICLE RUN
             Ashton Court Estate, Long Ashton, Bristol, Avon.

June 16–19   STAPEHILL ABBEY FLOWER FESTIVAL
             Stapehill Abbey, Crafts and Gardens, Wimborne Road West,
             Stapehill, Wimborne Minster, Dorset.

June 17   PORT OF BRIXHAM INTERNATIONAL TRAWLER RACE
             AND QUAY FESTIVAL
             New Fish Quay, The Harbour, Brixham, Devon.
             New Quay open to the public during the day, and the festival
             includes stalls, live bands and displays.

June 24   THE GLASTONBURY PILGRIMAGE
             Glastonbury Abbey, The Abbey Gate House, Glastonbury
             Somerset. (Anglican Pilgrimage.)

June 30 to   EXETER ARTS FESTIVAL
July 16   Various venues, Exeter, Devon.

July 1   TORBAY CHAMPIONSHIP SWIM
             Meadfoot Beach, Torquay, Devon.
             A race from Torquay to Brixham and return.

July 24 to August 4	INTERNATIONAL 505 SAILING CHAMPIONSHIPS Mounts Bay, Penzance, Cornwall.

July 29 to
August 6

COWES WEEK 1995
High Seas, Cowes, Isle of Wight.

July 30 to
August 6

BOURNEMOUTH REGATTA AND CARNIVAL
Pier approach, Bournemouth, Dorset.

August 4–11

INTERNATIONAL FESTIVAL OF FOLK ARTS –
SIDMOUTH
The Arena and other venues, Sidmouth, Devon.

August 12

OPEN AIR CONCERT: FIREWORK AND LASER
SYMPHONY CONCERT
Bowood House & Gardens, Calne, Wiltshire.

August 14–18

TORBAY ROYAL REGATTA
The Harbour, Torquay, Devon.

August 17–19

PLYMOUTH NAVY DAYS
HM Naval Base, Plymouth, Devon.
An opportunity to view the ships and aircraft.

August 20

VICTORY IN JAPAN SPECTACULAR
Various venues, Plymouth, Devon.

*September

375TH ANNIVERSARY OF THE SAILING OF THE
"MAYFLOWER"
Various venues, Plymouth, Devon.
Pilgrim banquets, exhibitions and street traders.

September 12

WIDECOMBE FAIR
Old Field, Widecombe-in-the-Moor, Devon.

October 14

GRAND ILLUMINATED CARNIVAL PROCESSION
Town Centre, Exeter, Devon. Approx. 90 floats plus street
entertainment.

November 4   OLD CUSTOM: ROLLING OF THE TAR BARRELS
              Town Centre, Ottery St. Mary, Devon.
              Carnival procession, lighting of the bonfire and the rolling of
              lighted barrels through the streets of the town.

November 10   WELLS GUY FAWKES CARNIVAL
              Town Centre, Wells, Somerset.
              Illuminated carnival floats visiting various towns in Somerset
              & Avon over an eleven-day period.

*Denotes provisional date

For further information contact:
The West Country Tourist Board
60 St. Davids Hill
Exeter, Devon EX4 4SY
Tel: 01392 76351

Southern Tourist Board
40 Chamberlayne Road
Eastleigh
Hampshire SO5 5JH.
Tel: 01703 620006

TREGLOS HOTEL
Constantine Bay, Nr. Padstow, Cornwall PL28 8JH

Telephone: 01841 520727   *Fax: 01841 521163*

London 256, Newquay 12, Padstow 3, Falmouth 36, Truro 25

R and R licence; 44 en suite bedrooms, all with telephone, colour TV, hairdryers, 3 rooms with sitting rooms (one ground floor); lift; meals to 9.30 p.m.; night service; off season conferences; diets; log fires; full central heating; bridge room; snooker and pool table; indoor heated swimming pool; spa bath; sea bathing; sailing; boating; golf and tennis by arrangement with Trevose Golf Club; special rates available at Treloy, Bodmin and the new Bowood Park golf courses; sea fishing; riding nearby; surfing; 4 self-contained luxury flats.

Treglos has been recommended by *Signpost* for many years. It is run as a country house hotel – the 'hotel' atmosphere being hardly apparent. It is a veritable model of elegance and luxury, standing in its own grounds overlooking the Atlantic. Personal consideration is the keynote to this splendid house, personally cared for by the owners, Ted and Barbara Barlow, their son Jim and his wife Rose, who retain loyal, cheerful and attentive staff. There are five lounges, all traditionally furnished to the highest of standards. The décor is pleasant and restful with freshly cut flowers and, in cooler weather, log fires. Upstairs is as sumptuous as down, with all the appointments expected here. In the newly refurbished dining room, Treglos has a great reputation for the excellence of the fare. A varied selection of interesting and carefully prepared dishes is offered, and local sea-food and vegetables are served whenever possible. All this good food is complemented by a wide selection of carefully chosen wines at moderate prices. The elegantly designed indoor swimming pool leads to open lawns and sunken gardens. Within a few hundred yards are the sandy beaches of Constantine, Treyarnon and Booby's Bay. Dinner, room and breakfast from £58.50 (single), demi-pension weekly from £320.00 per person including VAT. Closed mid November to early March; office open for enquiries.

ROYAL DUCHY HOTEL
Falmouth, South Cornwall TR11 4NX

Telephone: 01326 313042   *Fax: 01326 319420*

Redruth 10, Truro 11, Lizard 20, Penzance 25, Bodmin 34, London 267

F licence; 50 en suite bedrooms (1 suite suitable for the disabled), all with direct dial telephone and satellite TV; room service; baby listening; night service; lift; last orders for dinner 9.00 p.m.; bar meals; special diets; children welcome; dogs accepted at managers discretion; conferences max. 40; small snooker/billiards table; table tennis; indoor heated swimming pool; sauna; solarium; spa pool; sea bathing; free golf to hotel residents at Carlyon Bay; sailing, boating, riding, shooting and fishing all locally; open all year; most credit cards accepted.

With well kept gardens in the historic, maritime resort of Falmouth on Cornwall's famed riviera coastline, this is the ideal setting for a seafront hotel. It is just a short, level walk to the town centre and harbour, with views across Falmouth Bay to Pendennis Castle. Owned by the Brend family (who own other luxurious hotels, including the Carlyon Bay Hotel, near St. Austell – see page 8), the hotel is expertly managed by Darryl Reburn. With very good furnishing and colour schemes, both bedrooms and public rooms are comfortable and relaxing, with a friendly atmosphere. The food is distinguished by its high standard and the choice of interesting dishes. It is beautifully cooked and presented, and complemented by a well chosen wine list. I can thoroughly recommend a stay at the Royal Duchy in all seasons – whether for relaxation or a more active holiday, you will always enjoy first class service. Room and breakfast from £34.50 single, £45.50 double/twin, per person, and dinner, room and breakfast from £42.50 single, £53.50 double/twin, per person. Prices include VAT. Do write for their attractive brochure. Other terms, including special summer saver tariffs and autumn and winter breaks on application. Recent ground floor luxury refurbishment.

MARINA HOTEL
Esplanade, Fowey, Cornwall PL23 1HY

Telephone: 01726 833315   *Fax: 01726 832779*

London 270, Plymouth 35, Bodmin 12, Truro 22, St. Austell 9, Mevagissey 14

R & R licence; 11 en suite bedrooms, all with direct dial telephone and TV; baby listening; night service; last orders 8.30 p.m.; bar meals; special diets; dogs accepted; sea bathing; sailing/boating; golf and tennis 5 miles; riding, shooting 2 miles; fishing nearby; Visa and Mastercard accepted.

Tucked quietly away on the Esplanade, the Marina Hotel commands a unique waterfront position overlooking both the River Fowey and the sea. Guests have a bird's eye view of all that goes on in the estuary including the Regatta. Moorings are available to guests, and the hotel has its own access to the water from the secluded walled garden, a haven for sun worshippers. The hotel is Georgian and period features have been retained throughout. Four of the bedrooms have sun balconies, all are en suite and have colour television and direct dial telephone. The restaurant at the Marina has wonderful views and both the table d'hôte and à la carte menus include locally caught fish and shellfish. An interesting selection of wines is available to complement each dish. A special feature of this hotel is that bargain breaks of two days or more are offered throughout the season. Proprietors, John and Carol Roberts, provide a warm welcome at this attractive, small hotel and I know you will enjoy your stay. Room and breakfast from £31.00 per person, for 2 people sharing a double room (no singles). Weekly half board from £301.00.

POLURRIAN HOTEL
Mullion, Lizard Peninsula, Cornwall TR12 7EN

Telephone: 01326 240421   *Fax: 01326 240083*

Penzance 22, Truro 26, The Lizard 4½

*F licence; 39 en suite bedrooms (5 ground floor), all with direct dial telephone
and TV; room service; baby listening; night service; last orders for dinner 9.00
p.m.; special diets; children welcome; dogs accepted; conferences max. 100;
games room; snooker/billiards; outdoor and indoor heated swimming pools;
leisure centre; sauna; solarium; spa pool; gymnasium; squash; tennis; sea bathing
200 yards; golf ½ mile; shooting/fishing ½ mile; sailing/boating 5 miles; hotel
closed from 3rd Jan.–17th Feb. inc.; all major credit cards accepted.*

Three hundred feet above Polurrian Cove, and surrounded by wonderful National
Trust coastline, the Polurrian Hotel enjoys an enviable position overlooking some
of Cornwall's loveliest scenery. Steps lead down from the hotel to the sandy beach
where bathing is safe and clean, or there is an alternative of indoor or outdoor
heated swimming pools. In the hotel's leisure club, is a hairdressing and beauty
salon, sauna and solarium, a gym for the more energetic, and light snacks can
be enjoyed in the Aqua Bar. An inviting 18 hole golf course is nearby, and further
sporting activities at the Polurrian include tennis, badminton and croquet. Small
children can enjoy a safe-play area within the hotel's gardens, an indoor activity
room, and during my visit, a conjuror! The attractive restaurant romantically
overlooks the sea. The dishes are expertly cooked and presented, and seafood
is a speciality. Early rising guests can help catch the latter in a local fishing boat!
The bedrooms are luxurious and are all en suite, some having four-posters. The
Polurrian Hotel also has its own self-catering apartments and bungalows. Do
write for the brochure and enjoy a really exceptional family holiday. Dinner,
room and breakfast from £42.00 plus VAT.

HOTEL BRISTOL
Newquay, Cornwall TR7 2PQ

Telephone: 01637 875181　　　　　　　　　　　*Fax: 01637 879347*

London 255, Wadebridge 16, Bodmin 20, Penzance 38, Truro 16

F licence; 74 bedrooms, all with private bathrooms and colour TV, all with radio and room telephone; full central heating; lift; night service; meals to 8.45 p.m.; diets; children welcome; dogs welcome; sauna, solarium, indoor heated swimming pool; hair dressing salon; billiards (full size table); games room; dancing in season; sea bathing; sea fishing; sailing/boating; golf 1 mile; tennis and squash nearby; all credit cards accepted.

The Hotel Bristol enjoys an idyllic position directly overlooking Tolcarne Beach, which is acknowledged as being one of Europe's finest for surfing. It has been a great favourite of mine for many years and was featured in the 1939 Edition of *Signpost*. The hotel has remained under the ownership of the Young family since its foundation in 1927, and continues to be run under their personal care. This was evident when Mr. Stuart Young, Managing Director, took me round. The Bristol has a charm of its own, and very much the family home-from-home atmosphere with a wealth of hospitality for young and old alike. The décor throughout is pleasant and restful, the furnishings are very good, giving an air of comfort and quality. In the elegant and spacious dining room you are offered dishes that are interesting, varied and expertly prepared, complemented by a fine and carefully chosen wine list. I can thoroughly recommend this well run and comfortable hotel, where the service is friendly, courteous and efficient at any time of the year. Why not enjoy a break away from the hurly burly of the peak holiday months? Room and breakfast from £37.00 per person, weekly from £301.00 dinner, bed and breakfast, inclusive of VAT and service. Always open.

PORT GAVERNE HOTEL
Nr. Port Isaac, North Cornwall PL29 3SQ

Telephone: 01208 880244   Freephone: 0500 657867   Fax: 01208 880151

London 236, Wadebridge 9

F licence; 19 en suite bedrooms all with colour TV, direct dial telephone; 7 self-catering cottages available; late meals by prior arrangement; bar meals, function room; Real ale St. Austell's H.S.D. and Flowers I.P.A., Bass Draught Bitter; children welcome; dogs welcome; sea bathing; boating; riding; sea fishing; 4 golf courses nearby; delightful walks – the Cornish coastal path passes the door; all major credit cards accepted.

This charming 17th century inn, situated in an unspoilt North Cornish coastal cove ½ mile from Port Isaac, offers the hospitality and welcome you would expect from a place of this character and from your hostess, Midge Ross who has owned Port Gaverne for over 20 years. The public rooms retain their old charm, the old baking oven is still to be seen, and many paintings and interesting objects will draw your attention in the two bars and the residents' drawing room. The bedrooms are well appointed with soft restful colour schemes. Port Gaverne has a high reputation for good food; in an attractive candlelit dining room, you will enjoy a delicious dinner from a choice à la carte menu, augmented by the chef's daily specialities. All dishes are well prepared, imaginative, nicely presented and served, and complemented by a good wine from a cellar kept with pride. Excellent bar meals are also available. The cottages across the lane from the hotel have been converted into self catering units, 6 with 2 bedrooms and 1 with 3 bedrooms. Now adjoining the "Green Door Cottages" is a most delightful, and thoughtfully designed Function Room, which used to be the "Old Fish Cellar" featuring many objets d'art from bygone days. It has a fully licenced bar and is ideal for receptions, conferences and private parties. Port Gaverne is noted for its hospitality, comfort, intimate atmosphere, good food, wine and willing attentive service, praised by visitors from all over the world. Terms on application. Special "Breather" rates out of season, and "Tourer" rates during season. A member of the Hospitality Hotels of Cornwall.

ROSE-IN-VALE COUNTRY HOUSE HOTEL
Mithian, St. Agnes, Cornwall TR5 0QD
Telephone: 01872 552202   *Fax: 01872 552700*
Truro 7, St. Ives 18, Falmouth 20, Land's End 28

R & R licence; 17 en suite bedrooms (3 ground floor, 1 of which is suitable for the disabled); all have direct dial telephone, TV, radio, hairdryer and hospitality tray; room service; baby listening; last orders for dinner 8.30 p.m.; bar meals; special diets; children welcome; dogs accepted; conferences max. 20; games room; bar billiards; outdoor heated swimming pool; solarium; lawn croquet; badminton; sea bathing, sailing, boating and riding 1 mile; tennis and coarse fishing 2 miles; golf by arrangement with Truro Golf Club; open all year; most credit cards accepted.

The Rose-in-Vale is quite one of the prettiest hotels I have ever seen. Romantically covered in climbing roses, it is situated just outside the picturesque village of Mithian, near to St. Agnes. Set in eleven acres of woods and gardens, this elegant Georgian house was originally built as the winter residence of a Cornish mine captain, and has recently been extended and sympathetically updated by the owners, Mr. and Mrs. Arthur. There are seventeen well appointed bedrooms, three on the ground floor, one of which is adapted for use by the disabled, and the Rose Suite offers a four-poster bed and a separate sitting room. Imaginative dishes including fresh fish from Newlyn and local vegetables, feature on both the table d'hôte and à la carte menus. These are served in Opie's Restaurant, the whole being complemented by an interesting wine list. Croquet, badminton and swimming can all be enjoyed in the grounds, and delightful walks have been designed to begin and end at the hotel. There are six golf courses nearby, and special arrangements for guests residing at the Rose-in-Vale are made with the Truro Golf Club. I know that *Signpost* readers will enjoy staying at this pretty hotel in such a charming corner of Cornwall. Room and breakfast from £35.50 per person and dinner, room and breakfast from £47.00 per person. Prices include VAT.

CARLYON BAY HOTEL

Nr. St. Austell, Cornwall

PL25 3RD

Telephone: 01726 812304

Fax: 01726 814938

Bodmin 11, Truro 14,

Falmouth 25, Exeter 75,

Bristol 147, London 242

F licence; 72 en suite bedrooms, all with direct dial telephone and satellite TV; room service; baby listening; night service; lift; last orders for dinner 9.00 p.m.; bar lunches; special diets; children welcome; dogs accepted at managers discretion; conferences max. 125; games rooms; 2 snooker/billiards tables; indoor and outdoor heated swimming pool; sauna; solarium; spa pool; sea bathing; golf free to residents; 2 tennis courts; sailing, boating, riding, shooting and fishing all locally; open all year; all major credit cards accepted.

Carlyon Bay Hotel, which 50 years ago was called St. Austell Bay Hotel, featured in the first edition of *Signpost* in 1935, and was described as "A perfectly equipped, splendidly conducted and entirely modern hotel . . . magnificent site overlooking fine sands . . . deluxe hotel atmosphere allied with first rate cuisine and a wide choice of indoor and outdoor sports". Today it is even better for it has been charged with new ideas, energy and attractions, under the efficient and expert ownership of the Brend family. Here indeed is a place with character, luxury and an atmosphere of well being. The public rooms are elegant, well furnished with pleasant décor and a lift to all floors takes you to the comfortable and well appointed bedrooms. In the recently refurbished dining room you can be assured of delicious food that is cooked and presented with skill and imagination. The wine list is well chosen and extensive. Carlyon is a sportsman's paradise for there is a wide range of sporting activities to pursue, and is especially recommended for Golf Society meetings. But it is, above all, recommended for a superb family holiday throughout the year. Room and breakfast from £62.00 single, £59.00 double/twin per person, and dinner, room and breakfast from £72.00 single, £69.00 double/twin per person. All prices include VAT. Other terms on application. See Bargain Break section.

TREGENNA CASTLE
St. Ives, Cornwall TR26 2DE

Telephone: 01736 795254   *Fax: 01736 796066*

Plymouth 50, Exeter 90, Bristol 170, London 280

F licence; 83 en suite bedrooms (4 for the disabled), all with direct dial telephone and TV; room service; baby listening; night service; lift; last orders for dinner 9.30 p.m.; Bistro; special diets; children welcome; conferences max. 250; games room; outdoor heated swimming pool; solarium; squash court; 18 hole golf course; 6 tennis courts; snooker room; croquet; putting; open all year; all major credit cards accepted.

Set amidst acres of private estate land in an idyllic location, Tregenna Castle was originally built as a private house in 1774. The spacious en suite bedrooms, some of which benefit from panoramic sea views across St. Ives Bay to Godrevy Lighthouse, have recently undergone refurbishment, and provide guests with comfortable accommodation in a superb setting. The hotel's Trelawney Restaurant, offers a mouth-watering selection of fresh local seafood dishes which feature on both the à la carte and table d'hôte menus. An extensive selection of world famous wines is also available to complement your meal. I would recommend this hotel, particularly for the traditional family holiday. Children are welcome, and during the high season, a full programme of entertainment and activities are provided including Kiddies Farm Corner, Outdoor Adventure Centre and indoor play rooms. Prices start from £30.00 per person bed and breakfast, and £45.00 per person, for dinner, bed and breakfast, and are inclusive of VAT and service. Tregenna Castle offers leisure breaks such as Golfing, Racket Breaks, Multi-Activity Breaks, Murder Mystery Weekends, Christmas and New Year programmes and many more.

BOSKERRIS HOTEL
Carbis Bay, Nr. St. Ives, Cornwall TR26 2NQ

Telephone: 01736 795295   *Fax: 01736 798632*

London 277, Helston 13, Penzance 8½, Redruth 14, St. Ives 1

R and R licence; 18 bedrooms (some ground floor), one apartment or suite,16 private bathrooms, remote control colour TV, direct dial telephone and tea/coffee making facilities; diets available; children welcome; drying and games rooms; heated outdoor swimming pool; putting green; golfing packages available; sea bathing, boating, surfing, rock climbing and tennis all nearby, ample car parking facilities.

Boskerris stands in attractive gardens above the safe golden sands of Carbis Bay, with fine views across St. Ives Bay. This delightful hotel is owned and personally cared for by the Monk family, who have created a friendly, happy atmosphere. The public rooms are attractive and furnished to a high standard and together with the Cocktail Bar have extensive views over the Bay. In the dining room a carefully chosen menu is offered. The dishes are interesting, well presented and nicely served. Similar care is given in the selection of wines, which is excellent. The majority of the comfortable and well appointed bedrooms, most with private bathrooms, enjoy sea views and overlook the well-kept gardens. Boskerris is an ideal centre for a wide range of activities, including a golfing package which enables you to play at 14 major golf courses in Cornwall, all within easy distances, plus the many beautiful moorland and coastal walks. Room and breakfast from £26.40 per person, or with dinner £40.00, including VAT. Other terms on application. Off season bargain breaks from two to four days. Open Easter till November.

BOSCEAN COUNTRY HOTEL
St. Just, Nr. Penzance, Cornwall TR19 7QP

Telephone: 01736 788748

Penzance 6, Land's End 6, Land's End Airfield 2, Truro 35

R & R licence; 12 en suite bedrooms (1 for the disabled); baby listening; dinner served at 7.00 p.m.; bar lunches; special diets; children welcome; dogs accepted by prior arrangement; putting; sea bathing 2 miles; golf, riding and fishing nearby; hotel closed from 1st Nov.–1st March; Mastercard and Visa credit cards accepted.

The Boscean Hotel is a charming, Edwardian house, superbly situated in almost three acres of peaceful gardens, which are often still flowering in October. Putting and croquet are available within the grounds, and the coastal scenery is superb, with many secluded coves and beaches. The hotel overlooks Cape Cornwall Golf Course, and surfing and sea angling can be arranged. The resident proprietors, Joyce and Roy Lee, offer their guests a warm welcome, excellent home cooking, and above all, wonderful value. In the panelled dining room, dinners comprise four courses, with only the freshest ingredients used, and menus are changed daily. Guests are invited to request their favourite dishes and also, if they are able to, try more than one of the delicious puddings! There is a large and sensibly priced selection of table wines available. When required, a lovely log fire blazes in the panelled lounge, and there is a small, but well stocked bar. Each of the twelve bedrooms is large, most have sea views, and all have full facilities. The hotel is situated up Boswedden Road, which is next to the bank in St. Just. Dinner, room and breakfast from £30.00, weekly rates from £195.00.

THE IDLE ROCKS HOTEL
Harbourside, St. Mawes, Cornwall TR2 5AN

Telephone: 01326 270771   Freephone: 0800 243020   Fax: 01326 270062

Truro 20, St. Austell 20, Plymouth 58, London 273

F licence; 17 en suite bedrooms, all with direct dial telephone and TV; room service; baby listening; last orders for dinner 9.15 p.m.; bar meals; special diets; children welcome; dogs accepted by prior arrangement; conferences max. 20; sea bathing, sailing/boating (own 55ft Ketch); sea fishing trips; golf course at Truro; riding 10 miles; car parking facilities diagonally opposite the hotel; open all year; Mastercard and Visa credit cards accepted.

The Idle Rocks Hotel stands in a magnificent position overlooking the picturesque estuary at St. Mawes, which enjoys Cornwall's mild climate and sub-tropical vegetation. This charming little town is an ideal place from which to tour one of England's most scenic and interesting areas. For the energetic, guests may hire the hotel's own 55 foot Ketch, with a salad lunch and wine being included in the charge. For the less energetic you can take the pedestrian ferry from St. Mawes to Falmouth, or the King Harry car ferry across the river, to visit the pleasant cathedral city of Truro. The bedrooms at The Idle Rocks are beautifully decorated, mostly with outstanding views of the estuary, and there is a ground floor bedroom which has access to the terrace. This proves a very popular venue for enjoying excellent "alfresco style" bar lunches and afternoon teas, seafood being a speciality both at lunchtime and in the evening. For a more formal atmosphere, the large, attractive dining room offers imaginative menus, prepared from the freshest of local ingredients, where, once again, you can enjoy the magnificent views. The lounges are tastefully decorated and furnished in pastel shades, and one is non-smoking. Do write for the hotel's brochure, and enjoy an interesting and relaxing holiday at The Idle Rocks. Room and breakfast from £35.00, dinner, room and breakfast from £47.00. Prices are per person and include VAT.

ST. MORITZ HOTEL
Trebetherick, Nr. Wadebridge, Cornwall PL27 6SD

Telephone: 01208 862242   *Fax: 01208 862262*

Wadebridge 7, Falmouth 39, Padstow 14, Newquay 23, Bodmin 14, Truro 31

R & R licence; 40 en suite bedrooms, all with direct dial telephone, colour TV, radio and full central heating; meals until 9.30 p.m.; diets; children welcome, baby listening; dogs allowed in hotel; indoor heated swimming pool; jacuzzi; sauna; Turkish bath; solarium; snooker; billiards; all weather tennis court; sea bathing; sailing, golf, boating, sea and river fishing all nearby; riding by arrangement; major credit cards accepted.

The St. Moritz Hotel, located on the B3314 from Wadebridge, stands on 8 acres of land overlooking the Camel estuary. It is an area of outstanding natural beauty, much beloved by the Poet Laureate John Betjeman, who now rests in the pretty little church of St. Enodoc. This highly recommended hotel is owned by Stephen Rushworth and his mother, and their partner Brad J. Trethewey. All the bedrooms are en suite and well appointed, whilst downstairs, the new and attractive dining rooms and lounges are comfortable and restful. Recently completed is phase one of the leisure centre which includes an indoor swimming pool and hotel guests will automatically become members during their stay. Recently completed are 1, 2, 3 and 4 bedroomed holiday villas for weekly rental in the grounds adjoining the hotel. Thanks to the expertise of Brad Trethewey, St. Moritz has a fine reputation for good food. Great care and consideration are taken in the preparation of English and continental dishes, using local sea-food and garden produce whenever possible. A well chosen and selective wine list is offered to complete a delicious meal. There are three beaches within walking distance, offering safe bathing, canoeing, surfing and sailing. For golfers, St. Enodoc Golf Club is ideally situated ½ mile away, with a choice of two 18 hole courses, and only a few miles away, the newly built Bowood Park Golf Course offers a full 18-hole course designed by Bob Sandow. The hotel is closed from 4th January to mid February, but the office is open for enquiries. Dinner, bed and breakfast from £49.00. Freephone 0500 121299 for brochures and reservations.

BLAGDON MANOR COUNTRY HOTEL
Ashwater, Beaworthy, Devon EX21 5DF

Telephone: 01409 211224   *Fax: 01409 211634*

Launceston 8, Bideford 25, Exeter 43, London 218

R & R licence; 7 en suite bedrooms (1 four-poster room), all with TV; dinner served at 8.00 p.m.; hotel not suitable for children; dogs accepted by prior arrangement; conferences max. 14 (7 couples); bar; billiard room; library; croquet; practice ground for golfers; riding and fishing nearby; shooting in season; 2 golf courses within 10 miles; open all year; most credit cards accepted.

Blagdon Manor Country Hotel is as charming and original as the owners, Tim and Gill Casey. Most of the building dates back to the 17th century, and the whole is set amidst peaceful countryside. The fabrics and wallcoverings used in the décor of Blagdon Manor are unusual, vibrant and tasteful, with antique furniture throughout. The seven bedrooms are exquisitely decorated, with many thoughtful touches to make guests feel instantly at home. They are all en suite with bath and shower. Guests dine together "dinner party style" in the elegant and well furnished dining room. Gill Casey supervises all the cooking which is superb and plentiful, the wines have been well chosen, and nothing is too much trouble for your hosts. The pretty sitting room is very comfortable, as is the library, and there is also a bar and delightful billard room. Blagdon Manor is ideally situated on the border of two counties in the heart of the West Country, and lends itself to varied journeys from the moors to the coast, encompassing many areas of natural beauty and historic interest. To find Blagdon Manor, leave Launceston on the A388 Holsworthy road. Pass both Chapman's Well and the first sign to Ashwater. Turn right at the second Ashwater sign, then first right at the Blagdon signpost. The hotel is then a few hundred yards further on, on the right. Room and breakfast from £45.00, dinner, room and breakfast from £70.00. Prices are per person and include VAT.

TYTHERLEIGH COT HOTEL
Chardstock, Axminster, Devon EX13 7BN
Telephone: 01460 221170   *Fax: 01460 221291*
Axminster 3, Chard 3, Lyme Regis 6, Taunton 15, Exeter 25, London 140
R & R licence; 19 en suite bedrooms, all with direct dial telephone, hairdryer, trouser press and TV; room service; baby listening; last orders for dinner 9.30 p.m.; special diets; children welcome; dogs accepted; conferences max. 25; outdoor heated swimming pool; gymnasium; sauna; solarium; rough and clay pigeon shooting; riding 1 mile; shooting/fishing 2 miles; squash, golf and tennis 3 miles; sea bathing, sailing/boating 6 miles; open all year; Visa and Mastercard accepted.

Just a few minutes off the A358 Axminster to Chard Road, an absolute gem of an hotel has been lovingly created by the resident proprietors, Pat and Frank Grudgings. Tytherleigh Cot is set within a 14th century, original village cider house, where the barns and outbuildings have been tastefully converted into 19 quite superb, rooms and suites. Each bedroom has been individually decorated in a traditional country style, full of warmth and charm. Beamed ceilings and four-poster and half tester beds are to be found in some rooms, whilst all provide every possible modern day comfort. The award-winning restaurant is set within a Victorian-style conservatory, and offers exquisite cuisine, service and atmosphere. For all meals, only the freshest of local fare is used, and the actual presentation of each dish is to be admired as a perfect work of art! A carefully selected wine list complements any menu and every palate. A conference suite with comprehensive audio visual aids can accommodate up to 25 delegates, and a separate syndicate room, up to ten. For a reception, small exhibition or conference, all the facilities at Tytherleigh Cot are excellent. For relaxation, there is a mini gymnasium, sauna, solarium and heated outdoor swimming pool. Accolades increase by the year, and simply compliment the first class creation, management and hospitality of the proprietors. This was a wonderful "find", which I highly recommend. Room and breakfast from £49.00 single, £38.75 per person sharing a twin/double room. Prices include VAT.

DOWNREW HOUSE
Bishops Tawton, Nr. Barnstaple,
North Devon EX32 0DY

Telephone: 01271 42497/46673   *Fax: 01271 23947*

Barnstaple 3, Bideford 8

R & R licence; 12 en suite bedrooms (3 ground floor), all with telephone, colour TV and full central heating; last orders 9.00 p.m.; bar snacks; diets; children welcome; dogs allowed; conferences up to 24; games room; billiards; outdoor heated swimming pool; solarium; golf; croquet and tennis; fishing 1 mile; sauna, squash, badminton and leisure centre 3 miles; riding 5 miles; shooting, sea bathing, sailing and boating 8 miles; Visa and Mastercard welcome.

Downrew is a small Queen Anne Country House with lodge, 3 miles south of Barnstaple, off the A377, on the slopes of Codden Hill. The original building dates from 1640 and was enlarged in 1705. It stands in 12 acres of meadowland and well kept gardens and has its own 5-hole 9 approach golf course. The resident proprietors have created a wonderfully warm and friendly atmosphere, which is peaceful and relaxing. Care and attention to detail are the hallmarks of this delightful house, with service of the highest order under the personal supervision of the owners. Downrew House is very comfortable; the elegant drawing room with its log fire overlooks the garden, and adjoins the sitting room. The dining room's magnificent 18ft bow window looks over the lawns, rose beds and the surrounding countryside, towards Dartmoor in the far distance. I enjoyed an excellent dinner, carefully cooked and well presented, with many of the fruits and vegetables being homegrown. A well stocked bar and specially chosen wines complement the delicious food. The hotel is open all year round. Dinner, room and breakfast from £45.00 per day including VAT. No service charge.

THE BERRY HEAD HOTEL
Berry Head Road, Brixham, S. Devon TQ5 9AJ

Telephone: 01803 853225   *Fax: 01803 882084*

Torquay 10, Exeter 30, Bristol 100, Birmingham 200, London 180

F licence; 12 en suite bedrooms all with direct dial telephone, TV; room service; baby listening; night service; last orders for dinner 9.30 p.m.; bar meals until 9.30 p.m.; special diets; children welcome; dogs accepted; conferences 100 max.; boules; sea bathing 30 yds.; outdoor seawater pool 200 yds.; indoor swimming pool and squash courts ½ mile; sailing and boating, shooting and fishing ¼ mile; tennis 1 mile; golf and riding 2 miles; Amex, Visa and Mastercard accepted.

The Berry Head Hotel is set in a superb water's edge position in six acres of its own gardens and woodland, in the seclusion of the Berry Head Country Park, which is noted for its bird life and rare wild flowers. The hotel is steeped in history. It was built as a military hospital in the Napoleonic Wars, and was later the home of the Reverend Francis Lyte, who wrote the famous hymn *Abide with Me* at the hotel, no doubt inspired by the glorious sunsets. The historic fishing port of Brixham, where William of Orange first landed on English soil, is only a short walk away. The hotel offers relaxing accommodation and all the en suite bedrooms have colour television, radio and tea and coffee making facilities. The comfortable lounge and the restaurant, which overlook the terrace, enjoy spectacular views of Torbay and the Devon coast. The emphasis here is upon good food, wine and company in a very special setting. Room and breakfast from £30.00, and dinner, room and breakfast from £35.00 including VAT. The hotel is always open.

THE HOOPS INN
Horns Cross, Nr. Clovelly, North Devon EX39 5DL

Telephone: 01237 451222   *Fax: 01237 451237*

Clovelly 4, Bideford 5, London 210

F licence; 12 bedrooms (10 en suite), all with direct dial telephone and 10 rooms with TV; room service; night service until 11.30 p.m.; last orders for dinner 9.30 p.m.; bar meals; special diets; children welcome; dogs welcome; conferences max. 60; riding, shooting/fishing nearby; sea bathing, sailing and golf 4 miles; leisure centre 5 miles; open all year; most credit cards accepted.

Built in the 13th century, The Hoops Inn is located on the A39 between Bideford and Clovelly, and three-quarters of a mile from the North Devon coast. It is surrounded by beautiful, unspoilt countryside, and is one of Devon's oldest and most famous inns, previously notorious as a meeting place for smugglers. It was regularly used by Sir Richard Grenville (born only a few miles away), Raleigh, Drake and Hawkins, who sponsored the 1556 bill, calling for the construction of Hartland Quay nearby, when potatoes and tobacco were first imported into this country. This perfect English inn is complete with thick Wheaton-Reed thatch, quaint semi-circular brick fireplaces and old baking ovens. It is currently being sympathetically up-dated and refurbished by the charming new owner, Gay Marriott. Seafood is a speciality, collected daily from the trawler in nearby Appledore, although delicious English fare with a taste of Devon is also offered with the plus of home-made bread. Individually decorated bedrooms are mainly en suite, some with four-poster or tester beds, and there is further accommodation in the bedroom wing, behind the old house. Room and breakfast from £35.00, dinner, room and breakfast from £50.00. Prices include VAT.

THE MAYPOOL PARK HOTEL
Maypool, Galmpton, Nr. Brixham, Devon TQ5 0ET

Telephone: 01803 842442   *Fax: 01803 845782*

Dartmouth 5, Torquay 8, Totnes 8, London 200

F licence; 10 en suite bedrooms, all with direct dial telephone and TV; room service by arrangement; last orders for dinner 8.45 p.m.; special diets by arrangement; conferences max. 30; sailing/boating and fishing ½ mile; golf 2 miles; sea bathing 3 miles; riding 4 miles; hotel closed November and February; most credit cards accepted.

This delightful, peaceful hotel, set 400 feet above the River Dart, has a new name and new owners, Alison and Raymond Taylor. Their enthusiasm was very evident as I was shown around – personal service and good food are their aims, and these they achieve. The ten bedrooms are attractively furnished, all having their own private and beautifully equipped bathrooms. The Garden Room is available for conferences, banquets and functions, with a 30 person maximum. Having spent some years in the wine growing region of Germany, the Taylors have a specialist knowledge of the country's wines and the result is a wine list with a leaning towards unusual wines. A gourmet menu is offered on Fridays and Saturdays, and country menus from Sunday to Thursday, with a splendid Sunday lunch also being available. All the menus are innovative, and the food is very attractively presented. Two excellent golf courses are within easy reach of The Maypool Park, salmon and trout fishing are available on the Dart, and there is still water trout fishing nearby. A trip on the Painton and Dartmouth Steam Railway is a must for enthusiasts! I can highly recommend a stay at The Maypool Park Hotel, and the Taylors will make you most welcome. Room and breakfast from £32.50, dinner, room and breakfast from £51.00.

COMBE HOUSE
Gittisham, Nr. Honiton, Devon EX14 0AD
Telephone: 01404 42756 and 43560   *Fax: 01404 46004*

London 155, Birmingham 149, Bristol 61, Exeter 16, Honiton 2, Airport 14

R and R licence; 15 en suite bedrooms (one suite), 2 with four-poster beds, all with colour TV, direct dial telephone and hairdryer; diets available, including a vegetarian menu; children welcome; dogs welcome; small executive conferences; weekend house parties up to 20 welcome; small wedding receptions; croquet; trout fishing; riding by arrangement; tennis nearby; golf by special arrangement at Woodbury Park; sea bathing 7 miles; lovely walks and well kept gardens.

This 14th century Elizabethan mansion lies in 2000 acres of parkland adjoining the Otter Valley, off the A30 Honiton–Exeter road to Gittisham. John and Thérèse Boswell own and care for the hotel, and enhance the historic country mansion atmosphere with many antiques from the Boswell ancestral Scottish home. The staff work as a cheerful, efficient and attentive team. The spacious, restful bedrooms are dignified and well appointed. Among the magnificent rooms downstairs are the Entrance Hall – a fine example of Caroline grandeur – and the large, panelled drawing room. The cosy Cocktail Bar (adjacent to the smaller drawing room) features John's interest in horse racing. He owns some wonderful horses and pictures of them adorn the walls. A wonderful candlelit dinner is served in the two lovely dining rooms. Thérèse produces superbly cooked dishes, full of imagination, with her team. The wine list is excellent in its range and quality. Rates from 1st January 1995 which are subject to alteration without prior notice are, room and breakfast from £63.00 per person (single), £97.00 (double/twin), inclusive of VAT and service. Other terms on application, including out of season rate. Member of Pride of Britain. Open all year, but closed from 26th January to 9th February inclusive.

THE COTTAGE HOTEL
Hope Cove, Kingsbridge, South Devon TQ7 3HJ

Telephone: 01548 561555   *Fax: 01548 561455*

Totnes 18, Plymouth 25

F licence; 25 en suite bedrooms, all with direct dial telephone and colour TV; room service; baby listening; last orders for dinner 8.30 p.m.; bar meals; children welcome; dogs accepted; conferences max. 50; games room; sea bathing; sailing/boating; riding 3 miles; golf 4 miles; indoor heated swimming pool, tennis and squash courts 6 miles; hotel closed from 2nd Jan.–30th Jan. inclusive; no credit cards accepted.

The Cottage Hotel enjoys a superb position, overlooking the picturesque harbour and cove, with spectacular sea views and sunsets. The gardens descend to the beach, where you can bathe in safety. The hotel is delightful and has 35 beautifully furnished bedrooms, with 19 of them having private bathrooms / showers. I always enjoy visiting The Cottage; it has a happy and relaxing atmosphere thanks to the owners, John and Janet Ireland, who, with Patricia Bazzano, personally care for this pleasant and comfortable haven. The enticing dining room, which has lovely views of the cove and coast, offers table d'hôte and à la carte menus. I chose the former, which was excellent, cooked with great interest and attention, served by cheerful, efficient and courteous staff of many years standing. The meal was supported by a selective wine list. The ground floor rooms are comfortable and nicely furnished. This hotel still remains one of the best family hotels I visit, well illustrated by the preponderance of suntanned, well-fed families. Dinner, room and breakfast from £45.35.

BUCKLAND-TOUT-SAINTS HOTEL
Goveton, Kingsbridge, South Devon TQ7 2DS

Telephone: 01548 853055   *Fax: 01548 856261*

Salcombe 6, Plymouth 20, Exeter 30, Dartmouth 13

R & R licence; 12 en suite bedrooms, all with direct dial telephone and TV; room service; night service until 10.00 p.m.; last orders for dinner 9.30 p.m.; bar lunches; special diets; conferences from 12–16 people; putting green; croquet; 3 golf courses within 10 miles; open all year; all major credit cards accepted.

Although new to this hotel and the south of England, John and Tove Taylor are old hands at welcoming guests, having spent 15 years running the Taychreggan Hotel in Argyllshire. Buckland-tout-Saints is a beautiful Queen Anne manor house which was built in 1690, and lies in the heart of rural South Devon. "Far from the madding crowd," you will be able to relax in comfort, in elegant surroundings. The Great Hall boasts a glorious log fire on summer and winter nights, and personal pieces of antique furniture are on display. The newly decorated and refurbished drawing room overlooks the well-kept acres of garden, and the small bar offers a warm and friendly atmosphere. The panelled dining room serves imaginative, impeccably presented dishes from a daily-changing menu, and I highly recommend that you leave enough room for a pudding! There is an excellent choice of first class wines, suitable for the most experienced palate. Each of the 12 bedrooms is individually decorated with superb bathrooms, and good use has been made of the second floor, to create unusually shaped, smaller bedrooms, most of which overlook the grounds and surrounding countryside. Head Chef, Jeremy Medley, is responsible for the very high standard of the cuisine. The Taylors, together with their son, George, and the rest of the team, will make your stay happy and relaxed, and you will find you will want to return again and again. Room and breakfast from £50.00 single and £100.00 double, which also includes early morning tea, newspaper and VAT.

COMBE PARK HOTEL
Hillsford Bridges, Lynton, North Devon EX35 6LE

Telephone: 01598 52356

**Barnstaple 18, Tarr Steps 14, Porlock 12, Clovelly 31, Arlington 14,
Dunkery Beacon 16**

*R & R licence; 9 bedrooms with private bathroom, 8 en suite; last orders
7.15 p.m.; special diets; children over 12 welcome; dogs accepted; sailing /
boating, tennis and riding nearby; fishing; closed during the first week of
November until Easter, 4 nights full board at Christmas available; credit cards
not accepted.*

Combe Park is situated not only in the heart of the National Trust Watersmeet
Estate, but also by the Hoar Oak Water which gently winds its way through the
4½ acre gardens. This little corner of paradise is the perfect base for fishermen,
riders and walkers and dogs are most welcome in this friendly, family run hotel.
Only 2½ miles from Lynton and Lynmouth, it is surrounded by some of the
loveliest countryside in North Devon. Most of the charming bedrooms are en
suite with tea and coffee making facilities and a river view. Downstairs, are
comfortable lounges, log fires and an intimate residents' bar. There is also a television lounge with a piano for festive occasions. Cooking is offered in traditional
style with several choices for starters and a superb selection of puddings. Local
Devon produce is used whenever possible and standards are high. There are a
great many regular visitors to this pretty little hotel and I know that you too
will want to return again and again. Hosts, David and Shirley Barnes and John
Walley, always extend a very warm welcome. Dinner, bed and breakfast from
£45.00 per person, weekly from £265.00 per person.

THE WHITE HART HOTEL
The Square, Moretonhampstead, Nr. Newton Abbot, South Devon TQ13 8NF

Telephone: 01647 40406   *Fax: 01647 40565*
From Dec. '94   440406   *440565*

Exeter 12, Newton Abbott 12, Torquay 22, Plymouth 28

F licence; 20 en suite bedrooms, all with direct dial telephone and TV; last orders for dinner 8.30 p.m. in restaurant and 9.00 p.m. in bar; bar meals; special diets; children over 10; dogs welcome; conferences max. 90; golf by arrangement, 2 miles; open all year; most credit cards accepted.

Well known as the most famous coaching inn on Dartmoor, the 300 year old White Hart Hotel is a listed building, and was formerly a Georgian posting house where the horses were changed on the Exeter to Plymouth Mails. French officers who were taken prisoner also met here during the Napoleonic Wars. The hotel is well placed for exploring Dartmoor National Park with fishing and riding nearby, for racing at Newton Abbot, Devon and Exeter, and for visiting many of the South Devon seaside resorts. The bedrooms are attractive and well appointed, and the charming olde worlde dining room is graced with some lovely antique pieces. I was shown an immaculate kitchen – bar snacks and evening meals are exceptionally good value, which is why guests return to The White Hart again and again. Local meat and vegetables are delivered daily, and vegetarian dishes are clearly marked on the menus. Gorgeous traditional puddings with Devon clotted cream, are a feature of the hotel, and I would highly recommend any guest to sample one. Mine host, Peter Morgan, together with his well behaved canine friends and his excellent staff, ensure a warm welcome and a memorable stay. There is a small car park opposite the hotel, or a larger one on the right hand side, on the road to Bovey Tracey. Room and breakfast from £31.50, or dinner, room and breakfast from £45.00 per person, per night based on a 2 night stay. All prices include VAT.

THE BOLT HEAD HOTEL
Salcombe, South Devon TQ8 8LL

Telephone: 01548 843751   *Fax: 01548 843060*

London 214, Kingsbridge 7, Totnes 18, Exeter 43, Plymouth 25

F licence; 29 en suite bedrooms (4 ground floor), all with direct dial telephones, remote control colour TV with satellite, radio, tea/coffee making facilities; full central heating; meals to 9 p.m.; diets; children welcome, baby listening; dogs at Manager's discretion; games room; outdoor heated swimming pool; sailing, boating, private moorings; sea fishing; tennis ¼ mile; riding 7 miles; golf 8 miles; major credit cards accepted.

Blessed with a climate that is said to be the mildest in Devon, and set amid imposing scenery that ends with the fantastically shaped black rocks of mighty Bolt Head, this most southerly hotel in Devon commands a marvellous view of the Salcombe Estuary and coastline, and overlooks the sheltered golden cove of South Sands Beach. There are always yachts and fishing boats to be seen in this unspoilt estuary. The hotel has been completely refurbished to a very high standard under the ownership of Mr. Colin Smith. A sun terrace leads off the main lounge. The bedrooms are also very comfortable and equipped as one would expect of this well run hotel. The hotel is renowned for its warm welcome and friendly service and the staff are courteous, attentive and cheerful. The table d'hôte menu with specialities, is interesting and provides a splendid choice, carefully served, in an attractive restaurant which has panoramic views of the estuary. In spite of all that is offered at this first class establishment, it also provides peace and quiet with lovely walks in the National Trust property adjoining the grounds. Dinner, room and breakfast from £62.00 per person per night inclusive of VAT. Other items on application including Getaway Breaks. Closed mid November to mid March, but office open. A Best Western Hotel.

TIDES REACH HOTEL
South Sands, Salcombe, South Devon TQ8 8LJ

Telephone: 01548 843466   *Fax: 01548 843954*

London 214, Kingsbridge 7, Totnes 19, Exeter 43, Plymouth 26

F licence; 40 en suite bedrooms with col. TV, radio, direct dial telephone; some family suites; lift; children welcome over 8; games room; snooker room; some diets available; dogs by arrangement; indoor heated pool; solarium; sauna; Hydro Spa Bath; squash; indoor and outdoor water gardens; drying room; golf, tennis, riding nearby; sea bathing; boating; fishing, wind surfing, water sports from own boathouse.

The position of Tides Reach is perfect – a beautiful secluded sandy cove. The quiet luxury of the hotel strikes you as you enter the conservatory-style hall with its indoor water garden and the flower garden lounge-hall so full of sunshine and scented blooms. The décor throughout was chosen and supervised by Mrs. Edwards and the colours are wonderfully vibrant and original. The indoor heated swimming pool, around which has been built a new bar and coffee shop, is as glamorous as a Hollywood film set – there is an outdoor sun patio and sun deck leading off and below, a new hairdressing and beauty salon, multi gym., sunbed, Whirlpool Spa bath, sauna, steam baths and squash court. In addition to the new facilities the dining room has been extended and the bedrooms and public rooms have been re-furnished throughout in a most comfortable and luxurious manner. The food is superb, both à la carte and table d'hôte dishes being really first class. Dinner, room and breakfast from £53.00 to £98.00 per person including VAT, according to season and length of stay. Closed December–February inclusive. Resident Proprietor Roy Edwards FHCI.

HERON HOUSE HOTEL
Thurlestone Sands, Nr. Salcombe, South Devon TQ7 3JY

Telephone: 01548 561308/561600   *Fax: 01548 560180*

Kingsbridge 3, Salcombe 3, Plymouth 20, Torquay 20

F licence; 18 ensuite bedrooms, all with direct dial telephone and TV; room service; baby listening; night service; last orders for dinner 8.30 p.m.; bar meals; special diets; children welcome; dogs by arrangement; conferences max. 40; games room; pool table; outdoor heated swimming pool; solarium; sea bathing; special activities in autumn and spring; leisure centre 3 miles; sailing, boating, tennis, riding, shooting and fishing all nearby; golf by arrangement with Thurlestone Golf Club; open all year; Mastercard, Eurocard and Visa accepted.

Standing only fifty yards from the beach, the Heron House enjoys a prime location in South Devon, with magnificent views across to Plymouth Sound, Burgh Island, and on a fine day, Cornwall. Situated on the coastal path (incidentally, Britain's longest footpath), guests can either swim from Thurlestone's lovely sandy beach, the adjoining beaches, or in the hotel's large and exceptionally warm outdoor swimming pool. Thurlestone has the Premier Good Beach Award for 1994, which includes superior water quality. The Rowland family, together with their son-in-law, Paul Sanders, take great pride in running this hotel, and personally supervise the excellent meals that are freshly prepared in their well equipped kitchen. Dinner is five courses, and the menus feature vegetarian specialities and fish which is supplied locally. All of the eighteen comfortable bedrooms enjoy first class views, and have the facilities now expected by today's guest. Keen sailors can hire craft from nearby Salcombe, Newton Ferrers and Dartmouth, golfers are offered temporary membership of the Thurlestone and Bigbury Clubs, and there is riding and sea fishing available. Do ring for the hotel brochure which features a panoramic view of Heron House's superb position. Room and breakfast from £35.00, dinner, room and breakfast from £45.00 including VAT.

THE SAUNTON SANDS HOTEL
Saunton Sands, Nr. Braunton, Devon EX31 1LQ

Telephone: 01271 890212   *Fax: 01271 890145*

London 203, Barnstaple 8, Ilfracombe 9, Bideford 17, Exeter 48

*F licence; 92 en suite bedrooms, all with telephone, satellite TV, tea/coffee
making facilities; lift; 24 hour room service; last orders 9.30 p.m.; bar meals
(lunch); afternoon teas; vegetarian and vegan diets; children welcome; baby
listening; dogs by arrangement only; conferences max. 200; games room; dancing
frequently; full size snooker table; children's paddling pool; heated indoor and
outdoor swimming pools; sauna; solarium; hairdressing salon; mini cinema; 5
miles of beach below hotel; sailing; tennis; squash; riding; shooting; fishing;
helipad; golf nearby; Mastercard, Amex, Diners, Visa credit cards accepted.*

Lots of sun, miles of golden sands and tiered silvery waves advancing eagerly
up the beach is what you look down on from the warm and luxurious rooms
of The Saunton Sands, a member of the Brend Group of Exclusive Hotels. The
hotel is light and sunny as most of the rooms face the south, the sea and the
sands, and there are panoramic views from most. All the staff are efficient and
attentive, creating an air of warmth and friendliness. The furnishings are elegant
and comfortable, and the bedrooms have all the modern facilities that you could
want. Food is of a very high standard and the wine list is well chosen. Room
and breakfast from £56.00 single, £58.00 per person double, all inclusive of VAT.
Other seafront hotels in the Brend Group include Carlyon Bay near St. Austell,
and The Victoria Hotel in Sidmouth (see pages 8 and 30). This splendid hotel
provides a truly outstanding holiday for all the family, all year round. There is
a Christmas and New Year programme, see Bargain Break section. Open all year.

THE ROYAL GLEN HOTEL
Sidmouth, Devon EX10 8RW
Telephone: 01395 513221 / 578124 / 578125

London 161, Torquay 35, Birmingham 159

R & R licence; 34 bedrooms, 32 with bathroom/shower, 3 on ground floor; all have colour TV, radio, tea making facilities, telephone and full central heating; last orders 8.00 p.m.; children from 8 years; dogs allowed; indoor heated swimming pool; sea bathing; golf nearby; tennis 1 mile; Mastercard and Visa cards accepted.

Originally built in 1700 as a farmhouse, the Royal Glen Hotel has been managed by a member of the Crane family for over 100 years. This historic and lovely hotel stands in its own grounds, 200 yards from the sea-front at Sidmouth. The cricket club is nearby as well as the golf course and shopping centre. Overlooking the cricket club is the Royal Glen's sister hotel, The Torbay, managed by Mr. and Mrs. Martin Caldwell, daughter and son-in-law of the Cranes. Mr. Orson Crane proudly showed me around his lovely hotel, with its wonderful antique furniture and memorabilia from the time of Queen Victoria, whose family, the Kents, used it as a holiday cottage until the untimely death of the Duke. During the course of the young Victoria's stay, she came close to death when an apprentice boy who was shooting at birds in the garden, hit a window in the nursery, narrowly missing the future Queen. The hotel has a great deal of old world charm; the upstairs drawing room is oval with period furniture, and the dining room of the same shape houses an intriguing collection of period chairs. The food is excellent, including a superlative pudding trolley and an extensive wine list. It is possible for visitors to the hotel to stay in a Royal bedroom or Princess Victoria's nursery. The hotel also has a wonderfully up-to-date swimming pool. Prices start from £30.00 per night for bed and breakfast, and from £35.00 dinner, bed and breakfast in the winter. Open all year.

THE VICTORIA HOTEL
Sidmouth, Devon EX10 8RY

Telephone: 01395 512651   *Fax: 01395 579154*

London 161, Birmingham 159, Bristol 70, Exeter 15, Honiton 9, Torquay 35

F licence; 61 en suite bedrooms, all with telephone and TV; lift; night service; meals to 9.30 p.m.; diets and vegetarian menus; children welcome; dogs accepted at discretion of management; conferences max. 100; hairdressing salon; games room; entertainment; billiards; indoor and outdoor heated swimming pools and lido; sauna; solarium; spa bath; two, 18 hole putting courses; sea bathing; sailing; fishing by arrangement; squash, badminton and riding all nearby; major credit cards accepted.

Sidmouth was discovered as a resort by the affluent in Queen Victoria's day – hence the name of this imposing hotel which dominates the west end of the promenade, and has an uninterrupted view of the wide sweeping bay. The Victoria is owned by the Brend family who own other luxurious hotels, including the Royal Duchy at Falmouth (see page 2), Carlyon Bay at St. Austell (see page 8) and The Saunton Sands Hotel at Saunton Sands (see page 28). Mr. John Brend, Managing Director, is very much in evidence looking after the needs of the guests, with the help of his efficient and friendly staff. The ground floor creates an impression of space and good taste; everything is planned for your comfort and well-being. The restaurant has a first class reputation for its cuisine, the table d'hôte and à la carte menus reaching high levels in quality, presentation and service. The wine list is comprehensive and well chosen. Upstairs, the well appointed bedrooms are comfortable and pleasantly furnished. Set in 5 acres of landscaped gardens, with many outside attractions, I can recommend The Victoria to all ages. Room and breakfast from £66.00 single, £61.00 double per person (including VAT). Other terms on application, including special Out of Season breaks. Open all year.

GABRIEL COURT HOTEL
Stoke Gabriel, Nr. Totnes, South Devon TQ9 6SF

Telephone: 01803 782206   *Fax: 01803 782333*

London 198, Paignton Station 4, Totnes 4, Kingswear 7, Torquay 6

R & R licence; 19 en suite bedrooms (2 ground floor), all with telephone, colour TV, radio, hairdryer and tea/coffee making facilities; baby listening; TV lounge; diets; children welcome; dogs accepted; guests' laundry facilities; outdoor heated swimming pool; croquet; sea bathing; fishing; riding nearby; golf (Churston 3 miles); open all year.

Situated in the picturesque village of Stoke Gabriel on the River Dart, the Gabriel Court Hotel, a 15th century manor house, is a haven of peace and tranquillity. Early maturing gardens reflecting the climatic conditions of the area, are stocked with unusual plants, magnificent magnolias, box hedges and yew archways. The garden supplies the restaurant with fresh vegetables and herbs, whilst energetic guests will enjoy the heated outdoor swimming pool. Bedrooms are well furnished, with lovely peaceful views and all have full facilities. There are several good size family suites. Michael and Eryl Beacom, assisted by their son Ross, are wonderful hosts, nothing is too much trouble for them or their excellent staff. A delightful dining room has views of the gardens enhanced by a large magnolia. Gabriel Court has always had an excellent reputation for its food, and fresh fish from Brixham and Exmoor venison are specialities. This is a thoroughly comfortable and peaceful hotel, I can highly recommend it. Dinner, room and full English breakfast from £59.50 per person, inclusive of VAT.

HOMERS HOTEL
Warren Road, Torquay, Devon TQ2 5TN

Telephone: 01803 213456   *Fax: 01803 213458*

Exeter Airport 22, Plymouth 30, London 190, Birmingham 190

R & R licence; 14 en suite bedrooms (1 ground floor), all with direct dial telephone and TV; room service; baby listening; last orders for dinner 9.30 p.m.; bar meals; special diets; children welcome; dogs accepted by prior arrangement; conferences max. 50; sea bathing; sailing/boating; leisure centre, golf and tennis nearby; theatre trips, riding, archery, shooting/fishing by arrangement; open all year; all major credit cards accepted.

With one of the most superb views in Torquay, Homers Hotel is perfectly situated, with gardens sloping down, and its own path leading to the promenade and beach. Torquay is a lovely town in the heart of the English Riviera, offering theatre trips, good shopping, a wonderful leisure centre and much more. Gerry Clarke and Guy Mansell are the new resident proprietors of Homers, and their refurbishing programme has begun with the bedrooms. These are comfortable, individually designed, and the fabrics used are striking and most original. As you would expect, all are en suite, and many have sea views with some having balconies. The comfortable lounges also have views of the sea, as has the attractive south-west facing dining room. The cuisine at Homers offers a choice of à la carte or table d'hôte menus. To accompany your meal, the inexpensive wine list includes some special wines for the discerning palate! An added bonus for *Signpost* readers, is that this excellent hotel is also very good value for money – the price for dinner, room and breakfast is from £32.50 per person, including VAT. So, with good food, good prices and an ideal location, why not treat yourself to a relaxing and interesting break at Homers. This 3 star hotel, is 4 Crown Commended by the English Tourist Board.

IMPERIAL HOTEL
Torquay, Devon TQ1 2DG

Telephone: 01803 294301   *Telex: 42849*   *Fax: 01803 298293*

London 200, Birmingham 200, Bristol 100, Exeter 22, Plymouth 30

F licence; 167 en suite bedrooms, including 17 suites, all with telephone and colour TV; full central heating; lift; 24 hour room service; light bar meals; diets; children welcome; baby listening; dogs accepted; conferences max. 350; receptions and functions welcome; dancing Friday and Saturday; indoor heated swimming pool; leisure centre – solarium, sauna, gymnasium, massage, spa bath, slimming therapy; outdoor heated swimming pool; tennis; squash; croquet; sea bathing; sailing; golf, riding, shooting, including clay pigeon, fishing – fresh and deep sea – all by arrangement; all major credit cards accepted.

With its commanding cliff-top position, The Imperial offers superb panoramic views of Torbay and is set within five acres of beautifully tended sub-tropical gardens. The Prince of Wales – later King Edward VII – made numerous visits as have other Royal guests through the years. Managed by Mr. Charles Barker, The Imperial provides a peaceful haven for those wishing to relax, and the opportunity for the more active to sample many sporting activities in the hotel's own leisure centre. With a long and renowned tradition for its cuisine, The Imperial is the venue for the famous "Gastronomic Weekends" when world famous chefs present their own and regional specialities, accompanied by well-chosen wines. As you would expect, all the public rooms and bedrooms are spacious and luxuriously furnished, and most of the bedrooms have balconies. Many of the staff have given years of service and you can be assured of a warm and friendly welcome to this excellent hotel. Tariff on application. Open all year. A Forte Grand Hotel.

LIVERMEAD HOUSE HOTEL
Sea Front, Torquay, Devon TQ2 6QJ

Telephone: 01803 294361   *Fax: 01803 200758*

Plymouth Airport 26, Exeter 30, London 190

F licence; 64 en suite bedrooms, all with direct dial telephone and TV; room service; baby listening; night service; 2 lifts; last orders for dinner 8.30 p.m.; bar meals; special diets; children welcome; guide dogs only; conferences max. 300; snooker/billiards room; outdoor heated swimming pool; sauna; solarium; gymnasium; squash court; sea bathing; sailing/boating; leisure centre 900 yards; 18 hole golf course, 3 miles; open all year; most credit cards accepted.

Mrs. Sylvia Rew and family, own and personally run this excellent and wonderfully situated hotel on Torquay's seafront. A guest house in the last century, one of the hotels most famous visitors was Charles Kingsley, author of *The Water Babies*. Livermead House has been considerably enlarged and modernised since then, and guests can enjoy the extensive grounds and the hotel's many facilities which include an outdoor heated swimming pool, small gym, sauna, solarium and a squash court. The Kingsley Suite offers excellent conference facilities, and wedding receptions and banquets are also well catered for. The sixty four spacious bedrooms are all en suite, and are beautifully decorated and appointed, many having panoramic views of Torbay. There are also some charming four-poster rooms. Whilst staying at Livermead House, I enjoyed a delicious meal from the traditional menus, in the elegant silver service restaurant. Fresh fish is often available, the puddings are superb, and there is a wide choice of wines. I know that *Signpost* readers will enjoy this comfortable and first-class hotel, where I found the owners to be charming, and some of the most attentive staff I have ever encountered. Room and breakfast from £30.00, dinner, room and breakfast from £40.00. Prices quoted are low season rates, and include VAT.

WATERSMEET HOTEL
Mortehoe, Woolacombe, Devon EX34 7EB

Telephone: 01271 870333 *Fax: 01271 870890*

Taunton 62, Bristol 79, Barnstaple 14, Exeter 56

F licence; 26 bedrooms (1 ground floor suite) all with private bathroom, remote control colour TV; direct dial telephones; children welcome; meals till 8.30 p.m.; light lunches; diets; pool table; games room; outdoor heated swimming pool; grass tennis court; bathing, sandy beach – private steps to seashore; surfing and sailing, boating, sea and river fishing, riding and 3 golf courses all nearby; lovely walks – National Trust; all major credit cards accepted.

Watersmeet, with its south facing terraced gardens and private steps leading to the beach below, commands a unique position with extensive sea views from Hartland Point to Lundy Island. This lovely hotel is owned and personally looked after by Brian and Pat Wheeldon, both very experienced, who have taken great care preserving the comfort and style of a country house. All the public rooms and bedrooms are delightfully furnished with soft colour schemes complemented by lovely fabrics. There are two bars, one an exclusive cocktail bar with comfortable lounges leading off. Candles light the octagonal Pavilion Restaurant which is designed so that every table enjoys a spectacular view of the sea. The award winning cuisine, always imaginative, has gone from strength to strength, and is simply superb. The menus are changed daily, and guests may choose from an English or an International menu. The selection of wines is well chosen. I can thoroughly recommend this well run family hotel, where the service is efficient and conveys a happy atmosphere. Dinner, room and breakfast from £49.00. Other terms, including special breaks on application. Clay pigeon shooting, bridge and painting holidays arranged. Closed December to February but office open for enquiries. Do write for their most attractive and informative brochure.

WOOLACOMBE BAY HOTEL
Woolacombe, Devon EX34 7BN

Telephone: 01271 870388   *Fax: 01271 870613*

Taunton 62, Bristol 79, Exeter 56, Barnstaple 14

F licence; 59 en suite bedrooms, all with telephone and TV; room/night service; baby listening; lift; last orders for dinner 9.30 p.m.; bar meals in bistro; special diets; children welcome; conferences max. 200; games room; snooker/billiards; short mat bowls; masseur; tennis coaching; aerobic classes; indoor and outdoor heated swimming pools; leisure centre; sauna; steam room; solarium; spa pool; 2 squash courts; 9 hole approach golf course; 2 floodlit all weather tennis courts; sea bathing (blue flag beach); sailing/boating; own motor yacht; riding, shooting and fishing nearby; hotel closed Jan.–mid Feb.; all credit cards accepted.

Rugged moors, rocky tors, endless National Trust walks on both beach and headland; picturesque villages of "old worlde" charm are the feel and freedom of Devon. Set amidst this, in six acres of quiet gardens running to three miles of golden sand, is the luxurious Woolacombe Bay Hotel, built in the halcyon days of the mid 1800's. It exudes a relaxed air of friendliness, good living, comfort and traditional service. The hotel has been extensively but sensitively modernised, combining the discreet old fashioned ambience with modern charm. Dining is simply a delight. Head Chef, Michael, prepares the best of English and Continental cooking, using the freshest local produce, and vegetarian dishes and special diets are always available: to complement the menus, is an interesting wine list, and you can also enjoy a drink in one of the relaxed bars. Guests have unlimited free use of the extensive leisure and sporting amenities (see facilities above), and the hotel's MV Frolica boat is available for charter. A magnificent ballroom and spacious lounges, combined with the outstanding facilities at the Woolacombe Bay Hotel, enables everyone to have the holiday of their choice. Energetic or relaxed – the decision is yours. Room and breakfast from £50.00 per person, dinner, room and breakfast from £65.00 per person. Prices include VAT.

QUEEN'S HOTEL
Meyrick Rd., East Cliff, Bournemouth,
Dorset BH1 3DL

Telephone: 01202 554415   *Fax: 01202 294810*

London 100, New Forest 10, Southampton 35

R & R licence; 114 en suite bedrooms, with radio, TV, direct dial telephone, tea and coffee making facilities; lift; night service; dinner to 9.00 p.m.; diets; children welcome; baby listening; dogs accepted; wide range of conference facilities & new syndicate rooms; beauty salon; leisure club with indoor swimming pool, sauna, steam room, spa pool, trymnasium & solarium; games room; dancing; sea and sailing; open all year; all major credit cards accepted.

The Queen's Hotel, set in a prime position on Bournemouth's East Cliff, enjoys a southerly aspect, benefitting from wonderful views across Poole Bay. It is part of the Arthur Young Hotel Group, with The Cumberland, The Trouville and The Cliffside, all being "sister" hotels, within the central Bournemouth area. A truly warm welcome awaits guests. All the bedrooms are stylishly decorated, and have excellent en suite facilities. Many of the rooms have their own balconies (some with sea views), and a number of luxury four-poster bedrooms and family suites are available. The restaurant has established an enviable reputation for its excellent cuisine. Menus are well chosen with wide and varied combinations offered daily. A well selected wine list complements the culinary flair, and wines to suit every palate can be savoured. The Garden Room, leading out onto a sunny patio, is the ideal venue for either a coffee, or perhaps cocktails with friends. The new Queensbury Leisure Club is the most superb addition. Facilities including the indoor pool are of the highest standards, providing a truly luxurious fitness centre. Conferences are well accommodated for, with purpose built seminar and syndicate rooms available, providing for all your business needs. All in all, the Queen's Hotel is an excellent venue, whether your stay in Bournemouth is for business or pleasure. A fitting motto used by the group is "stay Young, stay happy", and I personally could not agree more! Room and breakfast from £39.50. An AA Rosette has been awarded to Queen's for their cuisine.

THE MANOR HOTEL
West Bexington, Dorchester, Dorset DT2 9DF

Telephone: 01308 897616   *Fax: 01308 897035*

**Bridport 7, Dorchester 10, Weymouth 11, Lyme Regis 14,
Bournemouth 50, Exeter 50**

*F licence; 13 en suite bedrooms, all with direct dial telephone and TV; room
service; baby listening; last orders 9.30 p.m.; bar meals; special diets; children
welcome; conferences 60 max; sea bathing; golf 5 miles; riding 2 miles; open
all year; credit cards accepted.*

The Manor Hotel, located amidst some of the most dramatic scenery on the south
Dorset coast, is somewhere very special just waiting to be discovered. This
ancient manor house steeped in history is well mellowed with age, offering a
wonderful combination of flagstone floors, panelled walls, beamed ceilings, cellar
rooms, yet has been provided with en suite bedrooms including every modern
comfort and facility that guests could require. The décor of the en suite rooms
certainly brings the vibrance of Dorset flowers and countryside through every
window. Views are breathtaking. The natural gardens of the hotel are colourful
and well established. Beyond, is the sweeping geographical landmark of Chesil
Bank with the clear seas of Lyme Bay lapping and ebbing over miles of pebbles.
A more dramatic and scenic, yet quiet and relaxing situation for an hotel, one
could not wish to better. The cellar bar provides a varied choice of bar meals
through the day and in the evening, the elegant restaurant enjoys a fine reputation
for well chosen culinary specialities, with fresh local produce, vegetables and
especially sea food being used by the chef to present an excellent menu. A fine
wine list satisfies all tastes. Historic Dorset, Weymouth, Lyme Regis and
Abbotsbury are all within easy reach of The Manor Hotel. With the owners,
Richard and Jayne Childs stating that, for their guests, ''nothing's too much
trouble'', please discover and pamper yourself with a visit to The Manor Hotel,
a real treat! Room and breakfast from £37.00, weekly charge from £330.00.

SALTERNS HOTEL
38 Salterns Way, Lilliput, Poole, Dorset BH14 8JR

Telephone: 01202 707321   *Fax: 01202 707488*

Kingston Lacey 9, Corfe Castle 14, Stonehenge 45, London 90

R & R licence; 20 en suite bedrooms, all with direct dial telephone and TV; room service; baby listening; night service; last orders for dinner 9.30 p.m.; bar meals; special diets; children welcome; dogs accepted; conferences max. 120; games room; snooker/billiards; sea bathing; sailing/boating; open all year; all major credit cards accepted.

The setting of this charming hotel never ceases to appeal. Located on the water's edge, Salterns has the most exceptional views of Brownsea Island with the Purbecks beyond, and Salterns Marina in the foreground. This lovely hotel has a well established business clientele, and is also the ideal place for that perfect weekend break. The use of natural ash wood throughout creates 20 well appointed bedrooms, all with excellent en suite facilities. Most rooms enjoy uninterrupted harbour views, with sunsets naturally being quite spectacular. Salterns restaurant is at the heart of the hotel, offering outstanding cuisine in a most elegant dining room with superb views. Head Chef, John Sanderson, who has returned to Salterns after a six year break, now rates amongst the top chefs in England. His constant attention to detail has earned Salterns a second rosette for food, taking their reputation from strength to strength. Lunch and dinner menus change daily, and interesting wines are available, including a good list of half bottles. Here you will also find one of the finest collections of armagnacs available in the south of England – all very tempting! The hotel has its own waterside patio and pleasant grounds. Salterns is set in an unrivalled position, and with high standards, a caring service and an ever present friendly atmosphere, this hotel is well worth a visit. Room and breakfast from £72.50, and dinner, room and breakfast from £80.00, including VAT.

KERSBROOK HOTEL
Pound Road, Lyme Regis, Dorset DT7 3HX
Telephone: 01297 442596

London 152, Exeter 28, Taunton 28, Bristol 66, Southampton 76, Birmingham 156

R and R licence; 14 en suite bedrooms (3 on ground floor), all with tea, chocolate & coffee making facilities; meals to 9 p.m.; diets; children over 12 welcome; well behaved dogs welcome; colour TV lounge; restaurant open to non-residents; receptions and conferences up to 20; sea bathing; wind surfing; sailing, boating, golf, riding, shooting, river and sea fishing all nearby; Visa and Mastercard accepted.

The Kersbrook Hotel is truly a gem set amidst the unspoilt beauty of Lyme Regis, nestling unobtrusively on the majestic Dorset coastline. Kersbrook Hotel is a charming 18th century house with 1½ acres of pretty "cottage style" gardens. The care and attention of the proprietors, Eric and Jane Stephenson, have made this hotel quite immaculate. Rooms are individually decorated and provide "welcoming packs", novels for reading and a basket of fresh fruit providing that "special something" for their guests. There is a fine 1820 oak panelled bar providing a splendid atmosphere, enhanced and decorated with well chosen antiques, all of which truly complement a connoisseur's selection of outstanding scotches, brandy and superb wines. The charming and spacious, split-level, pink and white dining room is a joy, providing the ideal surroundings in which to savour the superb cuisine. Norman Arnold, the talented chef, who has worked for our Royal Family, presidents of the U.S.A., and a host of famous stars, uses fresh produce daily, to prepare and present varied and comprehensive table d'hôte and à la carte menus, also catering admirably for vegetarians. The "Quiet Room" lounge too, is most charming, following the cottage-theme of this delightful hotel. The hotel truly deserves its datastar and blue ribbon accolades. Treat yourself to the charm of Kersbrook Hotel, a sojourn here is most highly recommended. Prices from £45.00 single, and £60.00 double.

THE HAVEN HOTEL
Banks Road, Sandbanks, Poole, Dorset BH13 7QL

Telephone: 01202 707333   *Fax: 01202 708796*

London 105, Southampton 28

F licence; 96 en suite bedrooms, all with telephone and TV; room/night service; baby listening; lift; last orders 9.30 p.m.; bar meals; special diets on request; children welcome; no dogs; conferences max. 200; indoor/outdoor heated swimming pools; American hot tub; sauna; spa pool; solarium; jacuzzi; gym; all weather flood-lit tennis court; squash court; aromatherapist/masseuse; sea bathing, sailing/boating; golf and riding 3 miles; shooting/fishing by arrangement; open all year; major credit cards accepted.

The Haven Hotel at Sandbanks must occupy one of the finest positions of any hotel on the south coast of England. It is situated on the deep water entrance to Poole Harbour where marine activity abounds. All 96 bedrooms are well-appointed, and décor reaches new heights of excellence. The public rooms, bars, sun lounge and Sea View Restaurant are tastefully presented, creating an aura of sophistication throughout, with friendly attentive service by a professional team of staff. The luxury of relaxing on leather sofas prevails in the Marconi Lounge from where Guglielmo Marconi sent his first wireless messages; the "message" transmitted today is of a first class hotel. The Sea View Restaurant's cuisine is supervised by an award winning chef, Carl Heinz-Nagler, who provides a buffet and carvery luncheon, and in the evenings, discerning diners can savour culinary delights from the table d'hôte and gourmet selected menus. La Roche Restaurant also serves excellent food from à la carte menus, and overlooks the sea. The purpose built Business Centre has individual suites and seminar rooms to cater for all requirements, and the numerous facilities of the Leisure Centre are again, superb. The ultimate luxury must be to charter the hotel's own yacht for a cruise around the bay. All in all, this is a first class hotel. Room and breakfast from £65.00 per night, and weekly, half board rates from £570.

KNOLL HOUSE HOTEL
Studland Bay,
Dorset BH19 2AH

Telephone: 01929 450251   *Fax: 01929 450423*

London 113, Swanage 3, Bournemouth 8, Studland 1, Corfe Castle 6

C licence; 79 bedrooms (many ground floor), comprising 30 family suites, 29 single, 20 twin bedded rooms; 57 private bathrooms; 5 lounges; children's dining room; self-service laundry; 3 games rooms; solarium; children's disco in season; colour TV room; 9 acre golf course; 2 hard tennis courts, playground, outdoor swimming and paddling pools; full leisure centre; gift shop; adjoins clean sandy beach, safe bathing; Isle of Purbeck Golf Club 2 miles, 2 courses; no credit cards.

This delightful hotel is situated on the finest stretch of Dorset heritage coastline, surrounded by some of the prettiest countryside in the West and it is well worth a visit. It is within a National Trust Reserve and overlooks three miles of golden beach with first class swimming, fishing, boating and wind-surfing. Knoll House is an independent country house hotel under the personal management of its family owners and is set in pine trees with the most attractive gardens where you can relax away from the cares of everyday life. The sporting facilities are numerous – tennis courts, a nine-hole par 3 golf course and outdoor heated

42

swimming pool. For relaxation there is a sauna, steam-room, Jacuzzi, plunge-pool, solarium and gym set in a marvellous health hydro complex with fruit juice and coffee bar. Many of the bedrooms are arranged as suites, ideal for families. Log fires and an attractive cocktail bar add to the unique atmosphere of this extremely efficiently run hotel. The quality, choice and presentation of the menus is excellent. At lunchtime a superb hors d'oeuvres selection and buffet table laden with cold meats, pies and salads is a speciality, followed by delicious puddings and a good English cheeseboard. Young children are catered for in their own dining room and there are many and varied facilities to keep them amused all day. Sandbanks and Bournemouth are easily reached by the nearby car ferry, with Dorchester, Corfe Castle and the picturesque villages of Dorset only a short drive away. The hotel is open from April to October. Half board from £53.00 daily, or full board (weekly) £380.00 (April) – £550.00 (August). Generous full board terms for five nights out of season.

Old Harry Rocks and Studland Bay. ↓ K.H.

← K.H.

MANOR HOUSE HOTEL
Studland Bay, Nr. Swanage, Dorset BH19 3AU
Telephone: 01929 450288

London 113, Swanage 3, Bournemouth 8, Dorchester 26, Corfe Castle 6

R & R licence; 18 en suite bedrooms, all with colour TV, radio, tea/coffee making facilities, telephone, hairdryer and full central heating; last orders for dinner 8.30 p.m.; bar lunches; vegetarian diets; children over 5 welcome; dogs allowed; sea bathing 3 miles, with sandy beach, sailing and boating; 2 tennis courts (hard); riding; golf within 2 miles; Mastercard and Visa cards accepted.

The site of the Manor House Hotel is mentioned in the Domesday Book, and parts of the present rambling Gothic House, date back to 1750. Set within 16 acres of elevated grounds, the hotel commands beautiful views overlooking the beaches and waters of Studland Bay. History and character are in abundance; the hotel's medieval carvings are said to have come from the residential quarters of Corfe Castle, home of the famous Mary Banks, who defended it so bravely against Cromwell's troops. The bedrooms are all en suite, and are individually decorated with great charm and style. Four rooms have four-poster beds, and most have spectacular views over the bay and out to Old Harry Rocks. Wall carvings in the Westminster Bedroom are of particular interest, reputed to have been from the old Palace of Westminster, circa 1636. All the reception rooms enjoy lovely views and those with old panelling, glow on winters evenings when the fires are lit. A delightful conservatory has extended the dining area, where décor is sophisticated, and the atmosphere and service is most warming. The menu has an excellent choice of fresh local produce and the delicious Studland Lobster is a must! The hotel has recently been awarded an AA Rosette for Good Food. The Manor House Hotel is the ideal base from which to explore the beauty of Studland, its conservation area, beaches, nature trails and in general, the many attractions of Dorset. Dinner, room and breakfast from £46.00. Hotel closed Christmas and January.

SPRINGFIELD COUNTRY HOTEL
& LEISURE CLUB

Grange Road, Wareham, Dorset BH20 5AL

Telephone: 01929 552177   *Fax: 01929 551862*

Poole 10, Bournemouth 15, Southampton 35, London 120

F licence; 32 en suite bedrooms with showers, all with direct dial telephone, TV, radio & tea/coffee making facilities; baby listening; lift; room service; night porter; last orders for dinner Sun.–Fri. 9.00 p.m. & Sat. 9.30 p.m.; bar meals; special diets; children over 2yrs welcome; dogs by arrangement; games room; snooker/billiards; tennis court; outdoor heated swimming pool; new sports and leisure club with indoor heated swimming pool, spa, saunas, steam rooms, solarium, gymnasium & squash courts; open all year; most credit cards accepted.

The Springfield Country Hotel, set in 6 acres of beautifully landscaped gardens at the foot of the Purbeck Hills, is situated one mile from the market town of Wareham. It is ideal for visiting local attractions such as Lulworth Cove, Corfe Castle, Dorchester and the nearby resorts of Poole and Swanage. For golf enthusiasts, there are three 18 hole golf courses within the locality, and a discount is arranged with one of the clubs. Each of the 32 bedrooms has delightful views across the grounds, which feature an ornamental lake and waterwheel. All types of rooms are available, including family suites and ground floor rooms, and there is a lift to take you to the first floor. Both the à la carte and table d'hôte menus offer a wide choice of delicious dishes, carefully cooked to perfection, and complemented by good value, quality wines from around the world. The oak beamed lounge bar leads out onto an attractive patio area, providing the perfect setting for bar meals, afternoon teas or evening aperitifs. The dining room and new large function suite can accommodate conferences, wedding receptions and business meetings. Syndicate rooms and audio visual aids are also available. Springfield's new leisure club enjoys a wealth of superb attractions, including a large gymnasium with the latest computerised equipment. This 4 Crown Commended hotel, is a first class family run establishment with outstanding facilities, where a warm Dorset welcome is always guaranteed. Room and breakfast from £58.00 single, £90.00 double, including VAT.

THE WALNUT TREE INN
North Petherton, Bridgwater, Somerset TA6 6QA

Telephone: 01278 662255   *Fax: 01278 663946*

Bridgwater 1½, M5 (exit 24) 1, Taunton 8, Wells 12, Bristol 35, Exeter 40

F licence; 28 en suite bedrooms (3 for the disabled), all with direct dial telephone and TV; room service; baby listening; night service; last orders for dinner 10.00 p.m.; bar meals; special diets; children welcome; conferences max. 70; solarium; extensive parking facilities; open all year; all major credit cards accepted.

The Walnut Tree Inn is a former 18th Century coaching inn, set in the heart of the pretty Somerset village of North Petherton, on the A38. Traditional values have been maintained here over the years. All the rooms are quietly located at the rear of the Inn, and every possible comfort is provided for guests. Each of the twenty eight bedrooms offer superb amenities. The décor is tasteful and warming, and the four-poster bed suite is a popular choice for those seeking a special or romantic weekend break. Three spacious meeting rooms are available, seating up to seventy people. These have all the usual support facilities, along with visual aids. Any business meeting here is bound to be successful! The Walnut Tree also specialises in receptions and parties – or whatever the celebration may be. The public rooms of the hotel have an abundance of charm and character. The popular bar with Cottage Room Restaurant, can tempt you with real ales, light bar snacks and succulent steaks. However, first class international cuisine can be savoured in the beautiful Sedgemoor Restaurant. Presentation, service and excellent wines complement this more formal setting in which to enjoy a memorable repast. The Walnut Tree Inn is a hostelry of high standards with friendly staff attending to your every need. Well located for touring the South West. Do sample the charm of this hotel, and you are bound to return. Room and breakfast from £31.00, dinner, room and breakfast from £44.00. Prices include VAT.

ALFOXTON PARK
Holford, Bridgwater, Somerset TA5 1SG

Telephone: 01278 741211

Bridgwater 11, Taunton 13, Minehead 15, London 167

R & R licence; 18 en suite bedrooms (1 for the disabled), all with TV; room service; last orders for dinner 8.45 p.m.; bar meals available for residents; special diets on request; children welcome; outdoor heated swimming pool; riding approx. 2 miles; 18 hole golf course approx. 7 miles; hotel closed during the winter; major credit cards accepted.

After a mile's drive through the lovely woodland, off the main A39 road, you arrive at Alfoxton Park. The hotel is a fine Queen Anne period house, set in fifty acres of undulating parkland and woods. From the position of Alfoxton, on the slopes of the Quantock Hills, the location commands the most spectacular and breathtaking views across the Bristol Channel and on to the distant Welsh coast. A thousand years of history can be directly traced to dwellings on the site, and dating from 1710, Alfoxton Park has many original features giving it a wonderful character and atmosphere. All the bedrooms are en suite and provide the facilities that ensure the comfort of guests. The décor is light and attractive, and complements the warm, historic, relaxing atmosphere that can be found throughout the hotel. The bar is set in a fine panelled room, and the dining room, of more classical style, commands beautiful views across the grounds. A wonderful walled kitchen and herb garden provide organically grown produce which is constantly used in the varied menus, based upon the best of British cooking. The well selected wine list, and friendly, attentive service is most welcoming. Alfoxton Park is a lovely hotel at which to stay, and for walking, swimming, or simply travelling through Somerset, I can thoroughly recommend it as a homely base. Room and breakfast from £38.00 and dinner, room and breakfast from £49.00. Prices are per person and include VAT.

COMBE HOUSE HOTEL
Holford, Nr. Bridgwater, Somerset TA5 1RZ

Telephone: 01278 741382, Guests 741213

**London 153, Birmingham 132, Bridgwater 12, Bristol 45,
Minehead 15, Dunster Castle 12**

*R & R licence; 20 bedrooms all with direct dial telephone and tea/coffee facilities;
colour TV; 17 with private bathrooms, four poster bed; central heating; children
welcome; meals to 8.30 p.m.; dogs welcome but not in public rooms; tennis;
croquet; indoor swimming pool; solarium; Visa, Mastercard, Amex accepted.*

This 17th century house is situated off the A39 at Holford amid romantic and
beautiful surroundings in the heart of the Quantock Hills, famous for their wildlife, red deer and ponies. Combe House Hotel, which was acquired in 1976 by
the resident proprietors, Mr. and Mrs. Bjergfelt, stands in its own grounds of five
acres half a mile from the main road, with lovely gardens and a wonderful 100
year-old monkey puzzle tree. For the actively inclined there is a hard tennis court,
croquet lawn and indoor heated swimming pool. The hotel is furnished to a high
standard with genuine period furniture and attractive décor throughout and there
is a fine collection of Royal Danish Christmas plates. Of the well appointed and
comfortable bedrooms, seventeen have private bathrooms en suite. Great care
is taken over the preparation and presentation of the meals, where fresh fruit
and vegetables feature prominently on the menu. Good riding stables nearby
provide suitable mounts for all ages to ride over the moors and forests of the
surrounding hills. Golf is available at Minehead and Enmore and a championship
course at Burnham-on-Sea. Room and breakfast from £35.00 (single) and £68.00
(twin). Open March to November. Write for colour brochure to R. S. Bjergfelt.

SWAN HOTEL
Sadler Street, Wells, Somerset BA5 2RX

Telephone: 01749 678877   *Fax: 01749 677647*

Glastonbury 6, Bath 21, Bristol 21

F licence; 38 en suite bedrooms, all with direct dial telephone and TV; room service; baby listening; night service; last orders for dinner 9.30 p.m.; special diets; children welcome; dogs accepted; conferences max. 100; 2 squash courts; leisure centre ½ mile; golf 1 mile; open all year; all major credit cards accepted.

The Swan is a charming coaching inn, dating back to the 15th century, and ideally located in Wells, Britain's smallest cathedral city. The hotel faces the magnificent west front of Wells Cathedral, and, as expected, the atmosphere at the Swan is historic, comfortable and friendly. Welcoming log fires fill large open fire places, mellow beams enhance the stylish, warm décor, and the furnishings are cosy and attractive. The original panelling gives a unique ambience to the Swan's fine restaurant, where guests have the choice of a good selection of dishes from either the à la carte or table d'hôte menus. The fresh local produce which is carefully prepared, is complemented by a well chosen and selective wine list. The Cocktail Bar adjoins the restaurant. All the bedrooms have either bath or shower facilities, and a few feature the most beautiful, original four-poster beds. Any of the eight Honeymoon Suites, are a tempting choice of accommodation, whatever the celebration or reason for your stay! The hotel's conference centre can host individual business meetings and seminars, and the friendly and helpful staff are most efficient. The Swan Hotel is perfectly located for touring Somerset and Avon, and is highly recommended in all respects. Room and breakfast from £62.50 single, £83.50 double, including VAT.

CRUDWELL COURT HOTEL
AND RESTAURANT
Crudwell, Nr. Malmesbury, Wiltshire SN16 9EP

Telephone: 01666 577194   *Fax: 01666 577853*

London 97, Cirencester 6, Swindon 12, Malmesbury 3

R & R licence; 15 en suite bedrooms, all with telephone, remote control colour TV, radio, tea/coffee making facilities, full central heating; night service until 12 midnight; last orders 9.30 p.m.; bar meals; diets; children welcome; baby listening; dogs accepted; conferences max. 25; heated outdoor swimming pool; croquet; leisure centre, sailing, golf, tennis, squash, badminton, riding, shooting, fishing all nearby; Mastercard, Visa, Amex, Diners credit cards accepted.

What a lovely surprise to find this enchanting little hotel on my travels near to Cirencester and Malmesbury. It is a 17th century former vicarage, set alongside a Saxon church in 3 acres of beautiful walled gardens. It is really like staying in a private home – I had the most warm welcome and I certainly look forward to a return visit. The house has recently been completely refurbished and all fifteen bedrooms are individually decorated. The gracious panelled dining room and the beautiful conservatory overlook the church. The excellent cuisine is freshly prepared to order, all complemented by an extensive wine list. Crudwell Court is run by its resident owners, who give that extra personal touch to the warm, country house atmosphere. Room and breakfast from £50.00 single, £90.00 double. Weekly terms on application. Hotel is open all year.

WHATLEY MANOR
Easton Grey, Nr. Malmesbury, Wiltshire SN16 0RB

Telephone: 01666 822888   *Fax: 01666 826120*

London 98, Chippenham 10, Swindon 16, Bristol 30

R and R licence; 29 en suite bedrooms (12 ground floor), all with telephone, TV, tea/coffee making facilities, radio; full central heating; night service; diets; children welcome, baby listening; dogs welcome; conferences; sauna; solarium; jacuzzi; croquet; billiards; heated outdoor swimming pool; tennis; golf 5 miles, squash 2 miles, riding 1 mile; Amex, Mastercard, Diners, Visa cards accepted.

Whatley Manor, located on the borders of Wiltshire and Gloucestershire and on the edge of the Cotswolds, is noted for the luxury and spaciousness of both the bedrooms and public rooms. It has a real feeling of comfort and opulence, backed by unobtrusive service and excellent cuisine. The dining room has lovely views over the gardens, beyond which paddocks run down to a peaceful stretch of the river Avon. The pine panelled lounge and oak panelled drawing room, both with log fires, are elegant and provide relaxing surroundings. The Library Bar offers drinks and volumes of *Punch* dating back to the 19th century. The Manor bedrooms are furnished to a very high standard indeed. The Court House, 70 yards from the Manor, has ten more bedrooms overlooking the tennis court and grounds. The hotel is within easy reach of Badminton, Westonbirt Arboretum, Stonehenge and Longleat, to name but a few places, and the towns of Bath, Bristol, Cirencester and Swindon. Convenient for M4 and M5. Bed and full English breakfast from £85.00 single, double £112.00, inclusive of VAT and service. Short breaks also available throughout the year.

BLUNSDON HOUSE HOTEL
& LEISURE CLUB
Blunsdon, Nr. Swindon, Wiltshire SN2 4AD

Telephone: 01793 721701   *Fax: 01793 721056*

London 91, Oxford 29, Reading 40, Bristol 41, Southampton 64, Birmingham 80

*F licence; 88 en suite rooms (29 ground floor), all with telephone, radio, TV;
lift; night service; late meals to 10.30 p.m.; diets; children welcome, baby
listening; no dogs; conferences; dancing by arrangement; sauna, solarium, spa
bath, gym, beauty salon; snooker room, games room; children's adventure
playground; heated indoor swimming pool; squash; tennis; petanque; 1 mile
woodland walk/jog; 9 hole, par 3 golf course; major credit cards accepted.*

Blunsdon House stands in 30 acres of grounds off the A419, just north of Swindon.
During the last thirty years, the Clifford family have worked hard, making this
hotel the fine, modern, four-star establishment it is today. In spite of the size
of the hotel, the emphasis is still on personal service, starting with the courteous
hall porter who escorts you to your room and explains the location and operation
of the many facilities. All the accommodation is spacious and comfortable, and
there is no extra charge for children sharing their parents' room. The Ridge
Restaurant offers a high standard of food, English and continental dishes, from
daily fixed price or à la carte menus. I found the dinner and service excellent.
For a more informal meal, try Carrie's Carverie, where there is a good choice
from a fixed price menu. Three bars provide a choice of venue for your pre-lunch
or dinner drink. The hotel is 7 miles from junction 15 on M4 and on the link
road to the M5. On the edge of the Cotswolds, it is an ideal centre for Bath,
Longleat, Stonehenge, Salisbury and many other interesting places. Room and
full English breakfast from £75.00; twin/double £92.50 inclusive of VAT and
service. Getaway Breaks and Honeymoon Breaks available. Open all year.

BARGAIN BREAKS

Readers are recommended to telephone the hotels to confirm rates and conditions prior to booking.

THE WEST COUNTRY

CORNWALL

TREGLOS HOTEL, Constantine Bay — page 1
Discounts or free golf offered the last weeks in May, July and August. Discounts are also offered for non seaview rooms throughout the season. Please enquire about our special 3 day breaks.

ROYAL DUCHY HOTEL, Falmouth — page 2
Winter Breaks from £82.00, Spring and Autumn Breaks from £98.00, Early and Late Summer Breaks from £108.00 and special July Breaks from £106.00. All prices are per person for the minimum stay of 2 nights, and include dinner, bed and breakfast.

MARINA HOTEL, Fowey — page 3
For any 2 or more consecutive nights including dinner, bed and breakfast, rates start from £44.00 per day.

POLURRIAN HOTEL, Lizard Peninsula — page 4
For a special occasion or a break from the stress of life, our Feature Breaks and Leisure Breaks in this most unspoilt part of Cornwall, will provide you with a memory to treasure. 3 day breaks – dinner, room and breakfast from £105.00 per person.

HOTEL BRISTOL, Newquay — page 5
Low season breaks from 24th September 1994 – 28th May 1995 (except Christmas and New Year). Bristol Breaks; 2 nights from £80.00 per person (no charge for children under 4 years). Five Day Bristol Break – any 5 nights from £185.00 per person (no charge for children under 4 years). Other children's prices available on request.

PORT GAVERNE HOTEL, Nr. Port Isaac — page 6
"Breather" breaks off season and "Tourer" breaks for 3 or 5 nights during the season. From 1st November – "Twofers" (2 persons, bed and breakfast for the price of one). "Four-for-two" – (2 nights, dinner, bed and breakfast at standard rate, and 2 nights bed and breakfast free of charge). Terms on application.

ROSE-IN-VALE COUNTRY HOUSE HOTEL, St. Agnes — page 7
Spring, Autumn and Winter breaks are available, together with Special Interest Breaks including Cornish Gardens, Golf, Riding, Wildlife Walks, Romantic and Painting. Full details on application.

CARLYON BAY HOTEL, Nr. St. Austell — page 8
Winter Breaks (Nov.–Easter) from £85.00, Spring Breaks (April–Whitsun excluding Easter) from £132.00, Early Summer Breaks (June–July) from £136.00, Late Summer Breaks (Sept.–Oct.) from £142.00, Autumn Breaks (Oct.–Nov.) from £134.00. All rates shown are per person for a minimum stay of 2 nights, to include dinner, room and breakfast.

TREGENNA CASTLE, St. Ives — page 9
Special 3, 4 and 7 day breaks available. Prices from £99.50 for room and breakfast for 3 nights plus one free round of golf. Special Interest Breaks include Murder Mystery, Golf, Culture Breaks, Glorious Garden Breaks and Activity and Racket Sporting Breaks. Please telephone 01736 795254 for full details. Christmas and New Year programmes also available.

BOSKERRIS HOTEL, Nr. St. Ives, Carbis Bay — page 10
Low season breaks – prices on application. Golfing packages available.

THE IDLE ROCKS HOTEL, St. Mawes   *page* 12
*3 day stays: room and breakfast from £30.00, and dinner, room and breakfast
from £42.00. 6 day stays: room and breakfast from £27.00, and dinner, room
and breakfast from £39.00. Prices are per person, per night. Christmas Breaks
and Low Season Special Breaks are available – prices on application.*

ST. MORITZ HOTEL, Nr. Wadebridge   *page* 13
*Low Season Breaks at very special prices: 3, 4 and 7 day break rates available
throughout the year. Please ask for details.*

DEVON

BLAGDON MANOR COUNTRY HOTEL, Ashwater   *page* 14
*Spring, Autumn and Winter Breaks. Weekend house parties. Please call for
further details.*

TYTHERLEIGH COT HOTEL, Axminster   *page* 15
*Two day breaks available all year. Bargain Breaks from October–April, for 3 or
more consecutive nights, 4th night at half price. Christmas and New Year Breaks.
Special rates not available over Bank Holidays.*

DOWNREW HOUSE, Barnstaple   *page* 16
*Reduced rates out of season, plus special Christmas and New Year packages.
Downrew is also the ideal venue for weekend house parties; details and tariff
on application.*

THE BERRY HEAD HOTEL, Brixham   *page* 17
*Set in national parkland at the waters edge, with miles of coastal walks, fishing,
birdwatching and sailing, yet close to the major resort of Torquay, this is an ideal
hideaway for a short break. 2 nights, dinner, bed and breakfast from £66.00.*

THE HOOPS INN, Nr. Clovelly   *page* 18
*Breaks available throughout the year (excluding Christmas and New Year),
minimum 2 night stay midweek from £45.00 per person, per night to include
dinner, bed and full Devon breakfast. Weekend Breaks, minimum 2 night stay,
from £48.00 per person, per night. Activity Breaks: Golf, Cycling, Walking, Fine
Art & Food & Wine Appreciation, Romantic/Valentine Breaks to include 6 course
candlelit dinner, room and breakfast.*

THE MAYPOOL PARK HOTEL, Galmpton   *page* 19
*Midweek 3 day breaks, Gourmet Weekends, and special terms for Christmas
and New Year are all available. Prices on application.*

COMBE HOUSE, Nr. Honiton, Gittisham   *page* 20
*Bargain breaks available in November, December and March (with the exception
of 23rd December–2nd January inclusive). A 2 night stay – 10% discount off
room and breakfast rate, and for a stay of 3 or more nights – 15% discount off
room and breakfast rate. January and February: a 2 or more night stay at the room
and breakfast rate, but will include table d'hôte dinner. Hotel closed 26th
January–9th February inclusive.*

THE COTTAGE HOTEL, Hope Cove   *page* 21
*Winter Breaks are available from 1st November 1994–13th April 1995
inclusive. 2 night stay £27.25–£42.00. 3–6 night stay £26.75–£42.50. 7 night
stay £26.75–£41.50 according to room. Prices are per person, per night, and
include accommodation, 6 course dinner plus coffee, full English breakfast,
service and VAT.*

BUCKLAND-TOUT-SAINTS HOTEL, Kingsbridge   *page* 22
*From October 1994–April 1995, rates are £60.00 per person, per night, to
include dinner, room and breakfast.*

BARGAIN BREAKS

THE WHITE HART HOTEL, Moretonhampstead page 24
Available throughout the year – any 2 days from £96.00, with the 3rd day at half price. Sleep free on a Sunday, when you stay 4 days or more (either on a holiday break or bed and breakfast), also available all year. Do mention Signpost *when making your reservation.*

THE BOLT HEAD HOTEL, Salcombe page 25
Getaway Breaks available, details on request.

TIDES REACH HOTEL, Salcombe page 26
Bargain breaks available from early March–26th May 1995 (excluding Easter) and 1st–31st October 1995. 2 day breaks from £120.00 for dinner, bed and breakfast. 4 day breaks from £224.00 for dinner, bed and breakfast. Extra days pro rata.

HERON HOUSE HOTEL, Nr. Salcombe page 27
Special Winter/Spring short breakaways are available from November to March: midweek and weekend stays from £60.00 per person for 2 nights. Rates include accommodation, breakfast, 5 course dinner, service and VAT.

THE SAUNTON SANDS HOTEL, Saunton Sands page 28
A Luxury Breaks Tariff is available in addition to the hotel's main tariff, with reduced rates for stays of 2 nights or more. Spring, June and Autumn Breaks represent excellent value with prices from £58.00 per person, per night, dinner, room and breakfast. Child reductions are also available. Telephone the hotel and ask for the Luxury Breaks Tariff – 01271 890212.

THE ROYAL GLEN HOTEL, Sidmouth page 29
November until the end of April, excluding Christmas and Easter, details on application.

THE VICTORIA HOTEL, Sidmouth page 30
Bargain Breaks available at various times of the year. Winter, Spring and Autumn Breaks are particularly good value with single rooms from £54.00 and double rooms from £49.00 per person, per night, dinner, room and breakfast (minimum 2 nights). Please telephone 01395 512651 for further details.

HOMERS HOTEL, Torquay page 32
House Party Weekends are available for a minimum of 8 doubles. Price per person is £65.00, and includes accommodation, an informal supper on Friday night once everyone has arrived, full English breakfast on Saturday, a gala dinner of 6 courses on Saturday night (sample menus on request), and brunch on Sunday. Special Weekend and Christmas Breaks are also available – details on request.

IMPERIAL HOTEL, Torquay page 33
Bargain breaks available, for a minimum stay of 2 nights to include dinner, accommodation in a sea-view room, full English breakfast, service and VAT. Discounts are offered for inland facing rooms. All prices on application.

LIVERMEAD HOUSE HOTEL, Torquay page 34
November–Easter: dinner, room and breakfast from £38.00 per person, per night for a minimum stay of 2 nights, excluding Christmas and New Year.

WATERSMEET HOTEL, Woolacombe, Mortehoe page 35
Spring and Autumn Breaks, 2–4 days. Terms on application.

WOOLACOMBE BAY HOTEL, Woolacombe page 36
Special seasonal offers are available. Please enquire for further details.

DORSET

QUEEN'S HOTEL, Bournemouth *page 37*
7th October 1994–9th April 1995; 2 night stay £92.50 per person, dinner, bed and breakfast. Mini breaks, Christmas, New Year and Easter programmes, details on application.

THE MANOR HOTEL, Dorchester *page 38*
2 day stay – dinner, bed and breakfast £108.00 per person. 5 day stay – dinner, bed and breakfast, £260.00 per person.

SALTERNS HOTEL, Lilliput *page 39*
"Getaway Break" – £66.00 per person, per night based on 2 people sharing. Papers and magazines included.

KERSBROOK HOTEL, Lyme Regis *page 40*
From mid February–end of October (including Bank Holidays); 2 nights – £80.00, 5 nights – £160.00 and 7 nights – £260.00. Prices are per person, on a dinner, room and breakfast basis. Single supplement £10.00.

KNOLL HOUSE HOTEL, Studland Bay *pages 42/43*
Special breaks: Family Five (2 adults, one or 2 children under 13), 5 nights full board in low season £696.00. Purbeck Five (single or twin rooms without private bathroom), 5 nights full board in low season £232.00 per person; September 24th–19th October, 2 nights full board £110.00–£127.00 per person. Prices include VAT, there is no service charge.

MANOR HOUSE HOTEL, Studland Bay *page 44*
Special 3 or 5 night breaks – 3 days 10% off daily rate and 5 days 20% off daily rate. Inclusive 2 and 3 night riding holidays are available. Longer periods by arrangement.

SPRINGFIELD COUNTRY HOTEL, Wareham *page 45*
Prices are per person, and include en suite accommodation, full English breakfast and table d'hôte dinner. 2 nights – £120.00, 3 nights – £177.00, 4 nights – £236.00, 5 nights – £290.00, 6 nights – £348.00 and 7 nights – £399.00.

SOMERSET

ALFOXTON PARK, Holford *page 47*
Special short breaks available throughout the year, for a minimum stay of 2 nights – £44.00 per person, per night, to include dinner, bed and breakfast.

COMBE HOUSE HOTEL, Holford *page 48*
Bargain Breaks available from September–May from £75.00 for 2 nights, dinner, bed and breakfast.

SWAN HOTEL, Wells *page 49*
Getaway Breaks available for stays of 2 nights or more, to include dinner, room and breakfast, from £99.00 per couple, per night, sharing a twin/double room. Singles available at weekends only from £69.50 including VAT.

WILTSHIRE

CRUDWELL COURT HOTEL AND RESTAURANT,
Crudwell, Nr. Malmesbury *page 50*
Bargain breaks available – tariff on application.

WHATLEY MANOR, Easton Grey, Nr. Malmesbury *page 51*
Two night break, including English breakfast and dinner from £119.00 per person. Special stay-on rates for longer breaks are available.

BLUNSDON HOUSE HOTEL & LEISURE CLUB, Nr. Swindon *page 52*
Luxury and hospitality await you at Wiltshire's first family-owned 4 star hotel. The leisure club is fantastic for the family. Explore Bibury and quaint Cotswold villages or visit Avebury and a host of historic attractions. Getaway weekend breaks from £59.50 per person, per night. 7 day break from £330.50 per person.

LONDON & THE SOUTH
SELECTED LOCAL ATTRACTIONS

Historic Houses, Gardens & Parks

LONDON
Carlyle's House, Chelsea
Fenton House, Hampstead
Kensington Palace, Kensington Gardens, W8
Osterley Park, Isleworth
Tower of London, Tower Hill, EC3N
Westminster Abbey Chapter House, SW1

BEDFORDSHIRE
Luton Hoo, Luton
The Swiss Garden, Old Warden
Woburn Abbey, Woburn
Wrest Park House & Gardens, Silsoe

BERKSHIRE
Beale Wildlife Gardens, Lower Basildon
Dorney Court, Nr. Windsor
Forbury Gardens, Reading
Highclere Castle, Nr. Newbury
Maplehurham House and Watermill, Nr. Reading
Stonor House, Henley-on-Thames
Stratfield Saye House, Nr. Reading

BUCKINGHAMSHIRE
Claydon House, Nr. Winslow
Hughenden Manor, High Wycombe
Stowe Landscape Gardens, Nr. Buckingham
West Wycombe Park, Nr. High Wycombe
Waddesdon Manor, Nr. Aylesbury

HAMPSHIRE
Breamore House & Museums, Nr. Fordingbridge
Broadlands, Romsey
Exbury Gardens, Nr. Southampton
Furzey Gardens, Minstead, Nr. Lyndhurst
Highclere Castle
Lymington Vineyard
Lymore Valley Herb Garden, Nr. Milford-on-Sea
Sir Harold Hillier Gardens & Arboretum,
   Ampfield, Nr. Romsey
Stratfield Saye House & Wellington Country Park

HERTFORDSHIRE
Ashridge Estate, Nr, Berkhamsted
Cedars Park, Waltham Cross
The Gardens of the Rose, Chiswell Green, St.
   Albans
Hatfield House
Knebworth House
The National Trust Wimpole Hall, Arrington, Nr.
   Royston
Priory Gardens, Royston
Verulamium Park, St. Albans

KENT
Bedgebury National Pinetum, Nr. Goudhurst
Chilham Castle Gardens, Nr. Canterbury
Doddington Place Gardens, Nr. Sittingbourne
Godinton House & Gardens, Godington Park,
   Ashford
Goodnestone Park, Wingham, Nr. Canterbury
Iden Croft Herbs, Staplehurst
Kent Garden Vineyard, Headcorn
Penshurst Place & Gardens, Nr. Tonbridge
Sissington Garden

OXFORDSHIRE
Basildon Park, Nr. Pangbourne
Blenheim Palace, Woodstock
Cliveden, Nr. Maidenhead

OXFORDSHIRE (continued)
Peoples Park, Banbury
Rousham House & Gardens, Steeple Aston
Waterperry Gardens, Wheatley

SURREY
Clandon Park, West Clandon
Claremont Landscape Garden, Esher
Ham House, Richmond
Hampton Court Palace, East Molesey
Hatchlands Park, East Clandon
Kew Gardens (Royal Botanic Gardens), Richmond
Polesden Lacey, Great Bookham, Nr. Dorking
The RHS's Garden, Wisley, Nr. Woking
The Savill Garden, Nr. Egham
Winkworth Arboretum, Hascombe, Nr.
   Godlaming

EAST SUSSEX
Alfriston Clergy House, Alfriston
Battle Abbey, Battle
Brickwall House & Gardens, Northiam, Nr. Rye
Carr Taylor Vineyards, Hastings
Great Dixter House & Gardens, Northiam, Nr.
   Rye
Michelham Priory, Upper Dicker, Nr. Hailsham
Merriments Gardens, Hurst Green
Pashley Manor Gardens, Ticehurst
Preston Manor, Preston Park, Brighton
Sheffield Park Garden, Danehill, Nr. Uckfield

WEST SUSSEX
Denmans Garden, Fontwell, Nr. Arundel
Goodwood House, Goodwood
Leonardslee Gardens, Lower Beeding, Nr.
   Horsham
Parham House & Gardens, Parham Park, Nr.
   Pulborough
Petworth House & Park
St. Mary's House, Bramber, Nr. Steyning
Standen, East Grinstead
Wakehurst Place Gardens, Ardingly, Nr.
   Haywards Heath

Walks & Nature Trails

BEDFORDSHIRE
Greensand Ridge Walk, from Leighton Buzzard to
   Gamlingay
Upper Lea Valley Walk, from Leagrave Common
   to East Hyde

BERKSHIRE
Riverside & Country Walk to Speen Moors
Heritage Walk, Reading
The Look Out Countryside & Heritage Centre,
   Nr. Bracknell
Reading Town Trails

HAMPSHIRE
Avon Valley Path, Salisbury to Christchurch
Itchin Way, Southampton to Hinton Ampner
Solent Way, Milford-on-Sea to Emsworth
Three Castles Path, Windsor to Winchester

HERTFORDSHIRE
The Lee Valley Walk, from Ware to Stanborough
   Lakes
Tring Reservoirs

WEST SUSSEX

Burton Pond Nature Trail
Worth Way Walk, from Worth Way to East
  Grinstead

KENT

Bewl Water Walks and Rides, Nr. Lamberhurst
Cobtree Manor Park Nature Trail
The Ecological Park, Elms Vale
Hastings Country Park, Hastings
Haysden Country Park Nature Trail
The Western Heights, Dover
White Cliffs Country Trail (various walks),
  around Kent

OXFORDSHIRE

Guided Walking Tours of Oxford
Oxford Ecology Trail

▮ Historical Sites & Museums

LONDON

British Museum, Great Russell Street, WC1B
Guinness World of Records, The Trocadero
  Centre
The London Dungeon, 28–34 Tooley Street, SE1
Mall Galleries, The Mall, SW1Y
National Portrait Gallery, St. Martin's Place,
  WC2H
Natural History Museum, Cromwell Road, SW7
The Queen's Gallery, Buckingham Palace, SW1A
Royal Mews, Buckingham Palace Road, SW1W
Science Museums, Exhibition Road, SW7
The Tate Gallery, Millbank, SW1P
Tower Bridge, SE1
Victoria & Albert Museum, Cromwell Road, SW7

BEDFORDSHIRE

Bunyan Museum, Bedford
Elstow Moot Hall, Church End
Stockwood Craft Museum & Gardens
Shuttleworth Collection, Biggleswade

BERKSHIRE

Blake's Lock Museum, Reading
Foxhill Collection of Historic Carriages, Nr.
  Reading
Newbury Museum
Reading Abbey
St. George's Chapel, Windsor Castle
Windsor Castle

BUCKINGHAMSHIRE

Buckinghamshire County Museum, Aylesbury
Chiltern Brewery, Terrick, Aylesbury

HAMPSHIRE

D-Day Museum, Portsmouth
Hurst Castle, Keyhaven
New Forest Museum & Visitor Centre, Ashurst,
  Nr. Southampton
Portchester Castle
The Sammy Miller Museum, New Milton

HERTFORDSHIRE

Berkhamstead Castle
Hertford Castle
Roman Baths, Welwyn Garden City
Roman Theatre, St. Alans
Verulamium Museum, St. Albans

EAST SUSSEX

Anne of Cleves House Museum, Lewes
Bodiam Castle, Bodiam
Brighton Museum & Art Gallery
Filching Manor Motor Museum, Polegate
Hastings Castle and 1066 Story, West Hill,
  Hastings
Hove Museum & Art Gallery
Quarry Farm Rural Experience, Robertsbridge

WEST SUSSEX

Arundel Castle, Arundel

KENT

Canterbury Cathedral
The Canterbury Tales, Canterbury
The Dickens Centre, Rochester
Dover Castle & Hellfire Corner
Eurotunnel Exhibition Centre, Folkestone
Guildhall Museum, Rochester
Leeds Castle, Nr. Maidstone
Lympne Castle, Nr. Hythe
Rochester Castle

OXFORDSHIRE

Banbury Museum & Art Gallery
Broughton Castle, Banbury
Cogges Manor Farm Museum, Witney
Didcot Railway Museum
Newbury District Museum
The Oxford Story, Oxford

SURREY

Brooklands Museum, Weybridge

▮ Entertainment Venues

LONDON

Madame Tussaud's & The London Planetarium,
  Marylebone Road, NW1R
London Zoo, Regent's Park, NW1

BEDFORDSHIRE

Stagsden Bird Gardens
Whipsnade Wild Animal Park, Dunstable
Woburn Safari Park, Woburn

BERKSHIRE

Bucklebury Farm Park, Nr. Reading
Crown Jewels of the World Exhibition, Windsor
Holme Grange Craft Centre/Art Gallery,
  Wokingham
Trilakes Country Park & Fishery, Sandhurst
Wyld Court Rainforest, Nr. Newbury

BUCKINGHAMSHIRE

Flamingo Gardens & Zoological Park, Olney
Glass Craft, Holtspur, Nr. Beaconsfield
West Wycombe Caves

HAMPSHIRE

Lepe Country Park, Exbury
Marwell Zoological Park, Winchester
New Forest Butterfly Farm, Ashurst
Paultons Park, Nr. Lyndhurst
Portsmouth Sea Life Centre

HERTFORDSHIRE

Maltings Centre, St. Albans
Paradise Wildlife Park, Broxbourne
Water Hall Farm & Craft Centre, Nr. Hitchin

EAST SUSSEX
The Bluebell Railway – Living Museum, Sheffield Park, Nr. Uckfield
Hastings Sea Life Centre

WEST SUSSEX
Butlins Southcoast World, Bognor Regis
Coombes Farm Tours, Lancing
Pulborough Brooks RSPB Nature Reserve

KENT
The Butterfly Centre, Swingfield, Dover
Kent & East Sussex Steam Railway, Tenterden

KENT (continued)
Port Lympne Wild Animal Park, Mansion & Gardens, Nr. Hythe
Toy & Model Museum, Lamberhurst

OXFORDSHIRE
Cotswold Wildlife Park, Burford
CuriOXiTy (Science Gallery) Oxford
The Oxford Story, Oxford
Waterfowl Sanctuary, Nr. Hook Norton

SURREY
Birdworld, Nr. Farnham
Gatwick Zoo, Charlwood
Thorpe Park, Chertsey

LONDON & THE SOUTH
DIARY OF EVENTS 1995

January 5–15	41st LONDON INTERNATIONAL BOAT SHOW Earls Court, London SW5.
February 11	HORSE RACING, TOTE GOLD TROPHY Newbury Racecourse, Berkshire.
March 16 to April 9	IDEAL HOME EXHIBITION Earls Court, London SW5.
April 1	OXFORD *v.* CAMBRIDGE BOAT RACE Putney to Mortlake, River Thames, London.
April 2	NUTRASWEET LONDON MARATHON Blackheath/Greenwich to the Mall.
April 14–15	THE THAME EASTER ANTIQUES FAIR The Spread Eagle Hotel, Thame, Oxfordshire.
April 16	EASTER PARADE Battersea Park, London SW11.
April 29	HORSE RACING, THE WHITBREAD GOLD CUP Sandown Park Racecourse, Esher, Surrey.
May 5	EASTBOURNE INTERNATIONAL FOLK FESTIVAL Various venues, Eastbourne, East Sussex.
May 7–8	MEDIEVAL FAIR Bodiam Castle, Bodiam, East Sussex.
May 10–14	ROYAL WINDSOR HORSE SHOW Home Park, Windsor, Berkshire.
May 20	FA CHALLENGE CUP FINAL Wembley Stadium, Wembley, London.
*May 21 to June 4	RAMSGATE SPRING FESTIVAL Various venues, Ramsgate, Kent.
May 23–26	CHELSEA FLOWER SHOW Royal Hospital, London SW3.
May 29	SURREY COUNTY SHOW Stoke Park, Guildford, Surrey.

June 9–11   HORSE RACING
             Epsom Racecourse, Surrey.
             The Vodafone Oaks (Fri. 9th)
             The Vodafone Derby (Sat. 10th)

June 7–8   BEATING THE RETREAT – MASSED BANDS OF THE
             HOUSEHOLD DIVISION
             Horse Guards Parade, London SW1.

June 8–10   SOUTH OF ENGLAND AGRICULTURAL SHOW
             Showground, Ardingly, West Sussex.

June 10   TROOPING THE COLOUR
             Horse Guards Parade, London SW1.

June 12–18   STELLA ARTOIS TENNIS CHAMPIONSHIPS
             Queen's Club, London W14.

June 17–24   BROADSTAIRS DICKENS FESTIVAL
             Various venues, Broadstairs, Kent.

June 19–25   EASTBOURNE INTERNATIONAL LADIES TENNIS
             CHAMPIONSHIP
             Devonshire Park, Eastbourne, East Sussex.

June 20–23   HORSE RACING, ROYAL WEEK
             Royal Ascot Racecourse, Berkshire.

*June 23–25 OPEN AIR CONCERTS IN PETWORTH PARK
             Petworth, West Sussex.

June 26 to   WIMBLEDON LAWN TENNIS CHAMPIONSHIPS
July 9   All England Lawn Tennis Club, London SW19.

June 28 to   HENLEY ROYAL REGATTA
July 2   Henley-on-Thames, Oxfordshire.

July 8   HORSE RACING, THE CORAL ECLIPSE STAKES
             Sandown Park, Esher, Surrey.

July 13–15   KENT COUNTY SHOW
             Showground, Detling, Kent.

July 18–29   ROYAL TOURNAMENT
             Earls Court, London SW5.

July 21 to   BBC HENRY WOOD PROMENADE CONCERTS
September 16 Royal Albert Hall, London SW7.

July 22   HORSE RACING, DIAMOND DAY
             Royal Ascot Racecourse, Berkshire.

July 25–27   NEW FOREST & HAMPSHIRE COUNTY SHOW '95
             New Park Farm, Brockenhurst, Hampshire.

July 25–29   HORSE RACING, GLORIOUS GOODWOOD
             Goodwood Racecourse, Goodwood, West Sussex.

August–October	BUCKINGHAM PALACE London. State apartments open to the public.
August18–25	BROADSTAIRS FOLK WEEK Various venues, Broadstairs, Kent.
August 25 to September 3	ARUNDEL FESTIVAL Various venues, Arundel, West Sussex.
September 2–3	ENGLISH WINE FESTIVAL & REGIONAL FOOD FAIR English Wine Centre, Alfriston, East Sussex.
September 26 to October 3	HORSE OF THE YEAR SHOW Wembley Arena, Wembley, London.
October 19–29	LONDON MOTOR SHOW Earls Court, London SW5.
November 5	LONDON TO BRIGHTON RAC VETERAN CAR RUN
*November 11	LORD MAYOR'S SHOW, CITY OF LONDON
November 12	REMEMBRANCE SUNDAY CEREMONY Cenotaph, London SW1.
November 25	HORSE RACING, HENNESSY GOLD CUP Newbury Racecourse, Berkshire.
December 26	HORSE RACING, KING GEORGE VI CHASE Kempton Racecourse, Sunbury-on-Thames, Middlesex.

*Denotes provisional date

For further details contact:

The Southern Tourist Board
40 Chamberlayne Road
Eastleigh
Hampshire SO5 5JH.
Tel: 01703 620006

The South East England Tourist Board
The Old Brew House
Warwick Park, Tunbridge Wells
Kent TN2 5TU.
Tel: 01892 540766

London Tourist Board & Convention Bureau
26, Grosvenor Gardens
Victoria
London SW1W 0DU.
Tel: 0171 730 3450

THE HOWARD HOTEL
Temple Place, Strand, London WC2R 2PR

Telephone: 0171 836 3555   *Fax: 0171 379 4547*

Heathrow 16, Gatwick 28, London City Airport 6

F licence; 135 en suite bedrooms, all with direct dial telephones, TV; 24 hour room service; 3 lifts; last orders 10.30 p.m.; special diets; children welcome; conferences 200 max; major credit cards accepted.

Ideally located for business or leisure, this unique, luxury hotel is imposingly situated on the Thames where the City meets the West End. Many of the elegantly designed bedrooms which feature French marquetry furniture and tasteful marble bathrooms, enjoy the stunning panoramic view of the river as it winds between St. Paul's and Westminster. All rooms are fully air conditioned and have every possible modern convenience, including 24 hour room service. The Surrey and Westminster suites cater for small parties, while larger meetings, to a maximum of 200, may be held in the Arundel and Fitzalan suites. One can relax over an aperitif in the Temple Bar overlooking an attractively landscaped terrace, planted with flowers and shrubs. I enjoyed an excellent luncheon, beautifully presented and served, in the justifiably famous Quai d'or Restaurant, where the Renaissance décor, domed ceiling and thoughtfully chosen paintings, complemented the French haute cuisine and wines. Attentive staff anticipate your every need, some having been at the hotel for many years. This rather special hotel is under the direction of Mr. Michael P. Day, Resident Director and Mr. Nicolino Martini, General Manager. Singles £215.00, twins/double £235.00 and suites from £265.00. Rates inclusive of 17½% VAT.

THE SWAN DIPLOMAT
Streatley-on-Thames, Berkshire RG8 9HR

Telephone: 01491 873737   *Telex: 848259*   *Fax: 01491 872554*

London 50, Reading 9, Oxford 20, Newbury 13, Windsor 30, Henley 20

F licence; 46 en suite bedrooms, all with telephone, colour TV with satellite channels, mini bar, hairdryer; 24 hour room service; last orders 9.30 p.m.; light lunches; diets; children welcome, baby listening; dogs by arrangement; conferences up to 90; indoor, heated fit-pool; spa bath; multi-gym; sauna; solarium; row boat and bicycle hire; beauty treatments; golf, tennis and fishing ½ mile; shooting 5 miles; riding 5 miles; Amex, Diners', Barclaycard and Mastercard accepted.

Set on the banks of the River Thames in 23 acres of grounds, this well established hotel offers a welcoming and caring service to its guests. The spacious bedrooms, some with balconies, are individually designed and furnished and many look on to the river or have views to the Streatley hills. The comfortable lounge overlooks the river and the hotel's own island. The Riverside Restaurant enjoys an enviable reputation for its classical French cuisine, wine list and high standard of service. In addition, the hotel operates the Duck Room Brasserie, in which guests may enjoy a variety of light, seasonal dishes. Other facilities include the Reflexions Leisure Club (free membership for hotel guests during stay) and the rebuilt 19th-century Magdalen College barge – a wonderful venue for meetings or cocktail parties. There are many short walks around the hotel, a number of National Trust properties and stately homes within easy reach and arrangements can be made for golf at local courses or the hire of a river cruiser. To sum up, this is a luxurious hotel in a marvellous setting which offers plenty to do and see – or you can even just relax by the river! Bed and full English breakfast from £96.00. Service charge at guests' discretion. Open all year.

THE GORDLETON MILL HOTEL
Silver Street, Hordle, Lymington, Hampshire SO41 6DJ

Telephone: 01590 682219   *Fax: 01590 683073*

**Lymington 1½, Southampton (Eastleigh Airport) 13,
Bournemouth (Hurn Airport) 18, London 90**

*F licence; 7 bedrooms with whirlpool bath and shower (1 with shower only),
all with direct dial telephone and TV; room service; last orders for dinner 9.30
p.m.; special diets by arrangement; children over 7; small dogs only; conferences
max. 30; gastronomic restaurant; extensive gardens; riding ¼ mile; sea bathing,
sailing/boating, golf, tennis and shooting/fishing 2 miles; open all year; most
major credit cards accepted.*

Situated just outside the charming town of Lymington, famous for its Saturday
market, yachting and marine interests, and bordering the New Forest National
Park, is The Gordleton Mill Hotel. This 17th century water-mill house, has been
sympathetically refurbished, providing seven exquisitely furnished bedrooms,
and the highly acclaimed, nationally famous Provence Restaurant. Décor and
facilities throughout, are nothing less than superb. Bedrooms provide every
possible comfort, including flowers from the garden, fresh fruit and a welcoming half bottle of champagne on arrival. These all demonstrate the true style of
Gordleton Mill. The ambience and magnificent style of the Provence Restaurant,
extends out on to the attractive, riverside terrace during summer months. The
cuisine, service and comprehensive wine list are all excellent, and presentation
and atmosphere, second to none. Up to 30 delegates can benefit from the use
of the well equipped meeting room, which can also serve as an ideal setting for
that special occasion. The character and charm of this spectacular riverside
location, coupled with the high standards throughout, make the Gordleton Mill
a truly wonderful place to relax and unwind. A visit here is most highly recommended – you will be bound to return again and again. Room and breakfast
from £92.00 including VAT.

PASSFORD HOUSE HOTEL
Nr. Lymington,
Hampshire SO41 8LS

Telephone: 01590 682398   *Fax: 01590 683494*

London 93, Lymington 2, Brockenhurst 3½, Bournemouth 17

F licence; 54 bedrooms (13 ground floor), 2 suites, all with private baths, telephone, radio, colour TV; children welcome; dogs by arrangement; diets on application; indoor leisure complex with swimming pool (details below); tennis court; croquet lawn; putting green; outdoor swimming pool – heated in season; sea bathing, sailing, golf, riding all nearby; major credit cards accepted.

This lovely country house hotel is set in nine acres of grounds on the edge of the New Forest and was originally the home of Lord Arthur Cecil. It has been carefully adapted to an elegant hotel run under the personal supervision of the owners, Mr and Mrs Patrick Heritage. Passford House is ideally suited for the pursuit of many interests and forest walks and drives begin at the hotel entrance. In addition to the many outdoor activities which include a new hard tennis court, swimming pool, croquet and putting green, a very comprehensive purpose-built leisure centre has been added recently, providing an indoor swimming pool, spa pool, sauna, solarium, multi-gym, including cycling, rowing and treadmill equipment, pool table and table tennis. In the hotel the spacious lounges are elegantly furnished and comfortable with wood fires in autumn and winter. The restaurant prides itself on its high standard of cuisine which is complemented by an extensive and varied wine list. All bedrooms have bathrooms en suite with shower and are maintained to a very high standard; trouser press and hair dryers are also provided. Room and breakfast from £81.00 single, £112.00 double. Hotel open all year.

SOUTH LAWN HOTEL
Milford-on-Sea, Lymington,
Hampshire SO41 0RF

Telephone: 01590 643911   *Fax: 01590 644820*

London 96, Lymington 4, Brockenhurst 5, Barton-on-Sea 3

R and R licence; 22 bedrooms and 2 deluxe all with en suite bathrooms, ground floor bedrooms available, colour TV, radio, telephone, trouser press, hairdryers; children over 7 years welcome; no dogs; diets; full central heating; sea bathing, sailing, boating, golf, tennis, squash, riding, shooting and fishing all nearby.

It was a letter of recommendation from a local resident that led me to South Lawn Hotel which is situated about a mile from the sea at Milford. Ernst Barten and his wife have owned the hotel since 1971 and are constantly effecting improvements. Mr. Barten can be justifiably proud of the standard of cuisine that is available. The quality is particularly emphasised and French, German and English dishes predominate. Mr. Barten supervises all the cooking himself and the kitchen is absolutely spotless. The spacious bedrooms are comfortably furnished and all have private bathrooms. Here, then, is a most attractive venue from which to explore the New Forest, or take advantage of the many sporting activities that are available in the vicinity. If you approach the hotel from the direction of Christchurch and Bournemouth, please note that you have to travel through the village of Milford-on-Sea, but then South Lawn is easily found on the left hand side of the road about half a mile beyond. The Bartens are always very helpful and courteous; they extend a warm welcome to every guest. Room and English breakfast from £47.50 single, £84.00 double, including VAT. Two day Winter Breaks (twin/double) Nov–Dec £97.50 (1994), Jan–May £99.00 (1995) except Easter and Bank Holidays. Closed mid-December to mid-January.

THE CHEWTON GLEN HOTEL
New Milton, Hampshire BH25 6QS

Telephone: 01425 275341   *Fax: 01425 272310*

London 97, Bournemouth 10, Lymington 7, Lyndhurst 12

F licence; 58 bedrooms with private bath and colour TV; satellite television; meals until 9.30 p.m.; no dogs; croquet and putting on the lawn; chauffeur service; indoor and outdoor heated swimming pools, en-tout-cas tennis court; 2 indoor tennis courts; health club; 9-hole golf course in grounds; squash, boating, fishing, shooting, riding, sea bathing nearby.

Undoubtedly Chewton Glen is one of the finest hotels that Great Britain has to offer – the only privately owned, 5 Red Star hotel in the U.K. It is somewhat off the beaten track, but is within easy reach of such places as Salisbury and Winchester with their famous cathedrals, Wilton House, Broadlands, Stonehenge, Exbury Gardens, the Mary Rose and Kingston Lacey. The bedrooms are beautifully furnished and spacious, and the décor and fittings in the public rooms are of an exceptionally high standard. The guest will particularly appreciate the friendly and attentive service, which is not to be found everywhere nowadays. The luxury health club incorporates two indoor tennis courts, indoor heated swimming pool, seven treatment rooms, gymnasium, saunas, steam room, spa and hairdressing salon. These are some of the finest facilities of their kind in the U.K. To locate this lovely old house, the traveller should find Chewton Farm Road in Walkford, off the Ringwood Road, which itself lies between the A35 and the A337. The hotel is at the end of a long drive, thus ensuring quiet and privacy. A member of The Leading Hotels of the World, Relais & Chateaux. Room and breakfast for 2 persons from £195.00, inclusive of service and VAT.

HOTEL DU VIN & BISTRO
14, Southgate Street, Winchester, Hampshire SO23 9EF
Telephone: 01962 841414   *Fax: 01962 842458*

Southampton 10, Heathrow 50, Gatwick 65, London 65

F licence; 13 en suite bedrooms, all with direct dial telephone and TV; baby listening; last orders for dinner 10.00 p.m.; special diets; children welcome; dogs accepted; conferences max. 30; walled city garden; golf, tennis, riding, shooting and fishing nearby; open all year; all major credit cards accepted.

The exciting and unique partnership of Robin Hutson, a progressive young hotelier, and Gerard Basset, the country's leading sommelier and wine celebrity, has created this new and most stylish hotel, located in the city of Winchester. A strong "wine interest theme" prevails throughout, with carved bunches of grapes on fire surrounds, decorative panelling and an abundance of wine and food books; even the rooms are named after wines! All this simply enhances the elegant and fun atmosphere you will encounter at the Hotel du Vin and Bistro. The bedrooms en suite facilities are of the highest standards and quality, with modern conveniences thoughtfully provided for, and the individual décor in each room gives them a sophisticated and romantic feel. The impressive function room can accommodate up to 30 people for business meetings or private parties, and its doors open out on to the delightful walled garden. The main reception area and grand Georgian drawing room are quite beautiful. The Bistro and bar come to life with the warmth and spontaneity of the young, attentive staff. Menus are constantly changed, incorporating only the freshest local produce, resulting in some quite superb dishes. With Gerard's expertise, the wines themselves are a true education, with an interesting selection available at all prices. The cellars and vaulted "tasting room" are yet further treats to discover in this exciting new hotel. A venture that I will personally support in years to come and recommend most highly in every respect. Room and breakfast from £70.00 and dinner, room and breakfast from £110.00. Prices are for 2 people and include VAT.

STOCKS HOTEL & COUNTRY CLUB
Stocks Road, Aldbury, Nr. Tring,
Hertfordshire HP23 5RX

Telephone: 01442 851341   *Fax: 01442 851253*

**Heathrow 29, Luton Airport 19, M1 & M25 9,
Tring station 2 (mainline Euston–London)**

F licence; 18 en suite bedrooms, all with telephone and TV; room service; night porter service; last orders for dinner 9.30 p.m.; bar meals; children welcome; conferences 65 max; 18 hole golf course; putting green; golf academy; snooker; outdoor heated swimming pool; sauna; solarium; jacuzzi; steam room; gymnasium; 4 tennis courts; croquet; riding; open all year; credit cards accepted.

Stocks, an historically elegant country house hotel, dates back to 1176, and was the former home of entrepreneur Victor Lownes who turned the house into a training school for his "Bunny Girls". The house is situated in 182 acres of parkland, surrounded by 10,000 acres of National Trust property. However, it is not only a peaceful house for unwinding and enjoying the delightful relaxing atmosphere and excellent cuisine, but also offers golf and an excellent range of sporting and leisure facilities. For companies who require corporate entertainment or hospitality days, hot air ballooning, laser shooting and off-the-road driving events are all available. One can take advantage of the riding and livery stables, four tennis courts (one flood lit), gymnasium or the recently opened 18 hole golf course. However, if you prefer more gentle pursuits, there is also the country's largest jacuzzi or a snooker table to while away an hour or so. The bedrooms are most luxurious and are beautifully furnished. The Tapestry Restaurant, inviting with its crisp linen, features a seasonal table d'hôte menu, changed daily, making good use of fresh ingredients and offers an exceptional cheese-board to finish. Breakfast can be taken here or in the Conservatory which has wonderful views of the Chilterns. A visit to Stocks is thoroughly recommended whether on business or pleasure, and you will find the staff are pleasant and helpful. Room and breakfast from £75.00.

REDCOATS FARMHOUSE HOTEL
Redcoats Green, Nr. Hitchin, Hertfordshire SG4 7JR

Telephone: 01438 729500   *Fax: 01438 723322*

London 35, Cambridge 25, Hitchin 3, Hatfield 10, Woburn 15, A1(M) 1

F licence; 12 en suite bedrooms, 2 with shared bathroom (9 ground floor), all with telephone, colour TV; last orders 9.30 p.m. for Club Suppers; children welcome; baby listening; conferences max. 20; garden suitable for marquees; tennis 1 mile; Mastercard, Amex, Visa and Switch credit cards accepted.

Near Little Wymondley village, set amidst the rolling Hertfordshire countryside, yet only a few minutes away from the A1, lies the 15th century Redcoats Farmhouse. It has been in the Butterfield family for generations and in 1971, Peter and his sister Jackie Gainsford converted the building into an hotel. Today, the hotel still retains its relaxed and easy-going country atmosphere. The bedrooms, where pictures abound, are in the main house or in the adjacent converted stables, and some have exposed beams. One room is particularly suitable for a long stay as it opens onto the very pretty country garden where marquees can be erected for weddings. There are three intimate dining rooms serving outstanding cuisine, and the new conservatory which offers a less formal type of menu, is very successful. The menus, which are changed every two weeks, include a good choice of delicious dishes such as Danish herring with dill sauce and new potatoes, half a Gressingham Duckling with peach and ginger sauce or a Fillet Steak Carpetbagger. Redcoats is ideal for visiting Knebworth and Woburn Parks, Hatfield House or the Shuttleworth Aircraft Collection. To find the hotel from Junction 8 of the A1(M), take the road to Little Wymondley – not the A602 to Hitchin. Redcoats is closed from December 24th to January 5th except for Christmas lunch and New Year's Eve dinner. Room and breakfast from £60.00, other terms on application.

ST. MICHAEL'S MANOR
St. Albans, Hertfordshire AL3 4RY

Telephone: 01727 864444   *Fax: 01727 848909*

London 20, Luton 8, Heathrow 35, Gatwick 60

F licence; 22 en suite rooms, all with telephone, radio, TV; night service; late meals to 9.00 p.m.; dogs by arrangement; conferences welcome; golf nearby; tennis 1 mile; Visa, Diners, Amex and Master Card accepted.

It was a delightful surprise to discover this manor house, which has celebrated over 400 years of history, in 5 acres of beautiful grounds at the heart of Roman Verulamium, offering guests complete tranquillity. The comforts, character and quality of the house combine the best of old and new in a way which has won praise from leading commentators on British Tourism, including an award from a 'Grounds for Delight' competition. They noted, as we did, the influence of Mr. and Mrs. Newling Ward, who have owned and lived on the premises for over 30 years. They are assisted by a very professional team, led by Residential Director, Mr. Martin Richardson, and his Manager Mr. Andrew Billington. All the staff are very proud of their hotel, and take great pains to ensure their guests have a happy stay. The restaurant, with its Victorian style conservatory, enjoys lovely views over the gardens. Head Chef, Mr. Steve Juett, provides delicious à la carte and table d'hôte menus, with a special Chef's Recommendation Menu in the evening. On Sunday evenings, there is also a very popular buffet supper. I noticed too, that everything was cooked traditionally, using fresh herbs from the garden. The bedrooms are interesting, as they are all so different, with picturesque views, and all have recently refurbished bathrooms. Tariff on application.

THE CASTLEMERE HOTEL
Western Esplanade, Broadstairs, Kent CT10 1TD

Telephone: 01843 861566   *Fax: 01843 866379*

Canterbury 19, Dover 20, Deal 15, Sandwich 9, London 76

F licence; 41 bedrooms (5 ground floor), 31 with private bath, 2 four posters and 2 twin canopy rooms; all rooms have colour TV, direct dial telephones, tea/coffee making facilities, hairdryers; golf and tennis nearby; sea bathing; boating; fishing; children welcome; late meals by order; diets; dogs accepted; conferences taken; large garden; sandy beach at Dumpton Gap; Dickens Festival.

On the Western Esplanade, overlooking the sea, and away from the noise of traffic – yet within easy walking distance of Broadstairs, stands the Castlemere Hotel. Mr. W. Hyde FCHI, the proprietor since 1960, maintains his hotel to a high standard of cleanliness, and you will always be greeted and looked after with quiet courtesy. The rooms are bright and tastefully furnished. Most have en suite bathrooms and all have amenities such as tea-making facilities, hairdryer, TV, radio and so on, provided. The menu, whilst small, is selective and carefully prepared, and there is a large choice of wines. For warm days, the beach is conveniently nearby, or you may prefer the well kept gardens, which are a pleasure to sit in on cooler days. There is much to see and do in Kent, many castles, gardens and churches to visit, and of course, golf courses for the more energetic. Bed and breakfast from £37.50 single, £35.50 twin per person, according to season. Weekly rates (one day free) from £267.00 per week, 2 day rates and reduced rates for the over 55's available.

THE SPREAD EAGLE HOTEL
Thame, Oxfordshire OX9 2BW

Telephone: 01844 213661   *Fax: 01844 261380*

Oxford 13, Aylesbury 10, High Wycombe 15

*F licence; 33 en suite bedrooms (1 ground floor twin room), all with direct dial
telephone & TV; room service; baby listening; night service; last orders for dinner
10.00 p.m. (Sunday 9.00 p.m.); bar lunches; special diets; children welcome;
conferences max. 250 non-residential; fishing, country walks, golf and horse
riding nearby; hotel closed 28th–30th December; all major credit cards
accepted.*

A country market town in the heart of Oxfordshire, Thame is easily accessible
from the North and Midlands by the M1 and M25, and now the M40 has been
extended, the journey from London or Birmingham is particularly fast and simple.
The Spread Eagle is situated centrally in the town, and is a traditional coaching
inn, made famous in the twenties by its owner, an eccentric, named John
Fothergill. Fothergill's innovative cuisine attracted a distinguished clientele such
as Augustus John, Shaw, H. G. Wells and Evelyn Waugh, and his unusual
management is chronicled in his well known book "An Innkeepers Diary". I
recently stayed in the new wing of this hotel known as the Brideshead Wing,
which has 2 suites, one with a four-poster bed and 12 new bedrooms. Mr. and
Mrs. David Barrington take a great personal interest in the hotel and employ
delightful and caring staff. My candlelit dinner was superb, with a choice of two
set menus and an à la carte. David Barrington is a great wine enthusiast, and
is justifiably proud of his wine list which features over 130 wines, a number of
which are French and Italian. I happened to be staying over Easter, and was able
to enjoy Sarah Barrington's most interesting Antiques Fair which was held in
their Banqueting Suite. Thame is central for visiting many places of interest,
such as Blenhein Palace, the manors of Hughenden and Claydon, the gardens
at Waterperry, and Mattocks Rose Nursery at Nuneham Courtney. This is a
genuine hotel, run by people who really care. Room and breakfast from £75.50
double, £69.00 single, dinner, room and breakfast from £112.00 double. All prices
include VAT.

THE FEATHERS HOTEL
Woodstock, Oxford OX7 1SX

Telephone: 01993 812291   *Fax: 01993 813158*

London 59, Stratford-upon-Avon 32, Oxford 8

F licence; 17 bedrooms, including 3 suites, all with private bath, room telephone, TV and radio; last orders 9.30 p.m.; diets; children welcome; dogs welcome; conferences; golf, riding and shooting 5 miles; squash and badminton 3 miles; tennis and fishing 1 mile; major credit cards accepted.

It is always a joy for me to go to The Feathers. It is simply a really cheerful hotel, where the standards are superb, and a friendly welcome awaits you. The lunch-time bar snacks in the Whinchat Bar are excellent – beautifully presented and great value for money. If you are lucky enough to visit The Feathers on a sunny summer's day as I was, lunch is served in the pretty little garden, surrounded by lovely hanging baskets and window boxes. Whatever time of year, there is a cosy atmosphere. The beautiful dining room, with interesting menus and an extensive wine list, is available for more formal eating. This 17th century building is privately owned, and is furnished throughout with antiques, chintzes and paintings. All the bedrooms are individually and tastefully decorated. Woodstock is one of England's loveliest country towns, and its location is an ideal centre from which to visit such places as Blenheim Palace, the birthplace of Sir Winston Churchill, and Oxford, which is only 8 miles away. I thoroughly recommend this charming hotel, and look forward to my return visit. Room and breakfast from £99.00 double, including VAT and service. Special winter terms on application. Open all year.

CHASE LODGE
10 Park Road, Hampton Wick,
Kingston-upon-Thames, Surrey KT1 4AS

Telephone: 0181 943 1862   *Fax: 0181 943 9363*

Kingston-upon-Thames ¼, Hampton Court 1½, Kew Gardens 4, London 7, Wimbledon 7, Heathrow 8

R & R licence; 9 bedrooms (6 en suite), all with direct dial telephone and TV; room service; baby listening; night service; last orders for dinner 9.30 p.m.; bar meals; special diets; children welcome; dogs accepted; conferences max. 50; gymnasium 500 yards; tennis ½ mile; indoor heated swimming pool, leisure centre, squash, golf and riding 1½ miles; open all year; all major credit cards accepted.

Nigel and Denise Stafford Haworth own and personally run this extremely popular little gem of an hotel, situated just 20 minutes from the heart of London. Chase Lodge has been cleverly amalgamated from two old cottages dating back to 1870, and Nigel himself has done most of the work. Whether you are in the pretty lounge and bar area, or in one of the gorgeous bedrooms, Denise has designed the style and décor of all the rooms with such flair and charm, that you will immediately feel relaxed and at ease. Nigel also runs the kitchen with equal aplomb. The menu is imaginative, and the food is cooked and presented to perfection. Avocado with crab, langoustine and pernod, followed by roast barbary duck with a kumquat or black cherry sauce are just an example of the delicious dishes available, which can be complemented by a bottle from the very fine wine list. Meals are served in the conservatory, which is surrounded by the prettiest little floodlit courtyard garden, and light bar snacks can also be enjoyed in the adjoining sitting room. I can thoroughly recommend this hotel to anyone who is looking for comfort, relaxation and good food. Having stayed here, I am sure guests will have no trouble in understanding the reason why Chase Lodge is so popular. Room and breakfast from £25.50, dinner, room and breakfast from £42.50, inclusive of VAT.

FLACKLEY ASH HOTEL
Peasmarsh, Near Rye, East Sussex TN31 6YH

Telephone: 01797 230651　　　　　　　　　　　　*Fax: 01797 230510*

Rye 3, Dover 36, Folkestone 29, London 60, Hastings 11

F licence; 32 en suite bedrooms, all with direct dial telephone and TV; last orders 9.30 p.m.; bar meals; children welcome; dogs accepted; conferences 80 max; indoor heated swimming pool; leisure centre; sauna; solarium; spa pool; steam room; gymnasium; open all year; all major credit cards accepted.

This is one of Sussex's charming, small country house hotels. It is set in 5 acres of beautiful grounds amidst a quiet rural setting. Rye is only a few miles away with its many historic buildings including the 15th century church, the Ypres Tower, the famous Landgate and Henry James' Georgian residence, Lamb House. Local activities are many and varied, with antique shops, potteries, local crafts and boutiques. There is a market on Thursdays. Camber Sands with its beautiful beaches and safe bathing is only a few miles further on; and of course there are castles, abbeys, a cathedral and many gardens to be visited, by those who are interested in places of beauty. The hotel has an indoor swimming pool and leisure complex, with whirlpool spa, mini gymnasium, steam room, sun bed, aromatherapy and beautician, new hairdressing salon, sun terrace and croquet lawn. There are endless sporting facilities in the vicinity of Flackley Ash including tennis, golf, riding, sea bathing etc, and it is easily accessible from London via the M25, A21 and A268 to Peasmarsh, or by train via Ashford to Rye. This Georgian house offers its visitors a warm and friendly atmosphere, comfortable bedrooms with en suite bathrooms or showers and all modern amenities, including hair dryers, colour TV and tea/coffee making facilities. The dining room has an AA Rosette for its food. Dishes are interesting and well presented by friendly and willing staff. Most vegetables are locally grown and emphasis is put on fresh local fish and seafood. Good conference and reception facilities for up to 100 are available. Room and breakfast from £49.00 per person, per night, weekly rate and "Getaway Break" rates on application.

THE BRICKWALL HOTEL
Sedlescombe, Nr. Battle, East Sussex TN33 0QA

Telephone: 01424 870253   *Fax: 01424 870785*

London 55, Battle 3, Hastings 7, Eastbourne 20, Rye 10, Dover 47

R and R licence; 23 en suite bedrooms (15 ground floor), all with colour TV, radio, alarm, telephone and tea/coffee making facilities; four four -poster bedrooms; private car park; children welcome; dinner until 9.00 p.m.; sea bathing and boating 6 miles; riding 2 miles; special arrangements made with the new 18 hole golf course in Sedlescombe; heated swimming pool from April to October; credit cards accepted.

Two acres of delightful gardens adjoining the village green and its surrounding charm, create an outstanding setting for this 16th century hotel. Retaining all its basic Tudor features, both outside and within, it still offers every modern comfort. Good food, served quietly but efficiently is presented in the oak-beamed dining room, there is a well-stocked cellar, and drinks are served from the recently extended bar lounge. The constant care and individual attention given by Mr. and Mrs. Pollio and their staff creates an atmosphere of welcome and the feeling that the comfort of their guests is their first consideration. The ground-floor rooms, often hard to come by, are in very constant demand and the generous provision of three fine lounges makes for unusual freedom. The heated swimming pool is a great asset, and there is a wealth of other garden features allowing each their own kind of pleasure. The splendid Sussex countryside is all around, with its kaleidoscope of beauty and interest inviting exploration. Room and full English breakfast from £40.00 (single) and £55.00 (twin) including VAT. Mini breaks available all year. Always open.

DALE HILL HOTEL AND GOLF CLUB
Ticehurst, Wadhurst, East Sussex TN5 7DQ

Telephone:
01580 200112

Fax: 01580 201249

**London 50,
Tunbridge Wells 10,
Eastbourne 30,
Hastings 11,
Gatwick 40,
Heathrow 45**

F licence; 32 en suite bedrooms, all with telephone and TV; room/night service; baby listening; lift; last orders 10.00 p.m.; bar meals; special diets; children welcome; dogs accepted; conferences max. 50; games room; snooker/billiards; indoor heated swimming pool; leisure centre; sauna; solarium; gymnasium; golf; tennis, riding, shooting and fishing available; open all year; Visa, Mastercard and Amex accepted.

Unique comfort, style and location, together with superb facilities, can be found at the Dale Hill Hotel and Golf Club. This modern hotel is set in 300 spectacular acres, on an established, highly acclaimed parkland golf course. From the covered portico entrance, through to the open plan, two storey classic reception area, the warmth and charm of this hotel is already established. The Fairway Restaurant, from its unusual elevated situation, commands wonderful views and serves outstanding cuisine, together with a fine selection of wines. The highest standards of décor are apparent throughout the hotel, creating a stylish, sophisticated atmosphere. Each of the attractive 32 bedrooms is appointed with every facility required by the discerning guest, and most of the rooms enjoy breathtaking views. The golf course itself has been up-graded over the past few years, and you can enjoy unlimited golf during your stay at Dale Hill. A second championship standard course, designed by Ian Woosnam, will be opened in 1996. Professionally coached golfing sessions can be arranged. The amenities in the luxurious health complex are all appointed to very high standards, including, massage and selected beauty treatments. Full conference facilities and technical equipment are ready for use, and the support and advice provided, ensures the success of any meeting. This truly first class hotel is within easy reach of Tunbridge Wells and the stunning Sussex countryside where you will find historic medieval forts and castles. A stay at Dale Hill is highly recommended, whether on business or pleasure. Room and breakfast from £45.00.

CHEQUERS HOTEL
Church Place, Pulborough, West Sussex RH20 1AD

Telephone: 01798 872486   *Fax: 01798 872715*

London 49, Brighton 20, Arundel 8, Gatwick 23, Worthing 12, Chichester 12

R & R licence; 11 bedrooms (10 en suite), all with direct dial telephone, colour TV, trouser press, hair dryer and tea/coffee making facilities; room service; last orders 8.30 p.m.; bar meals; special diets to order; children welcome; dogs welcome; small meeting facilities; golf 2 miles; tennis ¼ mile; riding and clay pigeon shooting by arrangement; open all year; all major credit cards accepted.

Whilst driving through West Sussex, it is enchanting to find this small country house hotel, built during the reign of Queen Anne, situated overlooking the beautiful Arun Valley. John and Ann Searancke, proprietors of this elegant family owned hotel, which was first recorded as changing hands in 1548, extend a warm welcome to their guests. The addition of a conservatory, which looks out over the attractive and secluded garden, provides a delightful location in which to enjoy morning coffee (with delicious Danish pastries), imaginative light lunches and afternoon cream teas. In the Restaurant, recently awarded an AA Rosette, the menu changes every evening and offers a good selection. On Sunday evenings, a fine cold buffet is laid out for guests to help themselves. The wine list is varied and interesting. Every bedroom is attractive and comfortable; some have four poster beds and each is individually named and decorated, with en suite bath or shower. There are plenty of leisure and sporting facilities to enjoy within easy reach of the hotel. Of interest to the visitor to West Sussex are Arundel Castle (home of the Duke of Norfolk), Chichester, "glorious" Goodwood and of course the open countryside of the South Downs. Room and English breakfast from £47.50 single, £36.00 double per person. Bargain Breaks are also available throughout the year.

BARGAIN BREAKS

Readers are recommended to telephone the hotels to confirm rates and conditions prior to booking.

LONDON AND THE SOUTH

BERKSHIRE

THE SWAN DIPLOMAT, Streatley-on-Thames *page 63*
Please apply for our newsletter for information on our many weekend breaks and activities. From 1st April 1995–30th September 1995, Summer Weekend Breaks from £158.00 per guest. Winter Weekend Breaks from £139.50 per guest.

HAMPSHIRE

THE GORDLETON MILL HOTEL, Lymington *page 64*
All year (subject to availability): Mid Week Breaks are available Sunday–Thursday. Three course Provence dinner (including wine and coffee), accommodation and full English breakfast – from £75.00 per person, per night. Christmas, New Year and Easter packages are also available. Please enquire for prices.

PASSFORD HOUSE HOTEL, Nr. Lymington *page 65*
Special 2 day breaks, October–May excluding Bank Holidays from £115.00 per person, dinner, bed and breakfast.

SOUTH LAWN HOTEL, Milford-on-Sea *page 66*
2 day breaks; November–December 1994 twin/double £97.50, deluxe £107.50, single £102.50. January–May 1995 twin/double £99.00, deluxe £109.00, single £105.00. Additional days pro rata. Prices are per person and include full English breakfast, dinner and VAT.

HOTEL du VIN & BISTRO, Winchester *page 68*
A variety of different short breaks are available from time to time, including "wine themed weekends". Please enquire for further details.

HERTFORDSHIRE

STOCKS HOTEL & COUNTRY CLUB, Aldbury *page 69*
Weekend Package – 2 nights accommodation, full English breakfast, dinner each evening and use of all the leisure facilities from £110.00 per person inclusive of VAT.

REDCOATS FARMHOUSE HOTEL, Redcoats Green, Nr. Hitchin *page 70*
Friday and Saturday, or Saturday and Sunday in this old farmhouse, with open fires, super food and interesting wine list; what more is needed for a winter break? Prices from £95.00 per person for 2 nights. Maybe you could leave after Sunday Lunch in the conservatory at £17.50 per head.

KENT

THE CASTLEMERE HOTEL, Broadstairs *page 72*
Any 2 nights from Friday to Monday from £78.00, and over 55's from £112.50 for any 3 nights. Tariff includes accommodation with private bathroom with all usual facilities, 3 course dinner and coffee and English breakfast.

OXFORDSHIRE

THE SPREAD EAGLE HOTEL, Thame *page 73*

Easter Weekend 14th and 15th April – £149.95 per person to include meals, accommodation and entrance to hotel's own Antique Fair. Short break stays available all week from £52.00 per person, sharing accommodation, inclusive of dinner and breakfast. Country pursuits. Good centre for visiting National Trust properties and the towns and villages of Oxfordshire and the Vale of Aylesbury. Murder Mystery Weekends also available.

THE FEATHERS HOTEL, Woodstock *page 74*

Bargain breaks available –tariff on application.

SURREY

CHASE LODGE, Kingston-upon-Thames *page 75*

Discounts are available for stays of 3 nights or more. Special Christmas and New Year programmes are also on offer. Please contact the hotel for further details.

EAST SUSSEX

FLACKLEY ASH HOTEL, Peasmarsh *page 76*

Getaway half board breaks from £59.50 per person, per night – minimum 2 nights. Winter Price Buster £141.00 per person for 3 nights. Summer Price Buster £169.00 per person for 3 nights or £275.00 per person for 5 nights.

THE BRICKWALL HOTEL, Sedlescombe *page 77*

Bargain breaks available throughout the year. Further details on application.

DALE HILL HOTEL & GOLF CLUB, Ticehurst *page 78*

Superb hotel with luxury health and leisure club, situated on an established 6,200 yard golf course of gently undulating weald country in an area of outstanding natural beauty. Breaks are available from £75.00 per person, per night, to include dinner, bed, breakfast and all day golf.

WEST SUSSEX

CHEQUERS HOTEL, Pulborough *page 79*

Any 2 nights – £87.00 per person, any 3 nights – £127.00 per person, any 5 nights – £212.00 per person and any 7 nights – £290.00 per person. All prices include dinner, bed and breakfast.

EAST ANGLIA & THE EAST MIDLANDS
SELECTED LOCAL ATTRACTIONS

■ Historic Houses, Gardens & Parks

CAMBRIDGESHIRE
Anglesey Abbey, Nr. Cambridge
Burghley House, Stamford
Chilford Hundred Vineyard, Linton
Docwra's Manor Garden, Shepreth
Elton Hall, Elton
Hinchingbrooke House, Huntingdon
Kimbolton Castle
Peckover House, Wisbech
University of Cambridge Botanic Garden
Wimpole Hall, Arrington

DERBYSHIRE
Calke Abbey, Park & Gardens, Ticknall
Chatsworth House & Garden, Bakewell
Eyan Hall, Eyam
Haddon Hall, Bakewell
Kedleston Hall, Derby
Hardwick Hall, Doe Lea
Lea Gardens, Matlock
Melbourne Hall Gardens & Craft Centre
Sudbury Hall & Museum of Childhood, Sudbury

ESSEX
Audley End House & Park, Saffron Walden
BBC Essex Garden, Abridge
Bridge End Gardens, Saffron Walden
Felstead Vineyard
New Hall Vineyards, Purleigh
Ingatestone Hall
Layer Marney Tower
Priory Vineyards, Little Dunmow
RHS Garden, Rettendon, Chelmsford

LEICESTERSHIRE
Belgrave Hall, Belgrave
Stanford Hall, Lutterworth
Whatton Gardens, Loughborough

LINCOLNSHIRE
Belvoir Castle, Nr. Grantham
Belton House, Grantham
Burghley House, Stamford
Doddington Hall, Lincoln
Fulbeck Hall, Grantham
Grimsthorpe Castle, Bourne
Harlaxton Manor Gardens, Grantham
Springfields, Spalding

NORFOLK
Beeston Hall, Beeston St. Lawrence
Blickling Hall
Fairhaven Garden Trust, South Walsham
Felbrigg Hall
Fritton Lake Countryworld
Holkham Hall, Wells-next-to-the-Sea
Sandringham
Hoveton Hall Gardens, Wroxham
Mannington Gardens, Norwich
Norfolk Lavender Ltd., Heacham
Rainham Hall and Gardens, Tasburgh

NORTHAMPTONSHIRE
Castle Ashby Gardens, Castle Ashby
Canons Ashby House, Daventry
Cottesbrooke Hall, Cottesbrooke
Elton Hall, Peterborough
Deene Halll, Corby

NORTHAMPTONSHIRE (continued)
Elton Hall, Peterborough
Holdenby House Gardens, Holdenby
Hill Farm Herbs, Brigstock
Lamport Hall, Lamport
Rockingham Castle, Market Harborough

NOTTINGHAMSHIRE
Naturescape Wildflower Farm, Langar
Newstead Abbey, Linby
Wollaton Hall Natural History Museum

SUFFOLK
Blakenham Woodland Garden, Nr. Ipswich
Bruisyard Vineyard and Herb Centre
Euston Hall, Thetford
Haughley Park
Helmingham Hall Gardens
Ickworth House
Kentwell Hall, Long Melford
Melford Hall, Long Melford
Otley Hall
Somerleyton Hall & Gardens

■ Walks & Nature Trails

CAMBRIDGESHIRE
Bishops Way, north of Ely
Devil's Dyke, from north of Reach to south of Stechworth
Grafham Water Circular

DERBYSHIRE
Carsington Water, Ashbourne
Gulliver's Kingdom, Matlock Bath
Longshaw Estate, Hathersage

ESSEX
Epping Forest Centenary Walk
Essex Way, from Epping to Harwich
Forest Way, from Epping to Hatfield

LEICESTERSHIRE
Beacon Hill Country Park, Woodhouse Eaves
Bradgate Park, Newtown Linford
Burbage Common Visitor Centre, Hinkley
Melton Country Park, Melton Mowbray
Watermead Country Park, Syston
Rutland Water, Oakham

LINCOLNSHIRE
Chambers Farm Wood Forest Nature Reserve, Aply, Lincoln
Hartwholme Country Park, Lincoln
Tattershall Park Country Club, Tattershall, Lincoln

NORTHAMPTONSHIRE
Barnwell Country Park, Oundle
Brigstock Country Park, Kettering
Daventry Country Park, Daventry
Pitsford Water, Brixworth
Sywell Country Park, Exton

NOTTINGHAMSHIRE
Burntstump Country Park, Arnold
Clumber Park, Worksop
Colwick Park, Colwick
Portland Park & Visitor Centre, Kirkby-in-Ashfield
Rufford Country Park & Craft Centre, Ollerton
Rushcliffe Country Park, Ruddington
Sherwood Pines Forest Park, Edwinstowe

NORWICH
Peddars Way & Norfolk Coast Path with Weavers Way
Marriott's Way, between Norwich & Aylsham

SUFFOLK
Constable Trail
Painters Way, from Sudbury to Manningtree
Suffolk Coast Path, from Bawdsey to Kessingland
Suffolk Way, from Flatford to Lavenham

Historical Sites & Museums

CAMBRIDGESHIRE
Ely Cathedral
Imperial War Museum, Duxford
Fitzwilliam Museum, Cambridge
Oliver Cromwell's House, Ely
Cromwell Museum, Huntingdon

DERBYSHIRE
Arkwright's Cromford Mill, Matlock
Bolsover Castle, Bolsover
Blue John Museum Ollerenshaw Collection, Castleton
Hardwick Old Hall, Doe Lea
Midland Railway Centre, Ripley
National Trust Museum of Childhood, Sudbury Hall
The National Tramway Museum, Crich
Peveril Castle, Castleton

ESSEX
Central Museum and Planetarium, Southend-on-Sea
Colchester Castle
Hedingham Castle, Castle Hedingham
Maritime Museum, Harwich
National Motorboat Museum, Pitsea
The Working Silk Museum, Braintree

LINCOLNSHIRE
Bishop's Palace, Lincoln
Bolingbroke Castle, Spilsby
Lincoln Castle
Lincoln Guildhall
Tattershall Castle, Tattershall
Woolsthorpe Manor, Nr. Grantham
The Incredibly Fantastic Old Toy Show, Lincoln

NORFOLK
100th Bomb Group Memorial Museum, Dickleburgh
Alby Lace Museum and Study Centre
Ancient House Museum, Thetford
Bygones Collection, Holkham Hall, Wells-next-to-the-Sea
Bygone Heritage Village, Burgh St. Margaret

NORFOLK (continued)
Charles Burrell Museum, Thetford
City of Norwich Aviation Museum, Horsham St. Faith
Maritime Museum, Great Yarmouth
Muckleburgh Collection, Weybourne
Norfolk Rural Life Museum, Gressenhall
Shrine of our Lady of Walsingham, Walsingham
Wolverton Station Museum
Tales of the Old Gaol House, King's Lynn

NORTHAMPTONSHIRE
Boughton House, Nr. Kettering
The Canal Museum, Stoke Bruerne
Chichele College, Higham Ferrers
Lyveden New Bield, Oundle
Rushton Triangular Lodge, Rushton

NOTTINGHAMSHIRE
Holme Pierrepont Hall, Nottingham
Newark Castle
Newstead Abbey, Linby
Brewhouse Yard Museum of Social History, Nottingham
D. H. Lawrence Birthplace Museum, Eastwood, Nottingham
Nottingham Castle Museum & Art Gallery

LEICESTERSHIRE
Ashby-de-la-Zouch Castle
Bradgate House, Newtown Linford
Oakham Castle
Stanford Hall, Lutterworth
Bosworth Battlefield Visitor Centre & Country Park
Donington Collection of Grand Prix Racing Cars, Castle Donington

SUFFOLK
Bridge Cottage, Flatford
Dunwich Underwater Exploration Exhibition, Orford
Framlingham Castle
Gainsborough's House, Sudbury
Guildhall of Corpus Christi, Lavenham
Moot Hall & Museum, Aldeburgh
National Horse Racing Museum, Newmarket
Sizewell Visitors Centre, Sizewell B Power Station
Sue Ryder Foundation Museum, Cavendish
Tolly Cobbold Brewery, Ipswich
Woodbridge Museum

Entertainment Venues

CAMBRIDGESHIRE
Grays Honey Farm, Warboys
Hamerton Wildlife Centre
Linton Zoo
Peakirk Waterfowl Gardens Trust
Sacrewell Farm & Country Centre, Thornhaugh

DERBYSHIRE
American Adventure, Ilkeston
Cauldwell's Mill & Craft Centre, Rowsley
Bentley Fields Open Farm Longford
Denby Pottery Visitors Centre, Denby
Lathkill Dale Craft Centre, Bakewell
Royal Crown Derby Museum & Factory, Derby

ESSEX

Colchester Zoo
Dedham Rare Breed Farm
Layer Marney Tower
Mole Hall Wildlife Park, Widdington
Southend Sea Life Centre

LINCOLNSHIRE

Brandy Wharf Cider Centre, Gainsborough
Battle of Britain Memorial Flight, RAF Coningsby, Lincoln
The Butterfly & Falconry Park, Long Sutton
Skegness Natureland Sea Sanctuary, Skegness
Cobb Hall Craft Centre, Lincoln

NORFOLK

Banham Zoo
Kingdom of the Sea, Great Yarmouth
Norfolk Wildlife Centre & Country Park, Great Witchingham
Otter Trust, Earsham

NORFOLK (continued)

Park Farm & Norfolk Farmyard Crafts Centre, Snettisham
Pensthorpe Waterfowl Park
Thrigby Hall Wildlife Gardens, Filby

NORTHAMPTONSHIRE

Peakirk Waterfowl Gardens Trust, Peterborough

NOTTINGHAMSHIRE

The Lace Centre, Nottingham
The Tales of Robin Hood, Nottingham
Newark Air Museum, Winthorpe
Nottingham Industrial Museum, Nottingham
Patchings Farm Art Centre, Calverton
Sherwood Forest Visitor Centre & Country Park, Edwinstowe

SUFFOLK

East of England Birds of Prey and Conservation Centre, Laxfield
Suffolk Wildlife Park, Kessingland

EAST ANGLIA & THE EAST MIDLANDS
DIARY OF EVENTS 1995

April 1–2 **THRIPLOW DAFFODIL WEEKEND**
Thriplow, Cambridgeshire.

April 16–17 **THE SAXON MARKET**
West Stow Country Park & Anglo Saxon Village, West Stow, Suffolk.

April 17 **FAKENHAM RACES**
Fakenham, Norfolk.

April 18 **FLAGG POINT TO POINT RACES**
Flagg Moor, Flagg, Buxton, Derbyshire.

April 18–20 **HORSE RACING, THE CRAVEN MEETING**
Newmarket Racecourse, Newmarket, Suffolk.

May 5–6 **NOTTINGHAMSHIRE COUNTY SHOW**
Newark and Notts. Showground, Winthorpe, Newark, Nottinghamshire.

May 5–7 **HORSE RACING, THE GUINEAS MEETING**
Newmarket Racecourse, Newmarket, Suffolk.

May 6–8 **SPALDING FLOWER SHOW**
Streets of Spalding, Springfields Gardens and Festival Site, Spalding, Lincolnshire.

May 7–8 **THE KNEBWORTH COUNTY SHOW**
Knebworth House, Hertfordshire.

May 11–27 **BURY ST. EDMUNDS FESTIVAL**
Various venues in Bury St. Edmunds, Suffolk.

May 13–14 **HERTFORDSHIRE GARDEN SHOW**
Knebworth House, Hertfordshire.

May 20 **FAKENHAM RACES (EVENING MEETING)**
Fakenham, Norfolk.

May 25–31 **TISSINGTON WELL DRESSING**
(Ascension Day, service in church on May 25).
Tissington, Nr. Ashbourne, Derbyshire.

May 27–28	AIR FETE '95 RAF Mildenhall, Mildenhall, Suffolk.
May 27–29	FELLBRIGG COAST & COUNTY CRAFT FAIR Fellbrigg Hall, Fellbrigg, Norfolk.
May 31 to June 1	SUFFOLK SHOW 1995 Suffolk Showground, Ipswich, Suffolk.
June 9–25	48TH ALDEBURGH FESTIVAL OF MUSIC AND THE ARTS Snape Maltings (and various venues), Aldeburgh, Suffolk. World renowned festival including operas, concerts, recitals and exhibitions etc.
June 21–22	LINCOLNSHIRE SHOW Showground, Grange-de-Lings, Lincoln.
June 28–29	ROYAL NORFOLK SHOW 1995 (agricultural) Norfolk Showground, Norwich, Norfolk.
July 7–9	BRITISH GRAND PRIX '95 Silverstone Race Circuit, Towcester, Northamptonshire.
July 12–30	BUXTON INTERNATIONAL FESTIVAL Various venues, Buxton, Derbyshire.
July 26	SANDRINGHAM FLOWER SHOW Sandringham, Norfolk. Large flower show held in the grounds of H.M. The Queen's country retreat.
July 30 to August 11	GILBERT & SULLIVAN FESTIVAL Various venues, Buxton, Derbyshire.
*July 31 to August 6	ROBIN HOOD FESTIVAL Sherwood Forest Visitor Centre & Country Park, Edwinstowe, Mansfield, Nottinghamshire.
August 2–3	165TH BAKEWELL SHOW The Showground, Coombe Road, Bakewell, Derbyshire.
August 10–14	ENGLAND v WEST INDIES 5TH TEST MATCH Nottinghamshire County Cricket Club, Trent Bridge, Nottinghamshire.
August 31 to September 3	BURGHLEY REMY MARTIN HORSE TRIALS Burghley Park, Stamford, Cambridgeshire.
September 23–24	N.A.F.A.S. FESTIVAL OF FLOWERS The Story of Knebworth House. Knebworth House, Knebworth, Hertfordshire.
October 8	WORLD CONKER CHAMPIONSHIP Village Green, Ashton, Nr. Northampton.
November 27 to December 10	THE BONNIE PRINCE CHARLIE FESTIVAL IN DERBY – 250TH ANNIVERSARY Various commemorative events, Derby city centre.

*Denotes provisional date

For further information contact:

East Anglia Tourist Board
Toppesfield Road
Hadleigh
Suffolk IP7 5DN.
Tel: 01473 822922

East Midlands Tourist Board
Exchequergate
Lincoln
LN2 1PZ
Tel: 01522 531521

HASSOP HALL HOTEL
Hassop, Nr. Bakewell, Derbyshire DE45 1NS

Telephone: 01629 640488   *Fax: 01629 640577*

Bakewell 2½, Sheffield 14, Buxton 14, Chesterfield 14

R & R licence; 13 en suite bedrooms, all with radio, telephone, TV; full central heating; lift; phone only night service; meals to 9.30 p.m.; diets; children welcome; dogs at hotel's discretion; small conferences; dancing over New Year; all weather tennis; golf, riding and fishing nearby. Most credit cards accepted.

Mr. and Mrs. Chapman, owners of Hassop Hall Hotel, are justifiably proud of their beautiful and historic home. The original house was mentioned in the Domesday Book and the Chapmans have lived there since 1975. The gardens are beautifully stocked and have breathtaking scenery, including a lake view. Restoration is underway on a magnificent and historic ballroom in the hotel grounds. The panelling in the elegant bar is reputed to be from Sheffield Castle. The staff are charming and courteous and nothing is too much trouble for them. Conference rooms are available, as well as a very special bridal suite. Golf and fishing are nearby, and croquet and a hard tennis court are in the grounds. There are helicopter landing facilities. The excellent dinner menu is most comprehensive, and the wine list varied. From Tuesday to Friday a special two course luncheon is offered at £9.90 including coffee and VAT. Single room from £65.00, twin from £75.00, both plus breakfast which is normally served in the room. Winter breaks are available from 1st November to 31st March. Always open except for 3 days at Christmas.

RIBER HALL
Matlock, Derbyshire DE4 5JU

Telephone: 01629 582795   *Fax: 01629 580475*

**Derby 20, Nottingham 26, Chesterfield 11, Sheffield 25,
M1 Motorway (exit 28) 20 minutes**

Take the A38 from Junction 28, M1 motorway, turn on to A615 and follow 7
miles to Tansley, turn left at lane signposted Riber.

*R and R licence; 11 en suite bedrooms (7 ground floor), with radio, tea/coffee
making and bar facilities, colour TV, direct dial telephone; children over 10
welcome; meals to 9.30 p.m. (last orders); service to 11.00 p.m.; breakfast from
7.00 a.m.; small conferences; all weather tennis court; indoor swimming pool
and golf 2 miles; fishing and clay pigeon shooting by arrangement; all credit cards
accepted.*

This lovely peaceful Elizabethan manor house is set in the heart of the Derbyshire
countryside, surrounded by woods and meadows with a beautiful walled garden
to stroll in or sit and soak up its enchantment. Situated on the border of the Peak
National Park, and close to five of the finest stately houses in England, Riber
Hall is a delightful and luxurious hotel in a most tranquil setting. The bedrooms
are set around the courtyard and are of the highest standard. Five rooms have
whirlpool baths, and nine have antique four-poster beds. There are three luxury
double rooms, and all have individual colour schemes, the exquisite work of
Gill Biggin, the wife of proprietor Alex Biggin. Since it was established in 1972,
Riber Hall has been renowned for its outstanding cuisine and extensive wine
list. There is no room to describe all the pleasures at Riber Hall, so do try it, and
I am sure you will return for more. Room and Continental breakfast from £79.50
single and £98.00 double including VAT. Other rates, including 'Away
Weekends', on application. Hotel and restaurant open seven days a week
throughout the year.

MAKENEY HALL COUNTRY HOUSE HOTEL
Makeney, Milford, Derbyshire DE56 0RU

Telephone: 01332 842999   *Fax: 01332 842777*

Derby 7, Manchester 38, London 125

R & R licence; 45 en suite bedrooms, all with direct dial telephone and TV; room service; baby listening; night service; lift; last orders for dinner 9.45 p.m.; special diets; children welcome; dogs accepted at the discretion of the management; conferences max. 180; games room; table tennis; croquet; mountain bikes; golf 1 mile; tennis 2 miles; riding 3 miles; shooting/fishing 15 miles, taken by minibus; open all year; all major credit cards accepted.

Originally a wealthy mill owner's mansion, Makeney Hall stands in six acres of lovely, mature gardens overlooking the peaceful Derwent Valley. This is a wonderful base from which to explore the Peak District, several National Trust properties and so many other places of interest. A fully equipped conference room with adjoining bar caters for up to 180 business delegates, or for weddings, for which the hotel has an excellent reputation. Other smaller boardrooms are available, all equally well equipped. Breakfast and lunch is served in an elegant glass garden room overlooking the grounds. Lavinia's Restaurant, attractively panelled, provides the discerning diner with imaginative and delicious dishes, beautifully cooked and presented under the supervision of head chef, Ronnie Wyatt-Goodwin. Suites and bedrooms are traditionally and tastefully decorated with sumptuous fabrics, and eighteen of the rooms are in a covered courtyard. All the bedrooms have luxuriously equipped bathrooms and every conceivable amenity. This lovely hotel is owned by Mrs. Sonia Holmes, and I can thoroughly recommend a visit. Rooms from £65.00 inclusive of VAT, weekly rates available on application.

WASHINGBOROUGH HALL
COUNTRY HOUSE HOTEL
Church Hill, Washingborough, Lincoln LN4 1BE

Telephone: 01522 790340   *Fax: 01522 792936*

Lincoln 3, Hull 37, Peterborough 60, York 75, London 150

F licence; 12 en suite bedrooms, all with telephone, TV, hairdryer & trouser press; limited room service; last orders for dinner 8.30 p.m.; special diets; bar meals; children welcome; dogs accepted; conferences max. 50; croquet/boules; outdoor heated swimming pool (summer only); leisure centre & squash 3 miles; water skiing centre 7 miles; golf, tennis, riding & fishing nearby; closed over Christmas; all major credit cards accepted.

Washingborough Hall is a charming Georgian manor house, peacefully situated on the edge of the village, just three miles from historic Lincoln. I received a warm welcome from the owners Brian and Mary Shillaker who are very congenial hosts. The Hall is furnished and decorated throughout to create a friendly and comfortable atmosphere. Each of the 12 bedrooms is different; all are most attractive, and equipped to a very high standard. Some have four-poster beds, some spa baths, and they are named according to the décor. Mary Shillaker is a first-class chef. In the Wedgwood Restaurant, I enjoyed a delicious dinner from the table d'hôte menu, which was cooked to perfection. However, there is also an interesting à la carte available, together with a very good choice of wines. After dining, the hall, with its huge fireplace, is a most comfortable and relaxing place in which to enjoy a drink. Mary must also be congratulated on the beautiful 3 acres of gardens which she is responsible for, with her speciality being the wide variety of fuschias that she grows. Within the grounds, sheltered from the wind, is a small swimming pool which is heated in the summer months, and croquet can be played on the lawn when the weather is fine. A pleasant function room is also available to cater for up to 50 delegates. Washingborough Hall is an ideal base, as the pretty Lincolnshire Wolds are a short drive away, and the walled medieval city of Lincoln is well worth the visit. Twin room and breakfast from £69.00 including VAT, no service charge.

THE BLAKENEY HOTEL
Blakeney, Nr. Holt, Norfolk NR25 7NE

Telephone: 01263 740797   *Fax: 01263 740795*

**London 127, Cambridge 60, Norwich 25, King's Lynn 30,
Brancaster 15, Cromer 15**

*F licence; 60 en suite bedrooms (10 ground floor, 5 of which have own patio
suitable for dogs and 1 for wheelchairs), all with telephone and TV; night service;
diets; children welcome; baby listening; dogs accepted; banquet and conference
facilities; car parking; most credit cards accepted.*

The Blakeney Hotel is a traditional, privately owned and friendly hotel with
magnificent views across the estuary and salt marshes to Blakeney Point, an
area of outstanding beauty owned by the National Trust. North Norfolk is an
ideal region for relaxation. There are lovely walks, birdwatching, cycling, sailing
and fishing to enjoy. Other activities include shooting, tennis and golf which
are all nearby. The lovely city of Norwich and the port of King's Lynn are each
within an hour's drive, and close by are stately homes such as Sandringham,
pretty villages, market towns and sandy beaches. The Blakeney offers a wide
choice of accommodation. All rooms have private bathroom, colour TV and
tea/coffee making facilities. There are suites, 4 rooms with four poster beds,
a room with a balcony and a ground floor room suitable for wheelchairs. A few
bedrooms are in an adjacent annexe, some with their own patios. The restaurant
which serves a choice of good fresh food, and the cocktail bar both overlook the
quay. There are comfortable lounges, fine south facing gardens in which to relax
and new gardens overlooking the marshes. For the more energetic, the hotel has
an indoor heated swimming pool, spa bath, sauna and mini gym. Two day breaks
to include dinner, bed and breakfast from £51.00 per person, per night. See
Bargain Break section for further details. Open all year.

SOUTH WALSHAM HALL
South Walsham, Norwich, Norfolk NR13 6DQ

Telephone: 01603 270378   *Fax: 01603 270378*

Norwich 9, London 120, Great Yarmouth 11, Cromer 25

R & R licence; 17 en suite bedrooms all with colour TV and radio/alarm clocks; full central heating; meals to 10.00 p.m.; bar meals; children welcome; ideal for weddings and conferences; outdoor heated swimming pool; 2 double tennis courts; 2 squash courts; horse-riding school; sea bathing 11 miles; sailing and boating on the Broads 1 mile; golf 6 miles; credit cards accepted.

The first impression of South Walsham Hall is magnificent; having driven through a beautiful avenue of rhododendrons and yews, one suddenly sees this lovely building which stands back with lawns running down to the lake. This most attractive country mansion has been completely renovated and re-decorated under the present Swiss management. The original part of the Hall is steeped in Norfolk's history, being Elizabethan with further additions up to Victorian times. The most impressive interior feature is the beautiful 17th century staircase which leads up to ten bedrooms all named after European cities, with one magnificent bridal suite opening up to the most sumptuous bathroom. Three of the rooms can be used for a family let, and the other seven are chalet-type rooms in the courtyard. The restaurant offers a wine list for the connoisseur and an extensive menu for the gourmet. In the garden behind the Hall is a rose garden and heated swimming pool with existing plans for future sporting improvements to the 34 acre surrounds. The Hall is nine miles from Norwich and within easy reach of Yarmouth, so is an ideal place to stay, away from the bustle of the city, where one can completely relax in this wonderful setting. Free to residents, is the adjacent Fairhaven Garden Trust, a delightful, natural woodland and water gardens. Single room and breakfast from £40.00, double from £60.00 including VAT and service. Open all year.

LANGAR HALL
Langar, Nottinghamshire NG13 9HG

Telephone: 01949 860559   *Fax: 01949 861045*

Nottingham 12, London 120, York 90

R licence; 10 en suite bedrooms, all with direct dial telephones, TV; room service; baby listening; last orders for dinner 9.30 p.m.; children welcome; dogs by arrangement; conferences 20 max; own coarse fishing; golf 4 miles; Mastercard, Visa and Amex credit cards accepted.

I always love my visits to Langar Hall. The close proximity of Nottingham never ceases to amaze me, as Langar is beautifully situated overlooking the Vale of Belvoir. It is a lovely country house, built in 1837, which stands beside an early English church, with glorious views over the gardens, moat and parkland. The Hall is the family home of Imogen Skirving, where her father used to entertain famous cricketers of the 1930's. Langar Hall has delightful rooms, bursting with fine antiques and interesting pictures to be enjoyed by all. Imogen, a charming lady, and her excellent team, make every effort for their guests' happiness. Together with her chef Toby Garratt, she works to produce excellent, reasonably priced à la carte menus of French and English food. The menus, priced between £15.00 and £30.00 are kept small and varied, and include such dishes as chargrilled tuna steak with balsamic vinaigrette, local lamb, turbot, steak and chips with bernaise sauce or lobster. Recently, Imogen has extended one of her rooms to accommodate small conferences and private dinner party bookings. All the bedrooms are charming and uniquely furnished, and one has a four-poster bed. Family rooms are available in the stable block. This is a truly lovely place to stay, with a peaceful and relaxing atmosphere. Single room and breakfast, £60.00–£75.00, double room and breakfast from £80.00–£125.00.

THE OLD ENGLAND
Sutton-on-Trent, Nr. Newark,
Nottinghamshire NG23 6QA

Telephone: 01636 821216   *Fax: 01636 822347*

London 128, Newark 8, East Retford 12, Leicester 41, Lincoln 24

R & R licence; 10 en suite bedrooms (1 ground floor), all with TV; room service; last orders for dinner 9.00 p.m.; special diets; children welcome; dogs accepted; conferences max. 45; grass tennis court; shooting/fishing 4 miles; golf 8 miles; open all year; Mastercard and Visa credit cards accepted.

The Old England is a real home from home. The Pike family have run the hotel since we first published *Signpost* and, more than 55 years later, we are still pleased to recommend it. You will find Sutton Village just off the A1, north of Newark. A "Hotel" sign on the main road points in the direction of the quiet village High Street, and approximately ½ mile down on the left stands this most attractive country house. Situated in a large very well kept garden, which must be a haven of peace on a fine day, the house is continually being updated by its owners. All bedrooms have their own private bathrooms and are cheerful, cosy and well furnished. Those of you who appreciate good furniture, will be delighted with the beautifully polished antique tables and chairs in the dining room, and the many other interesting pieces and lovely old china throughout the hotel. The kitchen door is always open, for they have nothing to hide, and the food supervised by the Pike family, is really good British fare, such as steak, roasts and poached Scotch salmon, and always plenty of it. Later, I was assured by regular diners at the hotel that their high standard of food never varies. If you are travelling north or south, you can be assured of a very warm welcome at this lovely hotel. Single room and breakfast from £47.00, double from £57.00 including VAT.

THE SMOKE HOUSE
Beck Row, Mildenhall, Suffolk IP28 8DH

Telephone: 01638 713223   *Fax: 01638 712202*

**Bury St. Edmunds 10, Cambridge 20, Ipswich 30, Norwich 35,
Peterborough 45, London 70**

F licence; 105 en suite bedrooms (3 for the disabled), all on the ground floor, with direct dial telephone, TV and video; room service; baby listening; night service; last orders for dinner 10.00 p.m.; bar meals; special diets; children welcome; guide dogs only; conferences max. 150; games room; pool table; tennis court; golf, riding, shooting/fishing nearby; open all year; all major credit cards accepted.

Named after the proprietors Tony and Inez Warin's previous home in Malaya, The Smoke House is an ideal base for touring Suffolk and Cambridgeshire. The original 17th century main building is furnished in keeping with character and history, with inglenook fireplaces and oak beams, whilst the bedrooms and conference rooms are modern additions. There are two cosy bars where snacks are available and the Sunderland Lounge is used for live music and dancing. This leads onto a pretty paved patio surrounded by tubs of flowers, which is a pleasant spot to enjoy a quiet drink, and barbeques are held here in the summer months. The restaurant, adjacent to the cocktail bar, offers very good table d'hôte and à la carte menus. The latter has a limited choice but every dish is imaginative and nicely cooked, with steaks a speciality. I found the staff to be pleasant and attentive. All the bedrooms are on the ground floor and each is very well equipped with trouser press, hairdryer, tea tray, television and video player. You can choose from the selection of over 2000 films from the hotel's video library. The conference centre is first class and offers facilities for up to 120 delegates with many smaller rooms suitable for use as board rooms or syndicate rooms. Cambridge, Bury St. Edmunds, Newmarket, Thetford and Ely are all within half an hour's drive and visits to RAF Mildenhall which is close by, can be arranged. Do send for their imaginative and amusing brochure. Room and breakfast from £68.00, and dinner, room and breakfast from £80.00. Prices include VAT.

UFFORD PARK HOTEL, GOLF & LEISURE

Yarmouth Road, Ufford, Woodbridge, Suffolk IP12 1QW

Telephone: 01394 383555   *Fax: 01394 383582*

Ipswich 12, Colchester 29, Norwich 40, Stansted Airport 60, London 91

F licence; 37 bedrooms (1 for the disabled and 30 en suite), all with telephone and TV; room/night service; baby listening; last orders for dinner 9.30 p.m.; bar meals; special diets; children welcome; guide dogs accepted; conferences max. 150; 18 hole, par 70 golf course; beautician; steam room; indoor heated swimming pool; sauna; solarium; spa pool; gymnasium; open all year; all major credit cards accepted.

Suffolk is a lovely county with pretty towns and villages, and areas of outstanding natural beauty. Conveniently situated, just a few minutes from the main A12, is this unusually designed hotel – a peaceful retreat for the holidaymaker and businessman alike. Ufford Park's leisure facilities are excellent. The 18-hole parkland golf course includes 11 water hazards and a 6 acre conservation area. Resident PGA golf professional, Stuart Robertson, offers varying types of tuition breaks suitable for the novice to the scratch player. The hotel's spacious lounge bar overlooks and opens on to the course (spikes are allowed in one particular area!). During my stay, I enjoyed using the wonderful indoor swimming pool, and followed my swim with a relaxing visit to the beauty salon. There is a gym with all the necessary equipment and aerobic and step classes are available. What impressed me most was the friendliness and efficiency of all the staff throughout the hotel. Because of Ufford's unusual design, the bedrooms are of differing shapes and sizes. Some have their own small balconies overlooking the golf course, and all are well equipped and attractively furnished. The Cedar Room restaurant offers a good choice of dishes with a self-service breakfast and you can choose from the carvery or à la carte menu for dinner. The hotel has meeting facilities for 150 delegates and it is ideal for groups who wish to combine business with sport and leisure. With "Constable Country" only a short drive away, Ufford Park is well worth a visit. Twin room and breakfast from £70.00, dinner, room and breakfast from £50.00 per person. Prices include VAT.

BARGAIN BREAKS

Readers are recommended to telephone the hotels to confirm rates and conditions prior to booking.

EAST ANGLIA AND THE EAST MIDLANDS

DERBYSHIRE

RIBER HALL, Matlock *page 87*
Hideaway Break: 14th October 1994–30th April 1995, 2 nights, 2 dinners (£25.25 per dinner allowance), 2 full English breakfasts and 1 luncheon from £143.00 per person. Bank Holidays and Christmas excluded.

MAKENEY HALL COUNTRY HOUSE HOTEL, Milford *page 88*
Discover the delights of the Derbyshire countryside. From the splendour of Chatsworth to the rugged beauty of The Peak District National Park. Dinner, bed and breakfast – £95.00 for 2 days, Christmas and New Year excepted.

LINCOLNSHIRE

WASHINGBOROUGH HALL COUNTRY HOUSE HOTEL, Lincoln *page 89*
Weekend or midweek breaks are available for stays of 2 nights or more. Rates are £40.00 per person, per night.

NORFOLK

THE BLAKENEY HOTEL, Blakeney, Nr. Holt *page 90*
2 day midweek breaks from £51.00 per person, per night, special 4 day holidays from £184.00, and 7 day holidays from £322.00. Prices include dinner, bed and breakfast, per person, per day, and free use of all facilities.

SOUTH WALSHAM HALL, South Walsham, Norwich *page 91*
Weekend breaks – 1 day full board from £90.00 per couple, 2 days full board from £170.00 per couple, weekends only. Special half board terms from £50.00 single, £80.00 double for minimum of 3 nights, and from £345.00 single, £490.00 double for any 7 days. All rates apply until March 1995. Further details on application.

NOTTINGHAMSHIRE

LANGAR HALL, Langar *page 92*
Weekend breaks – room and breakfast (Main House): 2 night stay for 2 people from £135.00.

THE OLD ENGLAND, Nr. Newark *page 93*
Midweek Breaks: £39.50 per person, per night (for a minimum stay of 2 nights), including dinner, bed, breakfast and VAT.

SUFFOLK

THE SMOKE HOUSE, Mildenhall *page 94*
Short break/weekend rates for 2 nights or longer, to include dinner, room and breakfast, from £42.50 per person, per night, sharing a twin or double room.

UFFORD PARK HOTEL, GOLF & LEISURE, Woodbridge *page 95*
Two night golf and leisure breaks from £114.00 per person, inclusive of accommodation, 3 course table d'hôte dinner, full English breakfast, and use of extensive leisure facilities, including indoor deck level swimming pool, sauna, steam room, solarium, jacuzzi and fully equipped gymnasium. Christmas and New Year breaks available, as well as golf tuition breaks.

HEART OF ENGLAND
SELECTED LOCAL ATTRACTIONS

Historic Houses, Gardens & Parks

GLOUCESTERSHIRE
Berkeley Castle
Barnsley House Garden
Buscot House, Nr. Lechlade
Hidcote Manor Garden, Hidcote Bartrim
Painswick Rococo Garden
Snowshill Manor, Nr. Broadway
Stanway House, Nr. Winchcombe
Sudeley Castle & Gardens
Westonbirt Arboretum, Nr. Tetbury

HEREFORD & WORCESTERSHIRE
Abbey Dore Court Gardens
Berrington Hall, Nr. Leominster
Burford House Gardens, Burford
Eastnor Castle, Nr. Ledbury
Eastgrove Cottage Garden Nursery, Nr. Shrawley
Hagley Hall, Nr. Stourbridge
Hanbury Hall, Nr. Droitwich
Hergest Croft Gardens, Kington
Hill Court Gardens, Nr. Ross-on-Wye
How Caple Court Gardens, How Caple
Moccas Court, Moccas
The Picton Gardens at Old Court Nurseries, Colwall Village
Queenswood Country Park, Nr. Leominster
Spetchley Park, Nr. Worcester

SHROPSHIRE
Attingham Park, Nr. Shrewsbury
Benthall Hall, Broseley
Boscobel House, Nr. Albrighton
Goldstone Hall Garden, Market Drayton
Hawkstone Hall, Weston
Weston Park, Nr. Shifnal

STAFFORDSHIRE
Biddulph Grange Garden & Country Park, Biddulph
Chillington Hall, Codsall Wood
Greenway Bank Country Park, Nr. Biddulph
Hanch Hall, Lichfield
Shugborough, Milton
Trentham Gardens

WARWICKSHIRE
Arbury Hall, Nr. Nuneaton
Baddesley Clinton House
Charlecote Park, Nr. Wellesbourne
Coughton Court
Harthill Hayes Country Park, Nr. Nuneaton
Jephson Gardens, Leamington Spa
Kingsbury Water Park
Middleston Hall
Packwood House, Nr. Hockley Heath
Ragley Hall, Nr. Alcester
Ryton Organic Gardens, Coventry

WEST MIDLANDS
Aston Hall, Birmingham
Birmingham Botanical Gardens & Glasshouses, Edgbaston
Clent Hills Country Park, Nr. Stourbridge
Coombe Abbey Country Park, Nr. Coventry
Moseley Old Hall, Fordhouses
Selly Manor & Minworth Greaves, Bourneville
Sutton Park, Sutton Coldfield
Wightwick Manor, Nr. Wolverhampton

Walks & Nature Trails

GLOUCESTERSHIRE
Cotswold Water Park, South of Cirencester
Crickley Hill Country Park, Nr. Great Witcombe
Dean Heritage Centre, Nr. Cinderford
Great Western Railway Museum, Coleford
Forest of Dean Trails, starts at Cannop Ponds
Gloucester Guided Walks
Symonds Yat Forest Trail, SW of Ross-on-Wye

HEREFORD & WORCESTER
City of Hereford Guided Walks
Croft Garden Estate, Nr. Leominster
Kingsford Country Park, Wolverley
Malvern Hills Walks & Trails
Many short walks from Ross-on-Wye
The North Worcestershire Path
The Worcestershire Way

SHROPSHIRE
Broadway Tower Country Park
Cardingmill Valley, Long Mynd
Clee Hills, Cleobury Mortimer
Offa's Dyke, Clun Forest
Historic Hawkstone Park & Follies, Weston

STAFFORDSHIRE
Cannock Chase Country Park
Codsall Nature Trail
Deep Hayes Country Park, Nr. Longsdon
Manifold Valley, Nr. Waterhouses
The Wildlife Sanctuary, Nr. Cheadle

WARWICKSHIRE
Crackley Wood, Kenilworth
Edge Hill, Nr. Kineton
Hatton Locks, Nr. Warwick
Ufton Fields Nature Reserve

WEST MIDLANDS
Birmingham City Centre Canal Walk
Longmore Nature Trail, Sutton Park
Wren's Nest National Nature Reserve, Dudley

Historical Sites & Museums

GLOUCESTERSHIRE
Chedworth Roman Villa, Nr. Cheltenham
Clearwell Caves, Nr. Coleford
Corinium Museum, Cirencester
Cotswold Motor Museum & Toy Collection, Bourton-on-the-Water
Gloucester City Museum & Art Gallery
Gloucester Folk Museum
Holst Birthplace Museum, Cheltenham
Tewkesbury Abbey

HEREFORD & WORCESTER
Avoncroft Museum of Buildings, Nr. Bromsgrove
Cotswold Teddy Bear Museum, Broadway
Elgar's Birthplace, Lower Broadheath
Goodrich Castle, Nr. Ross-on-Wye
Hartlebury Castle State Rooms, Nr. Kidderminster
Hereford Cathedral
The Droitwich Spa Brine Baths
Worcester Cathedral
Worcester Royal Porcelain Dyson Perrins Museum

HEART OF ENGLAND — SELECTED LOCAL ATTRACTIONS

SHROPSHIRE

Acton Scott Historic Working Farm
Aerospace Museum, Cosford
Blists Hill Open Air Museum, Ironbridge
The Childhood & Costume Museum, Bridgnorth
Coalbrookdale Furnace & Museum of Iron
Ludlow Castle
Midland Motor Museum, Nr. Bridgnorth
Wroxeter Roman City, Nr. Shrewsbury

STAFFORDSHIRE

Bass Museum, Visitor Centre & Shire Horse
    Stables, Burton-upon-Trent
The Brindley Mill & Museum, Leek
Gladstone Pottery Museum, Longton
Lichfield Cathedral
Lichfield Heritage Exhibition & Treasury
Samuel Johnson Birthplace Museum, Lichfield
Stafford Castle
Wall (Letocetum) Roman Site, Nr. Lichfield

WARWICKSHIRE

Anne Hathaway's Cottage, Shottery
James Gilbert Rugby Football Museum, Rugby
Kenilworth Castle
Shakespeare's Birthplace, Stratford
The Shakespeare Countryside Museum & Mary
    Arden's House, Wilmcote
Warwick Castle

WEST MIDLANDS

Bantock House Museum, Wolverhampton
Birmingham Cathedral
Birmingham Museum & Art Gallery
Birmingham Museum of Science & Industry
Black Country Museum, Dudley
Broadfield House Glass Museum, Kingswinford
Coventry Cathedral
Jerome K. Jerome Birthplace Museum, Nr.
    Walsall
The Lock Museum, Willenhall
Midland Air Museum, Coventry
Museum of British Road Transport, Coventry
National Motor Cycle Museum, Bickenhill
Walsall Leather Museum

Entertainment Venues

GLOUCESTERSHIRE

Bibury Trout Farm
Birdland, Bourton-on-the-Water
Cotswold Woollen Weavers, Nr. Lechdale

GLOUCESTERSHIRE (continued)

The Model Village, Bourton-on-the-Water
Cheltenham Hall of Fame, Cheltenham
    Racecourse
Gloucester Docks
House of Tailor of Gloucester
National Birds of Prey Centre, Newent
Prinknash Bird Park, Nr. Gloucester
The Wildfowl & Wetland Trust Centre,
    Slimbridge

HEREFORD & WORCESTERSHIRE

Cider Museum & King Offa Distillery, Hereford
The Hop Pocket Hop Farm Bishops Frome
The Jubilee Park, Symonds Yat West
Severn Valley Railway, Bewdley to Bridgnorth
West Midlands Safari Park, Nr. Bewdley

SHROPSHIRE

Dinham House Exhibition Centre, Ludlow
The Domestic Fowl Trust, Honeybourne
Lickey Hill Country Park
The Shrewsbury Quest, Shrewsbury
Twyford Country Centre, Nr. Evesham

STAFFORDSHIRE

Alton Towers, Alton
Drayton Manor Family Theme Park & Zoo, Nr.
    Tamworth
Stoke-on-Trent – many china factory tours

WARWICKSHIRE

Ashorne Hall Nicledodeon, Ashorne Hill
Heritage Motor Centre, Gaydon
Royal Shakespeare Theatre, Stratford
Stratford Open Top Bus Tours
Swan Theatre, Stratford
Twycross Zoo, Atherstone

WEST MIDLANDS

Birmingham Jewellery Quarter Discovery Centre
Cadbury World, Bourneville
Cannon Hill Park, Edgbaston
Royal Doulton Crystal, Amblecote

HEART OF ENGLAND
DIARY OF EVENTS 1995

February 18–26   NATIONAL BOAT, CARAVAN & LEISURE SHOW
National Exhibition Centre, Birmingham.

February 28   SHROVETIDE FAIR & PANCAKE RACE
Market Square, Lichfield, Staffordshire.

March 7–12   WORLD FIGURE SKATING CHAMPIONSHIPS 1995
National Exhibition Centre, Birmingham.

March 14–17   HORSE RACING, FESTIVAL WEEK
Cheltenham Racecourse, Cheltenham, Glos.

March 16–19   CRUFTS DOG SHOW
National Exhibition Centre, Birmingham.

March 18   HORSE RACING, TETLEY BITTER MIDLANDS
GRAND NATIONAL
Uttoxeter Racecourse, Staffordshire.

March 20–26   WORLD INDOOR TARGET ARCHERY
CHAMPIONSHIPS
National Indoor Arena, Birmingham.

April 22   SHAKESPEARE BIRTHDAY CELEBRATIONS
Town centre, Stratford-upon-Avon, Warwickshire.

April 25–30   BRITISH INTERNATIONAL ANTIQUES FAIR
National Exhibition Centre, Birmingham.

May 5–7   MALVERN SPRING GARDEN SHOW
Three Counties Showground, Malvern, Worcestershire.

May 6–8   BBC TOP GEAR CLASSIC & SPORTSCAR SHOW
National Exhibition Centre, Birmingham.

May 7   CONCERT V.E. DAY CELEBRATION
Symphony Hall, Birmingham.

May 19–20   SHROPSHIRE & WEST MIDLANDS
AGRICULTURAL SHOW
The Showground, Berwick Road, Shrewsbury, Shropshire.

June 13–15   THREE COUNTIES AGRICULTURAL SHOW
Three Counties Showground, Malvern, Worcestershire.

June 14–18   BBC GARDENER'S WORLD LIVE
National Exhibition Centre, Birmingham.

June 15–21   MIDSUMMER MUSIC FESTIVAL
Charlecote Park, Wellesbourne, Warwickshire.

June 23–25   UPTON JAZZ FESTIVAL
Throughout city, Upton-upon-Severn, Worcestershire.

July 1–16   CHELTENHAM INTERNATIONAL FESTIVAL OF MUSIC
Cheltenham Town Hall, Cheltenham, Glos.

July 1–16   WARWICK & LEAMINGTON FESTIVAL
Various venues throughout Warwickshire.

July 3–6   THE ROYAL INTERNATIONAL AGRICULTURAL SHOW
                National Agricultural Centre, Stoneleigh, Warks.

July 7–16   BIRMINGHAM INTERNATIONAL JAZZ FESTIVAL
                Various venues around Birmingham.

July 7–16   LICHFIELD FESTIVAL
                Various venues around Lichfield, Staffordshire.

July 8–22   STRATFORD-UPON-AVON FESTIVAL
                Town Centre, Stratford, Warwickshire.

August 11–12   SHREWSBURY FLOWER FESTIVAL
                Quarry Park, Shrewsbury, Shropshire.

August 11–13   BRITISH OPEN HORSE TRIALS CHAMPIONSHIP
                Gatcombe Park, Minchin Hampton, Glos.

August 19–26   THREE CHOIRS FESTIVAL
                Gloucester Cathedral, Gloucester.

September 3   30TH ANNIVERSARY OF LAST STEAM TRAIN
                G.W.R., Toddington, Glos.

September 11   ABBOTS BROMLEY HORN DANCE
                Abbots Bromley, Staffordshire.

*September 16   DR. JOHNSON BIRTHDAY CELEBRATIONS
                Market Square, Lichfield, Staffordshire.

October 6–15   *DAILY TELEGRAPH* CHELTENHAM FESTIVAL OF
                LITERATURE
                Cheltenham Town Hall, Gloucestershire.

October 7–8   DIVE – THE INTERNTIONAL SUB-AQUA &
                WATERSPORTS SHOW
                National Exhibition Centre, Birmingham.

November 10–12 HORSE RACING, THE MACKESON GOLD CUP
                Cheltenham Racecourse, Gloucestershire.

*Denotes provisional date

For further information contact:
The Heart of England Tourist Board, Larkhill Road, Worcester WR5 2EF.
Tel: 01905 763436.

BIBURY COURT
Bibury, Gloucestershire GL7 5NT

Telephone: 01285 740337   *Fax: 01285 740660*

**London 86, Burford 10, Cheltenham 17, Cirencester 7,
Kemble Station 10, Stow-on-the-Wold 14**

F licence; 20 en suite bedrooms (3 single, 17 double/twin); 10 have four-poster beds, and all have telephone, hairdryer, colour TV; dogs welcome; small conferences; children welcome; river fishing; golf and watersports 8 miles; hunting, shooting, riding, ballooning, aerial Cotswold trips available by arrangement; Amex, Diners, Mastercard and Visa accepted.

This gracious mansion started life in 1633, and it has preserved its lovely appearance and peaceful, charming setting in an 8½ acre garden, bordered by the River Coln, to this day. The hotel is run by Anne and Andrew Johnston, and Anne's sister Jane, who give it a welcoming and friendly atmosphere. A most lovely panelled lounge with stone mullion windows leads from the flagstoned hall and the abundant fresh flowers and the attractive and comfortable furnishings make one feel really at home. Continental breakfasts, light lunches and light dinners are served in the oak beamed conservatory. In the evening, you can choose from a wide range of dishes made from only the finest ingredients in the restaurant. Bibury is such a pretty village and there are many beautiful walks from the hotel itself. You can walk down the River Coln to Coln St. Aldwyn, another charming village, in about 45 minutes and of course there are many other places of interest nearby — Bath, Oxford, Cirencester and Stratford-upon-Avon. If you are looking for good food, relaxation in a friendly home, and a warm welcome in a most beautiful part of the Cotswolds, then I highly recommend Bibury Court. Room and breakfast from £57.00 single, £76.00 double. Closed 23rd December–30th December.

ON THE PARK HOTEL & RESTAURANT
Evesham Road, Cheltenham, Gloucestershire GL52 2AH

Telephone: 01242 518898   *Fax: 01242 511526*

London 96, Stratford-upon-Avon 30, Birmingham 49, M5 2, Bath 56

R & R licence; 12 en suite bedrooms (including 3 suites), all with direct dial telephone and TV; room service; last orders for dinner 9.30 p.m.; special diets; children over 8 years welcome; dogs by arrangement; golf and riding 2 miles; tennis 1 mile; all major credit cards accepted.

At last, Cheltenham has an exclusive town house hotel. On the Park has been lovingly and caringly restored and refurbished by its enthusiastic owners, Darryl and Lesley-Anne Gregory, who made me feel most welcome. Situated on the A435, Evesham road, just in Cheltenham (less than ½ a mile from the main entrance to the famous Cheltenham Racecourse), and opposite Pittville Park, this elegant Regency house offers excellent accommodation in a very homely atmosphere. The bedrooms are beautifully appointed, and all have the most luxurious bathrooms, antique furniture, paintings and every little comfort required by today's guest. Darryl and Lesley-Anne have just added a superb extension to their hotel, which is equally elegant and blends in so well with the existing building. This includes four new bedrooms of which three are suites, a library, a reception area and cloakrooms. The restaurant is an important feature of this hotel. It is a very stylish room with a most unusual décor and lots of fresh flowers. Dinner was excellent and beautifully presented, and there is a selection of wines to complement every meal. On the Park was a very happy experience and I look forward to returning. Cheltenham is a splendid town, and whether you are on business, exploring the Cotswolds, a racing fanatic, or you just feel like spoiling yourself, then I highly recommend this lovely hotel. Single room and continental breakfast £74.50, double room from £94.00.

THE WILD DUCK INN
Drakes Island, Ewen, Nr. Cirencester,
Gloucestershire GL7 6BY

Telephone/Fax: 01285 770310

Cirencester 3½, Kemble Railway Station 1, Gloucester 23, London 93

F licence; 9 en suite bedrooms (7 ground floor), all with direct dial telephone and TV; last orders for dinner 10.00 p.m.; bar meals; special diets; children welcome; dogs accepted by arrangement; gymnasium, riding, golf, sailing and boating all nearby; open all year; most major credit cards accepted.

Ideally situated in the middle of the picturesque Cotswolds area, with the source of the Thames just one mile away, is this most charming and attractive Cotswold stone Inn. The Wild Duck itself may not date back to the days when the Thames first flowed, but the main building is believed to have been built in the middle of the 16th century. The hotel, therefore, abounds with history, and has the welcoming and friendly atmosphere of a cosy country cottage. There is a super bar which has open log fires in the winter, where you can enjoy an aperitif before dinner, and delicious lunches are served here every day. The beamed restaurant offers the highest standard of cuisine, and to my mind, is good value for money. On the ground floor, you will find seven en suite bedrooms, which have all been recently refurbished, whilst upstairs, there are two beautiful four-poster rooms. The Wild Duck has a lovely secluded garden, which has twice been runner-up in a National Pub Garden of the Year competition. The hotel is an ideal base for exploring its wonderful surrounds, and is easy to reach as the M4 and M5 are both within an half an hour drive away. For guests arriving by train, the main line railway station, which is only a mile from the Wild Duck, offers journeys to and from London in just 70 minutes. Room and breakfast from £48.00 single, including VAT.

103

TUDOR FARMHOUSE HOTEL
Clearwell, Nr. Coleford, Gloucestershire GL16 8JS

Telephone: 01594 833046   *Fax: 01594 837093*

London 125, Birmingham 55, Cardiff 50

R & R licence; 10 bedrooms (3 for the disabled), 6 with en suite bath and 4 with en suite shower; all with direct dial telephone and TV; baby listening; last orders for dinner 9.00 p.m.; children welcome; dogs accepted; mountain bikes, canoeing, abseiling, rock climbing and riding all by arrangement nearby; 2 golf courses within 2 miles; hotel open all year; all major credit cards except Diners accepted.

What a wonderful find! Nestling in the small village of Clearwell, almost touching the border of Wales, is the Tudor Farmhouse Hotel. It is a haven of warmth and charm, where you can be sure to find a friendly welcome from Richard and Deborah Fletcher. Whether you are looking to relax for a few days, are on business, or simply want to tour this wonderful area, the Tudor Farmhouse is a must. The cuisine at the hotel is outstanding, with two menus to choose from, and a good wine list to complement all dishes. The night I stayed, I enjoyed an excellent dinner of local salmon and scallops, with an abundance of fresh vegetables. You will certainly not leave the table feeling hungry, I promise! The actual house was built in the 13th century, and features oak beams and original wall panelling, and a large roughstone fireplace roars in the lounge in winter months. Some of the bedrooms are reached by an original oak spiral staircase, and they have all been refurbished to an extremely high standard, including two beautiful four-poster rooms. The other bedrooms are located in cider makers cottages and barns, which are quietly situated in the garden and are suitable as family rooms. Clearwell Caves are just a few hundred yards away, and are definitely worth a visit. There is also a Midsummer and Haloween Ball held there, so why not make a weekend of it, but do make sure to book early so you don't miss out. Room and breakfast from £42.50 single, £49.00 double and corporate business rate from £55.00 single, to include dinner, bed and breakfast. All prices include VAT.

MANOR HOUSE HOTEL
Moreton-in-Marsh, Gloucestershire GL56 0LJ

Telephone: 01608 650501   *Fax: 01608 651481*

Broadway 8, Bourton-on-the-Water 8, Stratford-upon-Avon 17, Cheltenham 22, Oxford 27, Birmingham NEC 30, London 90

F licence; 39 en suite bedrooms (4 with four posters), all with direct dial telephone and TV; room service; baby listening; night service; lift; last orders 9.30 p.m.; bar meals (lunch only); special diets; children welcome; conferences 70 max; indoor heated swimming pool; sauna; spa pool; golf 8 miles; open all year; all major credit cards accepted.

Here, in Moreton-in-Marsh, you will find a large Cotswold stone house which is steeped in history. The Manor House was originally built in about 1545 and retains many of the 16th century features, such as a priest's hiding hole and a secret passage. Recently the majority of the bedrooms have been upgraded and totally re-decorated to a high standard. They combine old world charm with all the modern amenities. The small cosy bar looks over the well kept garden which was part re-modelled and planted in 1984 by Charlotte Evans. The restaurant offers both a fixed price and an à la carte menu. The cuisine is a combination of traditional and modern cooking, providing an excellent choice. Guests can enjoy good quality fresh produce that is supplemented by a wide variety of wines. The hotel has a custom built conference centre where the facilities do not interfere with the services of the other guests. For the more energetic, the swimming pool complex is a popular place. A relaxed atmosphere pervades the hotel, enhanced by the welcoming sight of log fires in the lounges. Duncan Williams and his staff do all they can to make sure your stay will be a memorable occasion. The Manor makes an excellent place to stay whilst visiting all the Cotswold villages and surrounding countryside. Single room from £67.00, double from £87.00 including VAT and English breakfast.

THE AMBERLEY INN
Amberley, Nr. Stroud,
Gloucestershire GL5 5AF

Telephone: 01453 872565 and 872777   *Fax: 01453 872738*

London 104, Stroud Station 3, Cirencester 10, Cheltenham 16, Bristol 32, Gloucester 12

F licence; 14 en suite bedrooms, all with colour TV, radio and telephone; children welcome; bar meals; late meals; diets; drying room; golf and riding nearby.

Scenically the Amberley Inn enjoys one of the finest views in the Cotswolds, for it is perched on the very edge of a wold. It is a splendid base for the walker, artist or photographer, for, at this southern end of the Cotswolds, the wolds are much more abrupt and curious than those in the north. For the golfer, Minchinhampton's old course adjoins the Inn, with its 18-hole new course 3 miles distant. The atmosphere of the Inn is one of complete informality. The lounge bar is adjacent to The Country Bar which is a popular meeting place for local people. The bedrooms are comfortable and spotlessly clean. A very pretty Garden House has four bedrooms, which are secluded and peaceful. The dining room is popular, both with the locals and residents alike. There are normally three menus available which is a good idea as people often just pop in for a quick bite and can order a steak or something similar in the bar. Room and breakfast from £55.00 single, £70.00 double, dinner from £15.50, inclusive of VAT and service. Always open. Owned by the Price family of the Hare & Hounds just a few miles away (see page 107). A member of Best Western Hotels.

106

HARE AND HOUNDS
Westonbirt, Nr. Tetbury, Gloucestershire GL8 8QL

Telephone: 01666 880233   *Fax: 01666 880241*

**London 100, Bath 19, Birmingham 78, Bristol 25, Cheltenham 26,
Cirencester 13, Gloucester 22, Severn Wild Fowl Trust 15**

*F licence; 30 en suite bedrooms, all with colour TV, radio and direct dial
telephones; tennis; squash; snooker; croquet in summer; table tennis; golf 1 mile;
children welcome; dogs welcome; drying room; conference rooms; large garden;
snacks; diets; Duke of Beaufort's Hunt Country.*

This most attractive Cotswold stone Country House has been owned by the Price
family for over forty years, and the two brothers, Martin and Jeremy, now run
the hotel. The house, set in ten acres of garden and woodland, stands well back
from the A433 which runs from the A40 near Burford towards Bath and Bristol.
There are beautiful fresh flowers everywhere, arranged by Mrs Price, which add
a lovely personal touch to this elegant hotel. The spacious lounges are
comfortable and relaxing, with views of the garden, and in the winter there are
welcoming log fires as well as full central heating. The bedrooms are attractive
and well furnished, with some particularly pleasant rooms in the adjacent garden
cottage, including two on the ground floor. The restaurant offers daily menus
with a good choice of varied and original dishes as well as à la carte. There is
also Jack Hare's bar which serves excellent hot and cold food at lunchtime –
and remember Westonbirt is the site of Britain's most famous arboretum and
one of the country's best-known girls' schools, as well as the Hare & Hounds!
Single room from £58.00, doubles from £80.00. Dinner from £17.75. Always
open. The family also owns the Amberley Inn, just a few miles away (see page
106). A member of Best Western Hotels.

DORMY HOUSE HOTEL
Willersey Hill, Broadway, Worcestershire WR12 7LF
Telephone: 01386 852711   *Fax: 01386 858636*

**London 95, Stratford-upon-Avon 15, Cheltenham 15,
Birmingham Airport 40, Oxford 40**

*F licence; 49 en suite bedrooms (22 ground floor and 3 suites), all with telephone,
TV, tea/coffee making facilities and hairdryers; night service; last orders 9.30
p.m.; bar meals; diets on request; children welcome; baby listening; dogs
accepted; conferences max. 74 residential; sauna/steam room; gym with cardio-
vascular equipment; games room; pool/billiards tables; mountain bikes for hire;
croquet lawn; putting green; adjacent golf course; major credit cards accepted.*

To write about the Dormy House is easy for me, for it is one of my favourite
hotels, tucked away high above Broadway and next to the golf course. The high
standard of this superb hotel has only improved over the years. The original part
of the building is a 17th century cotswold stone farmhouse with a charming
drawing room, warmed by log fires in winter and enhanced by fresh flowers
throughout the year. Head Chef, Alan Cutler, maintains the highest level of
cuisine. Alan has been classically trained and believes presentation to be very
important, but will not compromise on quantity. The Barn Owl Bar is extremely
popular with both locals and residents, and serves light lunches and dinners daily.
Each of the forty nine bedrooms are individually and beautifully decorated, and
have recently been upgraded to include televisions with teletext, and trouser
presses in all the rooms and suites. The Dormy House is under the personal
supervision of its Managing Director, Mrs. Ingrid Philip-Sorensen, whose
charming personality, together with her skilled team, give one the warmest
welcome to a most memorable hotel. Whether you just eat in the restaurant,
or visit on Sunday for lunch, The Dormy House will be an experience you will
wish to repeat. Room and full English breakfast from £58.00 per person. Hotel
closed at Christmas.

THE OLD VICARAGE HOTEL
Worfield, Bridgnorth, Shropshire WV15 5JZ

Telephone: 01746 716497   Telex: 35438 Telcom G.   Fax: 01746 716552

Bridgnorth 4, Telford 8, Kidderminster 12, Birmingham 25

R & R licence; 14 en suite bedrooms (1 for disabled), all with direct dial telephone and TV; baby listening; last orders for dinner 9.00 p.m.; special diets; children welcome; dogs accepted; conferences max. 30; Mastercard, Visa, Amex and Diners credit cards accepted.

Situated in the pretty conservation village of Worfield, The Old Vicarage Hotel is a peaceful retreat for travellers whether on business or pleasure. The style of this old parsonage has been preserved with subtle refurbishment in keeping with modern comfort, and pretty watercolours add an intimate and homely touch. An attractive Edwardian conservatory, with views of the gardens, provides a comfortable and pleasant sitting room at any time of the day. The small restaurant is renowned for its first class cuisine, excellent wines and efficient service. People travel from far afield, just to enjoy a superb dinner. I was very impressed with the bedrooms; those in the main house retain their Victorian charm with huge antique beds and wardrobes, and have lovely views over the quiet Shropshire countryside. Recently the old stables have been converted into beautiful large bedrooms, all furnished to a very high standard and exquisitely decorated using splendid colour schemes. There is a ground floor suite with twin beds, which has been adapted for disabled guests, and has a large bath and shower room with an adjustable washbasin, a level shower for wheelchair access and a good sized sitting area. Peter and Christine Iles, the resident proprietors, are attentive and welcoming hosts who endeavour to make your stay memorable. Room and breakfast from £65.00 single, £88.00 double. Weekly – dinner, room and breakfast for two people £833.00, and 2 night breaks from £59.50 per person, per night. English Tourist Board 4 Crowns Deluxe.

THE REDFERN HOTEL
Cleobury Mortimer, Shropshire DY14 8AA

Telephone: 01299 270395   *Fax: 01299 271011*

Bewdley 8, Ludlow 11, Bridgnorth 13, Worcester 23

F licence; 11 en suite bedrooms (1 four-poster, 2 with deluxe whirlpool bathrooms), all with direct dial telephone, colour TV and hair dryer; room service; baby listening; last orders 9.30 p.m.; bar meals; special diets; children welcome; dogs welcome; conferences 30 max; 7 golf courses within 15 miles; 3 tennis courts within 10 miles; riding 1 mile; clay pigeon shooting and fishing ½ mile; open all year; all major credit cards accepted.

The Redfern Hotel, owned by Jon and Lis Redfern, is a small, comfortable hotel which has been sympathetically modernized, providing all up-to-date facilities. It is located in the middle of Cleobury Mortimer, an attractive old tree-lined village with its famous crooked church steeple, which derives its name from the great Norman family of Mortimer, who came over to England with William the Conqueror. Good quality, fresh food is traditionally served in the English Kitchen Restaurant, which is enthusiastically run by the Redferns' son, Richard. He has steadily built up an excellent reputation both locally and nationally; you will find the 5 course table d'hôte menu well priced at £15.25. Also available is an extensive à la carte menu. Breakfast is served in the large airy conservatory, where a selection of hot and cold snacks are available throughout the day. The 11 bedrooms are well equipped and tastefully furnished, providing every comfort for the holiday-maker and business person alike. The Redfern makes an ideal base for visiting this historic area with its many places of interest, including The Ironbridge Industrial Museum, Severn Valley Steam Railway and Acton Scott Farm Museum. The Redfern's also have their own canal narrowboat for hire. There are numerous maps and brochures available in the hotel containing all the above and also the beautiful country walks in the area. Jon and Lis are always willing to give help and advice on where to go and what to see. Single from £45.00, double from £68.00 and half board from £44.00.

THE FEATHERS AT LUDLOW
Bull Ring, Ludlow, Shropshire SY8 1AA

Telephone: 01584 875261   *Fax: 01584 876030*

Hereford 25, Shrewsbury 30, Knighton 17, Leominster 11, Birmingham 37

F licence; 40 en suite bedrooms, several of which are four-poster suites, all with telephone, colour TV, radio, tea/coffee making facilities, mini-bars, some with fires and air conditioning; lift to all floors; night service; meals to 9.30 p.m.; bar lunches; diets; children welcome; ideal for incentive and reward conferences; receptions; billiards room; riding, golf, helicopters by arrangement; indoor heated swimming pool nearby; most credit cards accepted.

I have visited The Feathers at Ludlow for many years, and in my opinion, it doesn't seem to have changed. I was most impressed when I stayed recently, to find such very caring and attentive staff. The proprietor, Mr. Osmond Edwards, and the managers, Mr. and Mrs. Peter Nash, who have been here for over twenty five years, take great pride in running this delightful hotel personally, and always greet their guests with a warm welcome. This historic Jacobean building, has the most wonderful beamed façade, and inside, the hotel displays many fine antiques, pictures, and beautifully arranged fresh flowers. Each bedroom is comfortably furnished and spotlessly clean, offering tea making facilities, colour TV, mini-bar, and the added touch of bathrobes in the en suite bathrooms. The Housman Restaurant, which has an excellent reputation for its cuisine, serves both à la carte and table d'hôte menus, together with a carefully selected wine list. On sunny days, The Courtyard Restaurant opens, and offers delicious light meals. This is a very well-run hotel, with elegant, traditional furnishings and an exceedingly welcoming atmosphere. I can thoroughly recommend a stay at The Feathers, as Ludlow is such a beautiful town to visit, with the river nearby, and wonderful castle ruins and antique shops to browse around. Room and breakfast from £72.00 single, £49.00 per person, twin. Budget terms on application. Open all year.

HAWKSTONE PARK HOTEL
Weston-under-Redcastle, Shrewsbury, Shropshire SY4 5UY

Telephone: 01939 200611   *Fax: 01939 200311*

Shrewsbury 14, Birmingham 50, Manchester 55, Chester 28, London 160,

F licence; 59 en suite bedrooms (2 suites), all with every facility; dinner to 10.00 p.m.; children welcome; conferences; billiards; sauna, solarium & trimnasium; croquet; 18 hole Hawkstone golf course, practice range, 6 hole par 3 Academy course & golf centre with video room & golf shop; 1.5.95 – Championship 18 hole Windmill course designed by Brian Huggett; Shropshire's only English Heritage designated Grade 1 landscape – (Park with walks and follies open 1st April–31st Oct.); helipad; clay shooting by prior arrangement; open all year; major credit cards accepted.

For many years within these pages, Hawkstone Park has been described as a "golfer's and walker's paradise", and now has a great deal more on offer. The hotel's Grade 1 "walking centre", known as the Historic Park and Follies has already been host to over 5,500 visitors a month since its opening in April 1993. This attraction includes a gift shop, cafeteria, classroom and interpretation centre. Fascinating walks can be taken through the labyrinth of pathways containing antiquities and follies built in the 18th century. The mature "Hawkstone" golf course is set within this unique landscape, and the hotel's famous parkland now has a New Golf Centre, complete with extensive golf and leisure shop, complemented by their Head Pro, the Senior Coach to the English Golf Union, and assistant pro's, hi-tech golf video training room, reception and changing facilities. Here, you will also find the Terrace Restaurant which offers grills and snacks all day, with balconies and terraces overlooking the golf courses and 13th century Redcastle. A Practice Range has been added to the complex, together with an Academy course. Amidst this splendid scenic back-drop and with quiet efficiency, Hawkstone Park also accommodates business meetings and conferences for up to 200 delegates. For guests seeking total relaxation, a very warm and sincere atmosphere abounds and you will always be well looked after. The hotel's superb English cuisine is complemented by a competitively priced wine list. Bed and breakfast from £45.00 per night, per room, and other special breaks available (see Bargain Break Section).

NAILCOTE HALL
Berkswell, Nr. National Exhibition Centre,
Warwickshire CV7 7DE

Telephone: 01203 466174   *Fax: 01203 470720*

**Birmingham Airport, International Station & N.E.C. 8, Warwick 12,
Stratford-upon-Avon 17, Stoneleigh Deer Park Golf Course and N.A.C. 7**

*F licence; 40 en suite bedrooms (15 ground floor & 1 for the disabled), all with
every amenity; room/night service; baby listening; last orders for "Rick's Bar"
10.30 p.m.; bar meals; special diets; children welcome; no dogs; conferences,
res. max. 60, theatre style non-res. max. 100, dinner functions max. 130; live
music every Fri/Sat; indoor heated swimming pool; leisure complex; croquet;
petanque; 2 all weather tennis courts; 9 hole golf course & putting green; 18 hole
golf by arrangement with Stoneleigh Golf Course; riding, shooting & fishing by
arrangement, 2 miles; open all year; credit cards accepted.*

Nailcote Hall is an old Elizabethan country house with all today's amenities.
In the last 18 months it has undergone radical changes. There is now a leisure
complex which includes a 14 metre swimming pool, spa pool, sauna, solarium
and gymnasium. All the bedrooms are well appointed and tastefully decorated
in keeping with the period of the house. Conferences and private functions are
catered for, and the quiet, secluded setting provides an excellent venue, be it
for business or pleasure. The Oak Room Restaurant has an excellent reputation
and offers a daily-changing menu with a good variety of dishes; these are
complemented by a carefully chosen cellar which has a wide selection of wines.
For a totally different atmosphere and menu, you can now dine at the new
"Mediterranean" style cafe, "Rick's". Nailcote is found in 15 acres of peaceful
countryside on the B4101, 4 miles outside Knowle and 2 miles from Berkswell.
Transport can be arranged by the hotel, as it has its own, old fashioned courtesy
coach. The owner, Rick Cressman, is proud of his staff's attentiveness and how
they go out of their way to make your stay a memorable one. So, with good food,
fine wines, comfort and a relaxed atmosphere, I am certain you will return to
Nailcote. Double room and full English breakfast from £115.00, single room from
£95.00 inclusive of VAT.

NUTHURST GRANGE
Hockley Heath, Warwickshire B94 5NL

Telephone: 01564 783972   *Fax: 01564 783919*

N.E.C. 8, Birmingham 11, B'ham Int. Airport 8, Warwick 11, Coventry 15, Stratford-upon-Avon 13, London 104

R & R licence; 15 en suite bedrooms, all with spa baths, direct dial telephone, TV, hairdryer and trouser press; room service; night service until 1.00 a.m.; last orders for dinner 9.30 p.m.; special diets; children welcome; conferences, class room style max. 40 and theatre style max. 80; croquet, helipad; open all year; all major credit cards accepted.

Nuthurst Grange is found just off the A3400, between Birmingham and Stratford-upon-Avon, and is idyllically situated in 7½ acres of well kept gardens. David Randolph and his wife Darryl bought Nuthurst as a private house, converted it into an hotel, and have built themselves an excellent reputation, not only as hoteliers, but restaurateurs as well. The food is imaginative and well presented, and connoisseurs of gourmet cuisine will appreciate the large range of culinary treats, supported by a superb wine list. David and his team of chefs make sure only fresh, seasonal produce is used, and he makes a point of personally going to the markets. All the bedrooms are well proportioned and have views overlooking the garden and countryside. Each one is exquisitely furnished and provides you with all possible comforts, including the added personal touch of a fruit bowl, homemade biscuits and chocolates. Nuthurst Grange is the ideal place for business meetings as it is well placed at the heart of England's motorway network, and is also close to the International Airport and railway stations and the National Exhibition Centre. So whether on business or pleasure, treat yourself to some gracious living and self-indulgent luxury. Single room and continental breakfast from £89.00, double from £105.00. All prices are inclusive of VAT.

WELCOMBE HOTEL AND GOLF COURSE
Stratford-upon-Avon, Warwickshire CV37 0NR

Telephone: 01789 295252   *Telex: 31347*   *Fax: 01789 414666*

London 92, Banbury 20, Birmingham 24, Coventry 19, Oxford 40, Warwick 6

F licence; 76 en suite bedrooms (7 ground floor) all with showers, hairdryers, radio, TV, telephone & minibars; full central heating; night service; children welcome, baby listening by arrangement; dogs accepted in bedrooms; diets by arrangement; 18 hole private golf course and clubhouse; 2 hard all-weather tennis courts; conferences; credit cards accepted.

On the Warwick Road, only a couple of miles out of Stratford-upon-Avon, famous for Shakespeare's birthplace, you will find the Welcombe Hotel set in 157 acres of parkland. At the end of a winding drive lies this large country house hotel which was once the home of the famous historian Sir George Trevelyan. During the last three years, two and a half million pounds has been spent on refurbishing the entire place. The bedrooms vary from the high ceilinged spacious ones in the old house to those with twin beds in the modern Garden wing; all are now of an exceptionally high standard and the décor is truly unsurpassed. There are now 35 bathrooms all with Italian marble fittings. The restaurant overlooks the formal gardens and offers the best of French and English cuisine and the food is well complemented by an excellent wine list. Facilities include an 18-hole golf course (6202 yards, par 70) surrounding the hotel with a new Club House and also two all-weather tennis courts. Theatre tickets can be booked in advance through the hotel. Tariff on application. Open all year.

BILLESLEY MANOR
Alcester, Nr. Stratford-upon-Avon, Warwickshire B49 6NF

Telephone: 01789 400888   *Fax: 01789 764145*

Stratford-upon-Avon 4, Birmingham 23, Oxford 40, London 95

F licence; 41 en suite bedrooms (9 ground floor), all with direct dial telephone and colour TV, full central heating; night service; last orders 9.30 p.m.; diets; children welcome; baby listening by arrangement; conferences; large indoor heated swimming pool; tennis; croquet; pitch & putt; riding/shooting/ fishing by arrangement; Amex, Visa, Diners and Mastercard accepted.

Billesley Manor is situated just off the A46 in the heart of England and it would be difficult to find a more agreeable place in the midst of Shakespeare country. Here you will come across the old blending with the new. There is a large oak panelled bar with a carved fireplace, usually burning logs in the winter months. The dining room is also panelled and I thoroughly enjoyed the Sunday table d'hôte lunch which was very well priced. The award winning restaurant which has received 3 AA Rosettes, has a good selection of wines which complement the excellence of its cuisine and service. All the public rooms are lavishly furnished and very comfortable. There is a superb indoor swimming pool with sun patio, as well as tennis courts, croquet and pitch and putt in the grounds. The bedrooms, whether you choose a modern suite or one with a four poster bed, are all of the highest quality. Sixteen of these have been totally upgraded to a very high standard and all of these rooms overlook the well kept topiary which is a feature in the 11 acres of peaceful garden. Peter Henderson, General Manager, oversees his friendly staff well and you can be assured of a warm welcome. The hotel is an ideal base for visiting the Royal Shakespeare Theatre and the many other historical sites that Warwickshire has to offer. However, if it is a quiet time you are looking for, Billesley is a perfect retreat for total relaxation. Twin or double room and English breakfast from £140.00 including VAT. Weekend breaks and Christmas programme available. Open all year.

BARGAIN BREAKS

Readers are recommended to telephone the hotels to confirm rates and conditions prior to booking.

THE HEART OF ENGLAND
GLOUCESTERSHIRE

BIBURY COURT, Bibury *page 101*
Bargain breaks available – tariff on application.

ON THE PARK HOTEL & RESTAURANT, Cheltenham *page 102*
Bargain breaks are available for any 2 nights. Dinner, bed and breakfast £63.00 per person, per night inclusive of VAT, on the basis of 2 people sharing a twin/double room.

TUDOR FARMHOUSE HOTEL, Clearwell *page 104*
2 day breaks including dinner, room and breakfast from £75.00 per person in a standard room and from £82.00 per person in a luxury room.

MANOR HOUSE HOTEL, Moreton-in-Marsh *page 105*
2 night stay – £115.00 per person, for dinner, bed and breakfast, per night.

THE AMBERLEY INN, Nr. Stroud *page 106*
Two night breaks including dinner, bed and breakfast from £92.00 per person.

HARE & HOUNDS, Nr. Tetbury, Westonbirt *page 107*
2 night breaks including dinner, bed and breakfast from £99.00 per person.

HEREFORD AND WORCESTER

DORMY HOUSE HOTEL, Broadway *page 108*
Champagne Weekends and Carefree Midweek Breaks are available throughout the year – flyers available on application.

SHROPSHIRE

THE OLD VICARAGE HOTEL, Bridgnorth *page 109*
Leisure Breaks are available at any time, for stays of 2 or more consecutive nights, and include accommodation, full English breakfast, 3 course dinner and "Passport Tickets" to the Ironbridge Gorge Museums. The rate, based on 2 people sharing, is £59.50 per person, per night in a standard room and £69.00 per person, per night in a luxury room.

THE REDFERN HOTEL, Cleobury Mortimer *page 110*
"Let's go" 2 day breaks – dinner, bed and breakfast; single from £52.00 to £62.00 per person, per night. Double from £44.00 to £54.00 per person, per night including service charge and VAT. 10% reduction on the above for 5 days or more.

THE FEATHERS AT LUDLOW, Bull Ring, Ludlow *page 111*
Bargain breaks available for 2 nights and 4 nights – dinner, bed and breakfast. Tariff on application.

HAWKSTONE PARK HOTEL, Weston under Redcastle, Shrewsbury *page 112*
"Breaks with Tradition", inclusive of accommodation, breakfast, dinner, Park Entrance fees and other local attractions from £48.00 per person, per night, including VAT. 3 night Christmas and New Year Breaks from £215.00 per person, inclusive of 3 nights accommodation, 3 dinners, breakfasts, green/Park entrance fees and VAT. "Golf Breaks", inclusive of accommodation, breakfast, dinner and 1 round of golf on the Windmill or Hawkstone course, from £45.00 per person, per night.

WARWICKSHIRE

NAILCOTE HALL, Berkswell *page 113*
Romantic Package – £74.50 per person, per night, with a bottle of champagne and flowers on arrival. Weekend Break – £137.50 per person, for Friday and Saturday night, which includes champagne and flowers in your room on arrival. Golf Weekend – £162.50 per person to include 2 days (Sat. and Sun.) of golf at Stoneleigh Deer Park Golf Club. All breaks include dinner, bed and breakfast, and prices are inclusive of VAT. Murder Mystery Weekend – £165.00 per person, which includes accommodation, English breakfast on both days, buffet lunch on Saturday, and use of all leisure facilities. Always ask about special breaks during December, January, July and August.

NUTHURST GRANGE, Hockley Heath *page 114*
Weekend Breaks from £125.00 per person for 2 nights including dinner, bed and breakfast. Price is inclusive of VAT.

WELCOMBE HOTEL & GOLF COURSE, Stratford-upon-Avon *page 115*
Country House Weekends include free admission to Warwick Castle and one of six local National Trust properties. Golf Weekends include unlimited free golf. Prices on application.

BILLESLEY MANOR, Nr. Stratford-upon-Avon *page 116*
Minimum stay of 2 nights – dinner, bed and breakfast, per person, per night £82.00 until March 1995 and from 1st April 1995, £84.00. Bed and breakfast rates also available on request.

THE NORTH WEST
SELECTED LOCAL ATTRACTIONS

Historic Houses, Gardens & Parks

CHESHIRE
Arley Hall & Gardens, Nr. Great Budworth
Bridgemere Garden World, Nr. Nantwich
Brookside Garden Centre, Poynton
Cholmondeley Castle Gardens
Dunham Massey, Nr. Altrincham
Gawsworth Hall, Nr. Macclesfield
Little Moreton Hall, Nr. Nantwich
Ness Gardens, Neston
Stapeley Water Gardens, Nantwich
Tatton Park, Knutsford

CUMBRIA
Acorn Bank Garden, Nr. Temple Sowerby
Brantwood House, Coniston
Dalemain Historic House & Gardens, Nr. Pooley
  Bridge
Graythwaite Hall Gardens, Newby Bridge
Holker Hall & Gardens, Cark-in-Cartmel
Hutton-in-the-Forest, 6 miles from Penrith
Larch Cottage Nurseries, Melkinthorpe
Levens Hall & Topiary Garden, Nr. Kendal
Lingholme Gardens, Lingholme, Keswick
Mirehouse, Underskiddaw
Sizergh Castle, Nr. Kendal

LANCASHIRE
All in One Garden Centre, Middleston
Astley Hall & Park, Nr. Chorley
Catforth Gardens & Nursery, Nr. Preston
Gawthorpe Hall, Burley
Leighton Hall, Carnforth
Rufford Old Hall, Ormskirk
Williamson Park, Lancaster

MERSEYSIDE
Croxteth Hall & Country Park, Nr. Liverpool
Speke Hall, Liverpool

Walks & Nature Trails

CHESHIRE
Jodrell Bank Science Centre & Arboretum, Nr.
  Holmes Chapel
Styal Country Park
Walk the Walls, Chester
Wirral Peninsula

CUMBRIA
Cark to Cartmel Village
Dodd Wood
Dunnerdale Forest Nature Trail
Grange-over-Sands to Hampsfell
Grizedale Forest Park Visitor Centre, Hawkshead
Numerous fellwalks and trails throughout
  Cumbria
Ulverston Town Trail

LANCASHIRE
Carnforth Canal Circuit, from Carnforth Railway
  to Bolton-le-Sands
Pendle Way Walk at Pendle Heritage Centre,
  Nelson
The Weaver's Shuttle, around Pendle

Historical Sites & Museums

CHESHIRE
The Boat Museum, Ellesmere Port
Chester Cathedral
Experience Catalyst, Widnes
Macclesfield Silk Museum
Peckforton Castle, Nr. Tarporley
Quarry Bank Mill, Styal

CUMBRIA
Abbot Hall Art Gallery, Kendal
Appleby Castle, Appleby-in-Westmorland
Birdoswald Roman Fort, Brampton
Brough Castle, Kirkby Stephen
Brougham Castle, Nr. Penrith
Carlisle Castle
Cartmel Priory
The Cumberland Pencil Museum & Exhibition
  Centre, Keswick
Dove Cottage, Grasmere
Furness Abbey, Barrow-in-Furness
Heron Corn Mill & Museum of Papermaking,
  Milnthorpe
Laurel & Hardy Museum, Ulverston
Museum of Natural History, Kendal
Penrith Museum
Rydal Mount, Nr. Ambleside
Stott Park Bobbin Mill, Newby Bridge
Wordsworth Museum, Grasmere

GREATER MANCHESTER
Castlefield Urban Heritage Park, Manchester
Manchester Cathedral
Manchester United Football Museum
Museum of Science & Industry, Manchester

LANCASHIRE
Lancaster Castle, Lancaster

MERSEYSIDE
Liverpool Museum
Merseyside Maritime Museum, Albert Dock,
  Liverpool
Museum of Liverpool Life, Pier Head
Pilkington Glass Museum, St. Helens

Entertainment Venues

CHESHIRE
Cheshire Candle Workshops, Burwardsley
Chester Zoo, Upton-by-Chester
Gulliver's World, Warrington
Port Sunlight Visitor Centre, Wirral
Wetlands & Wildfowl Trust Centre, Martin Mere

CUMBRIA
Cumbria Crystal, Ulverston
Fell Foot Park, Newby Bridge
The Gem Den, Berrier, Penrith
Lake District National Park Visitor Centre,
  Windermere
Lakeland Bird of Prey Centre, Lowther
Ravenglass & Eskdale Railway, Ravenglass
Sellafield Visitors Centre, Seascale
South Lakes Wild Animal Park, Dalton-in-
  Furness
Ullswater Cruises
Webb's Garden Centre, Kendal
Windermere Lake Cruises
World of Beatrix Potter, Bowness-on-Windermere

GREATER MANCHESTER

Granada Studio Tours, Manchester

LANCASHIRE

Alexandra Craft Centre, Saddleworth
Blackpool Tower & Pleasure Beach
Butterfly World, Bolton
Camelot Theme Park, Chorley
Frontierland, Morecambe Bay

LANCASHIRE (continued)

Lakeland Wildlife Oasis, Nr. Carnforth
Noel Edmonds' World of Crinkley Bottom,
  Morecambe
Sea Life Centre, Blackpool

MERSEYSIDE

The Beatles Story, Albert Dock, Liverpool
Knowsley Safari Park, Prescot
Pleasureland Amusement Park, Southport
The Tate Gallery at the Albert Dock, Liverpool

THE NORTH WEST
DIARY OF EVENTS 1995

December 1 1994 to January 4
THE WORLD OF JIM HENSON MUPPETS, MONSTERS AND MAGIC
Warrington Museum and Art Gallery, Bold Street, Warrington, Cheshire.
All the work of Jim Henson, with displays, videos and photos to give a behind the scenes look at the making of all Henson's TV shows.

January 16
JANUARY RACE MEETING, CARLISLE
Carlisle Racecourse, Cumbria.

February 5–10
WORDSWORTH WINTER SCHOOL
The Wordsworth Trust, Dove Cottage, Grasmere, Cumbria.

February 25
HORSE RACING
The Greenall Gold Cup – Victor Ludorum Hurdle.
Haydock Park Racecourse, Newton-le-Willows, Merseyside.

*April 6–8
HORSE RACING, GRAND NATIONAL MEETING
Aintree Racecourse, Liverpool.

May 9–11
HORSE RACING
Chester Racecourse, Chester, Cheshire.
May   9 – Chester Vase.
May 10 – Chester Cup.
May 11 – The Ormonde Stakes.

May 11–14
REVELRY FLOWERS IN HOGHTON TOWER
Hoghton Tower, Hoghton, Lancashire.
Flower exhibitions/competitions, and craft stalls.

May 19–21
THE KESWICK JAZZ FESTIVAL
Keswick, Cumbria.

*May 24 & 27 & 29
CARTMEL STEEPLECHASES
Cartmel Racecourse, Cumbria.

May 26 to June 4
CONISTON WATER FESTIVAL
Coniston Water, Cumbria.

June 2–4 GREAT GARDEN & COUNTRYSIDE FESTIVAL
Holker Hall & Gardens, Cark-in-Cartmel, Grange-over-Sands,
Cumbria.

June 8–14 APPLEBY HORSE FAIR
(Selling Day is on final day)
Appleby-in-Westmorland, Cumbria.

June 17–18 WEEKEND FOR PEOPLE WITH DISABILITIES
Museum of Transport Manchester, Boyle Street, Cheetham,
Manchester.
An opening of the museum for people with disabilities, extra
guides available and free vintage bus rides.

June 18 KESWICK CARNIVAL
Keswick, Cumbria.

*June 20–21 CHESHIRE COUNTY SHOW 1995
Tabley House, Northwich Road, Knutsford, Cheshire.

June 29 WARCOP RUSHBEARING
Warcop, Appleby-in-Westmorland, Cumbria.
Ancient children's flower festival.

July 1 AMBLESIDE RUSHBEARING
Ambleside, Cumbria.

July 2 MUSGRAVE RUSHBEARING
Musgrave, Nr. Appleby-in-Westmorland, Cumbria.

July 15 CUMBERLAND SHOW
Carlisle, Cumbria.

July 28–30 CUMBRIA STEAM GATHERING
Cark Airfield, Flookburgh, Cumbria.

July 29 to LAKE DISTRICT SUMMER MUSIC FESTIVAL
August 11 Ambleside, Cumbria.

August 3 AMBLESIDE SPORTS
Ambleside, Cumbria.

August 4, 5 CLASSIC MOTOR BOAT RALLY
& 6 From Windermere Steamboat Museum, Windermere.

August 4–6 LOWTHER HORSE DRIVING TRIALS & COUNTRY FAIR
Lowther Park, Penrith, Cumbria.

August 17 RYDAL SHEEPDOG TRIALS
Rydal, Cumbria.

*August 17–19 SOUTHPORT FLOWER SHOW
Southport, Merseyside.

*August 20 CHESHIRE COUNTRY SPORTS FAIR
Peover Hall, Peover Estate, Over Peover, Cheshire.
Gun dogs, ferrets, parade of hounds, birds of prey and trade
stands.

August 25 to September 3	**BOLTON FESTIVAL 1995** Locations Bolton, Victoria Square, Bolton, Lancs. Arts and community festival, with artists of national and international repute and several days of street entertainment.
September 1 to November 5	**BLACKPOOL ILLUMINATIONS** Blackpool, Lancashire. Illuminations from 7 p.m. nightly.
September (1st 2 weeks)	**KENDAL GATHERING AND TORCHLIGHT PROCESSION** (Procession September 8th.) Kendal, Cumbria.
September 16	**EGREMONT CRAB FAIR** (World Gurning Championships.) Egremont, Cumbria.
October 17–21	**WINDERMERE POWER BOAT RECORD ATTEMPTS** Lake Windermere, Cumbria.
November 16	**BIGGEST LIAR IN THE WORLD COMPETITION** Santon Bridge, Whitehaven, Cumbria.
*November 18	**HORSE RACING, BECHER CHASE MEETING** Aintree Racecourse, Liverpool.

*Denotes provisional date

For further information contact:

The Cumbria Tourist Board
Ashleigh
Holly Road
Windermere
Cumbria LA23 2AQ.
Tel: 015394 44444

The North West Tourist Board
Swan House
Swan Meadow Road
Wigan
Lancashire WN3 5BB.
Tel: 01942 821222

ROWTON HALL HOTEL
Whitchurch Road, Chester, Cheshire CH3 6AD

Telephone: 01244 335262   *Fax: 01244 335464*

Chester 2, Liverpool 30, Manchester 40, Birmingham 80, London 200

F licence; 42 en suite bedrooms, 8 ground floor, all with radio, telephone and TV; full central heating; night service; meals to 9.30 p.m.; diets; children welcome; conferences and private parties; helicopter pad; leisure centre; heated indoor swimming pool, sauna-steam room; gym; tennis court; sea bathing and sailing 15 miles; tennis, squash, badminton, riding and fishing 1 mile.
Mastercard, American Express, Diners Club, Visa cards accepted.

Rowton Hall, originally a country manor house standing on the site of the Battle of Rowton Moor 1649, in eight acres of gardens, is two miles from the historic city of Chester, just off the A41 Chester to Whitchurch road. The hotel is now owned by Stuart and Diana Begbie. The public rooms are comfortable and distinctive, particularly the Cavalier Bar, where light lunches are served, and the attractive oak-panelled Langdale Restaurant. The bedrooms are decorated, furnished and appointed to a high standard. Rooms are available for conferences and private parties. For those seeking healthy relaxation, or indeed, for those of a sporting nature, the new leisure centre offers ample opportunity, with its gymnasium, solarium, steam room and swimming pool. It should be noted, however, that children under six are not allowed in the leisure centre, and those aged 6–16 have their own special hours. An ideal centre for touring and there are many sporting activities in the area. Room and breakfast from £72.00 single, £88.00 double including VAT. Other terms on application.

Hand Printed On Silk

Brocklehurst 1985

SUTTON HALL
Bullocks Lane, Sutton, Nr. Macclesfield, Cheshire SK11 0HE

Telephone: 01260 253211   *Fax: 01260 252538*

London 240, Macclesfield 1, M6 (J18/19) ½ hour, Manchester airport ½ hour

F licence; 10 en suite bedrooms, all with four poster beds, colour TV, direct dial telephones, tea/coffee maker & trouser press; full central heating; late meals to 10 p.m.; diets; dogs welcome; conferences up to 20; golf, tennis, riding nearby; Peak National Park adjacent; most credit cards accepted.

If like myself you enjoy staying at an hotel of character, then here at Sutton Hall is one of the finest in which to indulge yourself. A wealth of beams, log fires and four poster beds are all in evidence, and the ales, conditioned in cask, are matched by the choice of food from an excellent menu. As with the inns of old, there is an atmosphere of warmth, hospitality and good cheer. This, married to such modern conveniences as en suite bathrooms and colour TV, makes a very happy amalgam of past and present. To travel, even from afar, is well worth while and this is made easy by the fact that the M6 and Manchester Airport are less than half an hour away. Also in the area are many other famous old houses, as well as the scenic beauty of the Peak District. The hotel is personally run by Mr. and Mrs. Bradshaw. Room and breakfast from £68.95 single, £42.50 double, per person, inclusive of VAT and full English breakfast. Open all year.

LOWBYER MANOR
COUNTRY HOUSE HOTEL
Hexham Road, Alston, Cumbria CA9 3JX

Telephone: 01434 381230　　　　　　　　*Fax: 01434 382937*

Hexham 20, Carlisle 28, Penrith 20, Middleton-in-Teesdale 20

*R & R licence; 12 en suite bedrooms, 2 on ground floor; all with colour TV; full
central heating; last orders 8.30 p.m.; bar meals; diets; children welcome; dogs
by arrangement; conferences up to 20; Christmas and New Year programme;
sailing and boating, golf, riding, shooting and fishing all nearby; Visa, Mastercard,
Amex and Diners cards welcome.*

Although Alston is the highest market town in England, it lies in the sheltered
South Tyne Valley. Cobbled streets lead up to the Pennine Moor and Fells and
in a well wooded corner of the town, lies this small, friendly hotel. It has been
converted from a seventeenth century manor house to give the traveller or
holidaymaker the warmth and comfort appreciated after driving over or walking
through this superb moorland country. The bedrooms, all with private
bathrooms, tea/coffee making facilities and televisions are above average for this
type of hotel. There is an intimate bar, and the other public rooms are spacious
and well furnished. Mr. and Mrs. Hughes, the proprietors, ensure that a warm
welcome awaits you and that a meal in their dining room is a very pleasant
experience. The food is well prepared and presented and vegetarian dishes are
always available. To sum up, this is a quiet country hotel for those wishing to
sample the delights of this area of England, or to use as a base for touring the
Lake District, Hadrian's Wall or the Pennine Way. Always open. Room and
breakfast from £31.50 per night, or any 2 nights dinner, bed and breakfast from
£85.00 per person.

LOVELADY SHIELD COUNTRY HOUSE HOTEL
Nenthead Road, Nr. Alston, Cumbria CA9 3LF

Telephone: 01434 381203 *Fax: 01434 381515*

Alston 2¼, Penrith 20, Hadrians Wall 20, Carlisle 31, Newcastle 43, London 300

R & R licence; 12 en suite bedrooms, all with direct dial telephone, hairdryer and TV; room service; last orders for dinner 8.30 p.m.; bar meals; vegetarian diets; children welcome; dogs accepted; conferences max. 12; croquet; tennis; golf, riding and shooting/fishing nearby; hotel closed from Jan. 4th–Feb. 14th but office open for enquiries; all major credit cards accepted.

Lovelady Shield; the name conjures up an image of the peace and tranquillity that you will certainly find in this gracious country house hotel. Set beside a river in a wooded valley high in the Pennines, just 2¼ miles from Alston (England's highest market town), this quiet retreat is in an ideal situation for exploring the border country, the Lake District, Hadrians Wall and the Yorkshire Dales. Only 35 minutes from the Penrith exit on the M6, it is a very pleasant stop-over on journeys north and south. The owners, Mr. and Mrs. Lyons, together with their friendly staff, are keeping up the hotel's tradition of warm hospitality and service. The chef, Barrie Garton, produces imaginative and beautifully presented meals, and has been awarded 2 AA Rosettes for his cooking. Service in the pretty dining room is discreet and attentive. The hotel is well furnished and appointed, warm and comfortable, with welcoming log fires. The mature garden has croquet laid out on the lawns, and a tennis court. Shooting and fishing can be arranged, and riding and golf are available nearby; for the walker, there are miles of moorland tracks. To find the Lovelady Shield, take the Nenthead–Stanhope road out of Alston for 2¼ miles, and the hotel nestles down a long, tree-lined drive to your left. Room and breakfast from £47.50 per person, dinner, room and breakfast from £71.75. Weekly rates available. AA 2 Red Stars, RAC 3 Stars and E.T.B. "4 Crown Highly Commended".

KIRKSTONE FOOT
COUNTRY HOUSE HOTEL
Ambleside, Cumbria LA22 9EH

Telephone: 015394 32232

London 300, Kendal 13, Keswick 17, Penrith 30

R and R licence; 15 en suite bedrooms, all with direct dial telephone, TV, hair dryer and tea/coffee making facilities; full central heating; last orders for dinner 8.30 p.m.; special diets; children welcome; dogs in annexe only; sailing, boating, golf, tennis, squash, riding and fishing nearby; 16 self-catering units; all major credit cards accepted.

I have known this hotel for many years, and it seems to improve each time I visit it. The resident manager, Alison Magee has further developed an already well deserved reputation for comfort and good food, and the Kirkstone Foot still represents the best value in the area. The stylish décor and furnishings are comfortable, warm and homely, and the food is superbly prepared, cooked and presented, and is complemented by an excellent wine list. There is always an air of friendly efficiency without the pomp and stuffiness of the many, often more expensive, pretentious hotels, which believe themselves to be of a similar standard. As its name suggests, the hotel is situated at the foot of Kirkstone Pass, tucked away in a quiet backwater, far from the holiday crowds. This location makes Kirkstone Foot Country House Hotel the ideal venue from which to partake in all the pastimes and sports offered by the Lake District National Park. For guests who prefer self catering, there is a full range of cottages and apartments in the beautifully kept gardens, all of which are decorated to the same high standard of the hotel. Dinner, room and breakfast from £44.00 per person, per night. The hotel is closed for the first two weeks of December and for the month of January.

NANNY BROW COUNTRY HOUSE HOTEL & RESTAURANT
Clappersgate, Ambleside, Cumbria LA22 9NF

Telephone: 015394 32036   *Fax: 015394 32450*

Ambleside 1½, Windermere 4

F licence; 18 en suite bedrooms (including 9 suites), all with direct dial telephone and colour TV with satellite channels; room service; baby listening; last orders for dinner 9.00 p.m.; special and vegetarian diets; children welcome; dogs accepted; shooting/fishing; complimentary use of private leisure club with indoor heated swimming pool, squash, sauna, and gymnasium for hotel guests; open all year; Mastercard, Amex, Diners and Visa credit cards accepted.

The success of an hotel or otherwise, can be calculated by the remarks of guests in other hotels. The Nanny Brow Country House Hotel is one of those establishments that is repeatedly judged by guests as the standard by which other hotels should be compared. The consensus of opinion is nearly always that the standard of excellence rarely meets that of the Nanny Brow. In this I have to agree. Of all small country house hotels, few can match its restrained comfort, fewer still, its friendly efficiency, and only rarely, and this usually only in the most prohibitively expensive hotels, its standard of cuisine. The bedrooms are all individually designed and extremely comfortable. Let me just say that if you are looking for tranquillity within "an oasis of elegance", or if you are seeking to unwind and you want to do this whilst sampling excellent food and fine wines, then you can be pampered here, in the midst of the beautiful scenery of the Lake District, better than almost anywhere else I can think of. It is an experience that you will find very easy to get used to but very hard to forget. Room and breakfast from £90.00, dinner, room and breakfast from £124.00. Prices are for two people and include VAT. The Nanny Brow has been awarded a red rosette for its cuisine, and is 4 Crowns Highly Commended by the E.T.B..

ROTHAY MANOR HOTEL
Rothay Bridge, Ambleside, Cumbria LA22 0EH

Telephone: 015394 33605   *Fax: 015394 33607*

Kendal 13, Manchester 80, London 280

R & R licence; 18 en suite bedrooms (2 for the disabled) all with direct dial telephone and TV, room service; baby listening; last orders for dinner 9.00 p.m.; special diets; children welcome; conferences max. 20; free use of nearby leisure centre; tennis and fishing ¼ mile; sailing/boating ½ mile; open all year; all major credit cards accepted.

If you believe, as I do, that one of the main ingredients of civilised life is good food and wines taken in comfortable surroundings, then Rothay Manor is, without a doubt, one of the finest venues in which to enjoy that life. The hotel has been voted top of the list by a publication on hotel breakfasts, and the excellence of the lunches and dinners complements the sumptuous surroundings. Antiques and fresh flowers are abundant, and the feeling of warmth and well-being are everywhere. The whole ambience is orchestrated by Nigel and Stephen Nixon and their wives, and the reputation that they have gained for all round excellence is more than justifiably deserved. These impressions were echoed by many of the other guests to whom I spoke, and even from the elegant brochure, you too will begin to feel the atmosphere of Rothay Manor. It seems unnecessary to add that the surrounding mountains, lakes and the air of the Lake District, make a superb backdrop and atmosphere in which to indulge these pleasures. Double room and breakfast from £112.00 for 2 people, and dinner, room and breakfast from £141.00 for 2 people.

WATEREDGE HOTEL
Borrans Road, Ambleside, Cumbria LA22 0EP

Telephone: 015394 32332   *Fax: 015394 32332*

London 300, Kendal 13, Keswick 17, Penrith 30

R licence; 23 en suite bedrooms (5 ground floor), all with radio, TV and telephone, complimentary morning tea and coffee tray; TV lounge; full central heating; diets; children over 7 welcome; dogs not allowed in public rooms or suites; small conferences; lake bathing; boating; fishing; private jetty for guests' use; complimentary use of nearby leisure club; Mastercard, Amex and Visa credit cards accepted.

It is not often that one comes across a hotel that has excellent food, is immaculately and comfortably furnished and decorated, and yet is perfectly situated, but the Wateredge Hotel is exactly that. With its gardens running down to Lake Windermere, with its beautiful views from the public rooms, with its delightful bedrooms and delicious meals, it makes an idyllic venue for a holiday in the Lake District. Not only is there the peace and quiet of the hotel itself, but there is the tranquillity of a stroll on the nearby fells to be enjoyed. For those seeking a more active time, there is boating and fishing on the doorstep, there are sporting facilities of all kinds, both indoor and out, in the immediate vicinity. In addition, Ambleside is a lively and bustling town with everything that a holiday maker or tourist could need. The Wateredge is an unpretentious, "honest to goodness" hotel which makes any visit to the Lake District well worthwhile. Dinner, room and breakfast from £57.00 single, £98.00 twin. Closed mid-December to early February.

APPLEBY MANOR COUNTRY HOUSE HOTEL & LEISURE CLUB
Appleby-in-Westmorland, Cumbria CA16 6JB

Telephone: 017683 51571   *Fax: 017683 52888*

M6 (Junctions 38 & 40) 13, A1 Scotch Corner 38, Keswick 31, Kendal 25, Ullswater 15, Penrith 13

F licence; 30 en suite bedrooms (10 ground floor), all with telephone, hairdryer, colour TV, satellite and video film channels; last orders 9.00 p.m.; diets; children welcome, baby listening; dogs in coach-house bedrooms only; conferences 30 max; games room; snooker and pool; indoor heated swimming pool; jacuzzi; sauna; solarium; leisure centre; squash ½ mile; fishing locally; riding 8 miles; golf 2 miles; hotel closed 3 days at Christmas only; all major credit cards accepted.

Appleby Manor stands high, commanding views of the historic little town, its romantic castle and the sweeping countryside and fells beyond. Within, you will find relaxing and friendly courtesy, and most attractive and spacious public rooms. Facing south, the house gives shelter to its sunny gardens onto which some of the delightful rooms in the new wing have direct access. The bedrooms are comfortable and furnished in keeping with the period of the house. There is a coach house conversion, offering more contemporary accommodation which is also suitable for disabled people. The dining room is informal and you can relax over a good table d'hôte menu, well presented and satisfying, or choose from one of the three other menus available. The wine list offers a selection of wines from 20 countries and the bar stocks a broad range of malt whiskies. There is plenty to see and do locally, there are walks to suit all abilities and golf, fishing and riding are available nearby. Appleby is ideally situated for touring the scenic Lake District, and the Borders, Hadrian's Wall, the Roman Camps, the high Pennines and the Yorkshire Dales are all within easy motoring distance. Prices per person start at £43.00 for bed and breakfast, £49.50 for dinner, bed and breakfast; weekly rates from £297.00, including dinner, bed and breakfast.

THE PHEASANT INN
Bassenthwaite Lake, Nr. Cockermouth,
Cumbria CA13 9YE

Telephone: 017687 76234   *Fax: 017687 76002*

Cockermouth 5, Keswick 8, Carlisle 25, London 295

F licence; 20 en suite bedrooms (1 for the disabled); room service; baby listening; last orders for dinner 8.30 p.m.; bar meals at lunchtime; special diets; children welcome; dogs accepted in lounges and kennels; gardens and 60 acres of additional grounds and woodlands; fishing and riding nearby; golf locally; hotel closed on December 24th and 25th; Mastercard and Visa credit cards accepted.

Dating from the 16th century, The Pheasant Inn has kept abreast of modern standards of comfort without losing any of its character and charm. Guests can enjoy bar snacks and real ale in the original bar, and there are a further three lounges in which to relax; all are tastefully decorated and furnished. The bedrooms, likewise, are comfortable and each has its own character and décor. It is heartwarming to return from any of the activities that may have brought you to this beautiful part of the Lake District, and to relax in front of a welcoming log fire. The fact that many non-residents come from far and near to dine here, bears out that the food is prepared from the freshest ingredients, and cooked to the highest standards. The dining room is non-smoking, as is one of the resident's lounges. With pretty gardens and its own 60 acres of additional grounds and woodlands at the foot of Thornthwaite Forest, and with Bassenthwaite Lake only a few minutes walk away, The Pheasant Inn is a little step back in history. A nature lovers paradise and a gourmets delight. Room and breakfast from £34.00, dinner, room and breakfast from £54.00 including VAT.

OVERWATER HALL
Ireby, Nr. Bassenthwaite Lake, Cumbria CA5 1HH

Telephone / Fax: 017687 76566

London 310, Carlisle 22, Keswick 8

R & R licence; 13 en suite bedrooms, all with telephone, TV, hot drinks tray, hairdryer; full central heating; late meals to 9.00 p.m.; children welcome; dogs welcome; games room including billiards/snooker table; putting green; golf, riding, fishing, sailing all nearby; own nature trail; Access and Visa credit cards accepted.

To call Overwater Hall an hotel does not really do it justice. For here there is no cool receptionist to register you, hand you your key and then leave you to your own devices. No, here you are a guest in the beautiful Georgian mansion, and you are welcomed by the owners, Angela Hyde, Adrian Hyde the chef, and Stephen Bore. The furnishings and décor have been carefully chosen to give the comfort of the modern era while preserving the atmosphere of the gracious old building. The colour schemes are restful and blend in to add to the air of tranquillity. What more can one ask for after a hard day's motoring or a strenuous day in the Lake District? The Hall is set in eighteen acres of beautiful woodlands and gardens, and, further afield lie Bassenthwaite, Keswick, Caldbeck and the surrounding lakes and fells. An ideal venue for any *Signposter* who, if he doesn't mind travelling, also has the Solway coast, the Pennines and the Scottish border country all within easy reach. Room and breakfast from £38.00 per person. Two day breaks from £88.00 per person, per night, for dinner, bed and breakfast. Reduction for weekly terms. Open all year, including Christmas and New Year.

MARY MOUNT HOTEL
Borrowdale, Nr. Keswick, Cumbria CA12 5UU

Telephone: 017687 77223

Keswick 2½, Penrith / M6 21

F licence; 14 en suite bedrooms (4 for the disabled), all with TV and tea/coffee making facilities; last orders for dinner 9.00 p.m.; bar meals at lunchtime; special diets; children welcome; dogs accepted; sailing/boating; riding, shooting & fishing nearby; open all year; Mastercard and Visa credit cards accepted.

For "Signposters" looking for a smaller, quieter hotel, then you need look no further. The Mary Mount is one of those intimate hotels that offers little else but peace, comfort, good food, and in this case in particular, superb views and lovely wooded gardens. There are 14 attractively decorated bedrooms, 6 of which are in the adjacent Four Oaks bungalow. The proprietors, Mr. and Mrs. Peter Mawdsley, who also own the hugely successful Coledale Inn at Braithwaite, have transformed this small country house into everything that one looks for when unwinding from the cares of the city. Borrowdale itself, arguably the prettiest valley in the Lake District, offers the most spectacular, easy walking along the road or river, and, for the more energetic, there is rock climbing or fell walking. Having said all this, however, the Lodore Falls' landing stage is literally "at the bottom of the garden", and for those looking for the more traditional holiday pursuits such as boating, sailing and pony trekking, a boat will take them to Keswick where all this can be found. Room and breakfast from £26.00, price includes VAT.

HARE AND HOUNDS COUNTRY INN
Bowland Bridge, Nr. Grange-Over-Sands, Cumbria LA11 6NN

Telephone: 015395 68333

Newby Bridge 4, Windermere 6, Hawkshead 10, Cartmel Priory 10, Coniston 14, Grange-over-Sands 15, Keswick 20

F licence; 16 bedrooms (13 en suite), all with direct dial telephone and TV; baby listening; last orders for dinner 8.45 p.m.; bar meals; children welcome; dogs accepted; indoor heated swimming pool 1 mile; golf 8 miles; sailing/boating, riding and shooting/fishing 10 miles; open all year; all major credit cards accepted.

I have to thank an hotelier of great repute for guiding me to The Hare and Hounds. "It is my local, its marvellous and I often go there to eat" he said. How right he was. The hotel is personally run by Peter Thompson, an ex Liverpool and International football player, together with his wife Deborah. They have refurbished the building to modern standards, without detracting the ambience of the original 17th century coaching inn it once was. It is now extremely comfortable, warm, friendly, and the food is excellent. This however, is not all that The Hare and Hounds has to offer. It is hidden away in a superbly scenic valley at Bowland Bridge, and to me, its greatest asset is that one can enjoy the best of the Lake District in peace and quiet, and yet all the amenities for which this area is so famous for, are not far away. Only 15 minutes by car are Lake Windermere, Bowness and Kendal, and just a little further afield are Cartmel with its racecourse and all the other lakes. For anyone wanting to "get away from it all", this is one of the finest hotels in which to do so. Room and breakfast from £24.00, dinner, room and breakfast from £36.00 per person.

TARN END HOUSE HOTEL
Talkin Tarn, Brampton, Carlisle, Cumbria CA8 1LS

Telephone: 016977 2340   *Fax: 016977 2089*

**Hadrian's Wall 7, M6 (Junction 43) 9, Carlisle 11, Newcastle 45,
Manchester 130, London 290**

*F licence; 7 en suite bedrooms (1 ground floor), 6 with bath and 1 with shower,
all with TV; baby listening; last orders for dinner 9.00 p.m.; bar meals; special
diets; children welcome; dogs accepted in bedrooms only by prior arrangement;
conferences max. 30; sailing/boating; bird watching; superb walking; golf ¼
mile; riding 4 miles; shooting/fishing by arrangement; open all year; most major
credit cards accepted.*

Set in an idyllic situation at the end of Talkin Tarn, with the magnificence of
the Pennines on one side, and wooded farmland all around, the Tarn End House
Hotel is ideal for the nature lover and follower of outdoor pursuits alike. There
is sailing and rowing on the Tarn, a superb and picturesque golf course within
a few hundred yards, walks along the River Gelt, and, for the more ambitious,
there is fell walking, pony trekking, shooting and fishing all in the locality. For
the tourist, Hadrian's Wall, Lanercost Priory, Naworth Castle and the historic
city of Carlisle, are only minutes away. The Lake District, the Scottish Borders
and Northumberland are also easily accessible by car. For readers wishing to visit
such a beautiful area as the Eden Valley, with all the above amenities, the Tarn
End House must surely represent exceptional value for money. The restaurant,
which overlooks the Tarn, offers delightful meals from the à la carte menu, and
lighter meals can be enjoyed in the comfortable bar. All the bedrooms are en
suite, and have beautiful views over the gardens and the scenic countryside
beyond. In my mind, good food, good company and comfort count for everything
when selecting an hotel, and there is an abundance of all these ingredients at
Tarn End House, with the added bonus of the superb surroundings. Double room
and breakfast from £49.00 low season, £59.00 high season, including VAT.

WHEELGATE COUNTRY HOUSE HOTEL
Little Arrow, Coniston, Cumbria LA21 8AU

Telephone: 015394 41418

Kendal 30, Manchester 85, Edinburgh 150, London 270

R & R licence; 8 en suite bedrooms, all with TV; baby listening available; last orders for dinner 7.00 p.m.; special diets by arrangement; children welcome; attractive gardens; riding; lake bathing, sailing, boating and fishing nearby; hotel closed from Dec.–Jan.; only Amex credit card accepted.

Every now and again we find intimate, friendly, small hotels such as the Wheelgate Country House. Set in a pretty garden in this particularly quiet and beautiful part of the Lake District, the hotel offers peace and tranquillity. The building itself is an old farmhouse, and all the rooms have been sympathetically furnished with many antiques. Oak beams abound, and the cosy ambience is enhanced by the glow of the log fire in the lounge. The proprietors, Roger and Joan Lupton, take great pride in personally supervising the day-to-day running of this hotel, and are always around to help with holiday activity planning. There is an intimate bar for the pre-dinner drinker, and the dining room offers four or five course dinners which are very reasonably priced. Fresh sea fish and local game such as venison are featured on the menu, and these can be followed by delicious home-made rum truffles. All of the eight bedrooms are individually and tastefully decorated, and one has a four-poster bed. Coniston and its environs, is a lesser known part of the Lake District, but it has many of the famous locations within easy reach. The Lake itself is nearby, as is Tarn Hows, Grizedale Forest, the Langdale Pikes and the Duddon Valley. These can all be explored from here, and this makes the Wheelgate the ideal spot from which to enjoy the best of the National Park, without the bustle of the more popular venues. Room and breakfast from £27.50 per person, luxury bedroom from £32.50 per person, including VAT. Four course dinner £15.50 and five course dinner £17.00.

GRAYTHWAITE MANOR HOTEL
Grange-over-Sands, Cumbria LA11 7JE

Telephone: 015395 32001/33755   *Fax: 015395 35549*

London 261, Lake District (Windermere) 15, Carlisle 58, Liverpool 76

F licence; 22 bedrooms (some ground floor), 20 with private bathrooms and all with telephone, TV, tea/coffee making facilities, electric blankets; drying room; small conferences; billiards; attractive gardens; golf locally, putting green; hard court tennis; municipal sea water pool; riding nearby.

What first impressed me here was the courtesy and thoroughness with which one of the owners showed me round. As a result of what I saw and felt, I returned a few days later for a night's lodging and this is what I found. A largish and substantial house, beautifully appointed and with every indication that the detailed comfort of visitors had been most conscientiously achieved. The armchairs were cosy enough to go to sleep in. The dining room, an imposing affair, displays cut glass chandeliers and some fine oil paintings. There was a choice from the table d'hôte menu at dinner which was excellently cooked and served. I made a special note, too, of how pleasant and attentive the staff were, obviously taking their cue from the owners. Bedrooms, all with private baths, fulfilled the expectation of the downstairs comfort and elegance. Faithful guests return year after year for Graythwaite and Grange are within easy reach of the Lake District. Dinner, room and breakfast from £50.00 single, £90.00 twin. Special terms available on request from November to March.

NETHERWOOD HOTEL
Grange-over-Sands, Cumbria LA11 6ET

Telephone: 015395 32552   *Fax: 015395 34121*

London 262, Lake District (Windermere) 5, Carlisle 58, Liverpool 82, Kendal 12, Keswick 41

F licence; 29 bedrooms (1 for disabled); all with en suite bathroom, 2 pairs of intercommunicating bedrooms; all have radio, telephone, TV; night service; lift to 1st floor; late meals; special diets; children welcome; baby listening; dogs allowed; conferences; indoor heated swimming pool; spa bath; steam room; beauty area; parking for 160 cars; dancing; 11 acres of gardens; sea bathing and sailing 100 yds; tennis ½ mile; squash, badminton, riding, shooting and fishing all 5 miles; credit cards accepted.

This imposing hotel, set in its own topiary gardens on a woodland slope, dominates the main road into Grange-over-Sands. The house dates back to 1893, and it retains all the original panelling, wood-carvings and fireplaces. However, modern conveniences also have their place here, and you will find a lift servicing the first floor bedrooms, and all the dining areas are air conditioned. There is a honeymoon suite with all its original furniture, to help you re-live the romance of days gone by, and there are ten new bedrooms, all non-smoking, furnished in harmony with the rest of the hotel. The food at the Netherwood is excellent, being prepared from the freshest ingredients with imagination and flair. It is easy to over indulge in the dining room, but downstairs there is a heated swimming pool, spa bath, steam room and beauty salon where you can work off those extra inches gained, or simply relax after, perhaps a tiring day, having toured this lovely area. The southern Lake District offers much for the nature lover and tourists alike, and the delights of Morecambe Bay and the Lune Valley are on the doorstep. Room and breakfast from £42.75 single, £85.50 double. Open all year.

AYNSOME MANOR HOTEL
Cartmel, Nr. Grange-over-Sands, Cumbria LA11 6HH

Telephone: 015395 36653   *Fax: 015395 36016*

**London 263, Manchester 84, Ulverston 10, Coniston 15,
Bowness-on-Windermere 12**

R & R licence; 12 en suite bedrooms, all with direct dial telephone and TV; limited room service; baby listening; last orders for dinner 8.30 p.m.; special diets on request; children welcome, but no under 5's in the restaurant for dinner, high tea can be provided; dogs accepted; situated nearby: indoor heated swimming pool, riding, shooting and fishing; sailing/boating on Lake Windermere; 2 golf courses and tennis within 3 miles; hotel closed in January; Amex, Visa and Mastercard credit cards accepted.

This beautiful old manor house, parts of which date back to 1510, was once the residence of the Earl of Pembroke, founder of the historic Cartmel Priory. It is now in the experienced hands of its owners, Tony and Margaret Varley, their son Christopher, and his wife Andrea. The elegant, yet comfortable atmosphere has been retained by the tasteful furnishings and décor, which are to be found throughout the hotel. The superb candlelit dining room, with its views of the Priory, is an ideal setting in which to enjoy the imaginative and carefully chosen menu, offering the best of fresh local produce, well cooked and presented. The bedrooms, including the four-poster honeymoon suite, are quite charming in their individuality. After a day spent visiting the local places of interest, such as Holker Hall, Beatrix Potter's home, Sizergh Castle and Levens Hall, or after pursuing a day's sporting activities, the visitor can relax in the tranquil atmosphere that the hotel provides. Dinner, bed and breakfast from £52.00 including VAT. Other terms on application including special terms for winter breaks.

THE WORDSWORTH HOTEL
Grasmere, Ambleside, Cumbria LA22 9SW

Telephone: 015394 35592   *Fax: 015394 35765*

London 271, Ambleside 4, Kendal 17, Keswick 13

F licence; 35 en suite bedrooms (2 ground floor) and 2 suites, all with colour TV, telephone and full central heating; lift; night service; last orders 9.00 p.m., Fri–Sat 9.30 p.m.; bar meals; vegetarian diets; children welcome, baby listening; no dogs; conferences up to 100; games room; dancing by arrangement; indoor heated swimming pool; sauna and solarium; mini gym; jacuzzi; free golf on weekdays; squash, riding and fishing nearby; all major credit cards accepted.

Set in the centre of Grasmere, in 1½ acres of landscaped gardens, this hotel offers all that is best for a holiday in the Lakes. It is spacious, airy and has all the modern amenities to be expected by the discerning traveller. One bedroom has retained its original Victorian bathroom and is very much in demand, as the shower facilities must be seen to be believed. There are also three romantic four-poster rooms, one of which is a suite. The public rooms are tastefully furnished in keeping with the period of the buildings, without the gloomy atmosphere inherent in so many Victorian hotels. The swimming pool has large doors opening onto a patio and makes an excellent place in which to relax after a few days of walking, climbing or sightseeing. The hotel is owned by Reg Gifford of Michael's Nook Country House Hotel, so little more need be said of the food here, other than that the fame which he has gained as an hotelier is more than justified. What could be better than the fresh air of the Lake District and, maybe, a little exercise, coupled with the cuisine of the hotel's "Prelude Restaurant"? Christmas and New Year house parties. Winter breaks available; open all year. Prices from £59.00 per person.

DALE HEAD HALL LAKESIDE HOTEL
Thirlmere, Keswick, Cumbria CA12 4TN

Telephone: 017687 72478

Penrith 16, Keswick 4, Grasmere 5

R & R licence; 9 en suite bedrooms, all with direct dial telephone; room service; baby listening; last orders for dinner 8.30 p.m.; special diets; children welcome; conferences max. 20; sailing/boating; shooting/fishing; tennis; spa pool, gymnasium, squash courts and golf 5 miles; riding 7 miles; open all year; credit cards accepted.

If you turn off the A91 at the northern end of Thirlmere, and follow the private drive down to Dale Head Hall, you will find yourself at an hotel that is surely situated in the most idyllic position in the Lake District. Set in a clearing of trees, on the shores of the lake, and with Helvellyn rising majestically behind, you cannot help falling in love with the place. A small, yet luxurious, hotel this 16th century Hall is beautifully decorated in keeping with the age of the building. It exudes that intimate atmosphere of a true family home. The untiring enthusiasm, skill and innate sense of hospitality of the resident proprietors, Alan and Shirley Lowe, combine to make Dale Head Hall a very special place. Three red squirrels play on the lawn. The sun sets over the lake and fell, as I join fellow guests in the lounge for an aperitif; all in eager anticipation of yet another wonderful meal. The award winning cuisine is truly superb, lovingly prepared by one of the most dedicated mother and daughter teams I know. They even grow their own vegetables, fruit, herbs and flowers in the Hall's Victorian kitchen garden. Dale Head Hall is in an ideal position for exploring the Lake District, with all the major attractions not far away. Whether you are planning your ascent of Helvellyn, or walk from the hotel's grounds following paths through woods and past streams, I can highly recommend a stay at Dale Head Hall, and the hotel is possibly the best value in Cumbria. Room and breakfast from £30.00. Special breaks available. Cumbria Tourist Board 4 Crown Highly Commended.

LYZZICK HALL HOTEL
Underskiddaw, Keswick, Cumbria CA12 4PY

Telephone: 017687 72277   *Fax: 017687 72278*

Keswick 2, Edinburgh 128, Stranraer 139, Hull 169, London 300

F licence; 25 en suite bedrooms, all with direct dial telephone, radio, TV and tea/coffee facilities; baby listening; last orders for dinner 9.30 p.m.; special diets; children welcome; outdoor heated swimming pool; sailing/boating, golf, riding, shooting and fishing nearby; hotel closed from mid. Jan.–mid. Feb.; all major credit cards accepted.

Lyzzick Hall is set in an idyllic situation, with splendid views over the Derwent Valley, and has its own extensive grounds including a swimming pool on a sunny terrace. Everything is here for the visitor to the Lake District, whether on business or pleasure. Mr. and Mrs. Fernandez, who have been here for nine years, together with their staff, aim to provide a relaxing haven for guests, coupled with quiet and efficient service, which they do most successfully. The food, chosen from imaginative menus, is excellent, and is served in the spacious dining room which also enjoys wonderful views. The table d'hôte menu can be incorporated with dishes from the à la carte, and there are 140 bins on the wine list. These have been personally chosen by Mr. Fernandez, who is a most knowledgeable enthusiast of Spanish wines. I have rarely found more than one of my favourite Spanish wines on any list, but here, there are three amongst many that I had not heard of. Lyzzick Hall has made a well deserved reputation for itself amongst the many excellent hotels in this area and I can highly recommend a stay here. Room and breakfast from £35.00 per person, and dinner, room and breakfast from £45.00 per person, including VAT.

STAKIS KESWICK LODORE SWISS HOTEL
Keswick, Cumbria CA12 5UX

Telephone: 017687 77285   *Fax: 017687 77343*

Carlisle 42, Penrith 23, Keswick 3

F licence; 70 bedrooms all with en suite bathroom, satellite TV and telephone; room and night service; baby listening; lift; last orders 9.30 p.m.; bar lunches; special diets; children welcome; registered nursery with NNEB trained Nannies; conferences up to 80; games room; outdoor/indoor heated swimming pool; leisure centre; sauna; gymnasium; sunbed; squash and tennis; sailing, boating and riding nearby; fishing by arrangement; free golf Mon–Fri (18 hole course), Sat–Sun £15.00 per person; open all year; all major credit cards accepted.

The Keswick Lodore Swiss, situated overlooking Derwent Water and at the foot of the famous Lodore Falls, is an hotel of international class and reputation. It caters superbly for all manner of guests and their families. One of the most impressive aspects is the way in which children are looked after by N.N.E.B. nurses, with their own playroom and kitchen, providing parents with a welcome rest. The public rooms are all bright and airy, the bedrooms are spacious and well appointed, and the whole hotel is beautifully decorated and cheerful.Many of the excellent dishes served are from original Swiss recipes, and the staff are all courteous and friendly. The gardens are a delight, and the immediate environs have the most imposing views, yet there is also a gentler beauty in the land-scape. All the Lake District, with its sporting facilities, as well as its natural and historical features is easily accessible, so whether you are holidaying as a family or alone, there is something here to suit you. The hotel also has its own many and varied facilities for guests to enjoy. Dinner, bed and breakfast from £41.00, weekly rates (including dinner) from £287.00.

UNDERSCAR MANOR
Applethwaite, Nr. Keswick, Cumbria CA12 4PH

Telephone: 017687 75000   *Fax: 017687 74904*

Keswick 2, M6 (Junction 40) 16, Manchester Airport 120

F licence; 11 en suite bedrooms, all with direct dial telephone and TV; last orders for dinner 8.30 p.m.; boardroom max. 16; riding 1½ miles; 18 hole golf course 4 miles; fishing nearby; open all year; credit cards accepted.

Ranked as one of the best hotels in the North of England, it is surprising that we hear so little of Underscar Manor. This is because it is one of the most discreet hotels, and, hidden as it is up a secretive lane, it makes the perfect centre for discovering the Lake District, without encountering the crowds that so often mar such a visit. A guest here can wander in the hotel's own extensive and beautifully tended grounds, or up onto the fells without meeting a soul. The views are stunning. Inside, the décor can only be described as superb, the service is impeccable, and most importantly, the food is imaginative and delicious. For anyone contemplating a quiet break or a longer holiday, or for the businessman wanting to meet others without distractions, Underscar Manor is the perfect choice; the epitome of a country house hotel. Dinner, room and breakfast from £65.00 per person including VAT.

SCAFELL HOTEL
Borrowdale, Nr. Keswick, Cumbria CA12 5XB

Telephone: 017687 77208   *Fax: 017687 77280*

London 291, Keswick 6, Carlisle 36, Kendal 36, Penrith 24

F licence; 24 en suite bedrooms (8 ground floor); all with direct dial telephone, tea and coffee making facilities, TV; full central heating; children welcome and dogs accepted; bar meals; drying room; river bathing; boating; fishing; pony trekking; tennis 6 miles; golf 10 miles.

It is not surprising that the Scafell is becoming one of Lakeland's leading hotels following its recent improvements and the consistent efforts of its management. Situated almost at the head of the beautiful Borrowdale Valley, its position is as outstanding as the service and comfort which it provides for all its guests. There is an excellent table d'hôte menu and, for those wishing to dine later, a comprehensive à la carte supper menu. Both menus are accompanied by a well balanced wine list. Year after year guests return to walk and climb for they know that they are going to be comfortable and well looked after. For the less energetic there are cosy and homely lounges. The bedrooms are comfortable and attractively furnished, all of them having their own private bathroom. Pleasant views are to be had of the sheltered garden ringed by mighty mountains on which internationally famous climbers have learned their craft. Yes, this is a home for the visitor seeking peace or exercise and wishing to get away from it all. Hotel open all year except January. Special weekend and midweek breaks November to March. Dinner, bed and breakfast from £40.75–£52.25.

THE BARBON INN
Barbon Via Carnforth, Nr. Kirkby Lonsdale
Cumbria LA6 2LJ

Telephone: 015242 76233   *Fax: 015242 76233*

**Kirkby Lonsdale 3, Kendal 11, Lancaster 17, Windermere 25,
Preston 38, London 239**

*F licence; 10 bedrooms, 1 en suite and 4 bathrooms (2 more en suite planned
for Autumn 1994); all bedrooms have TV; last orders for dinner 8.45 p.m.; bar
meals; special diets; children welcome; dogs accepted; golf ½ mile; riding 2 miles;
shooting/fishing locally; open all year; Mastercard and Visa credit cards accepted.*

Nothing here is as it first appears. The Barbon Inn looks like a small, quiet village
pub. It is true that the bar is where you will meet the locals, but the restaurant
is no pub diner. It is furnished with antiques, and serves superb food, but it is
not wholly sophisticated. Drop any "façades" that you might have, and bring
out your sense of humour! This is a fun place. Relax, enjoy yourself, and you
will soon understand what it is that the owner, Mrs. MacDiarmid is aiming at
– and succeeding. The bedrooms are all in keeping with the building; old,
creaking and crooked, but they are all prettily furnished with antiques and
comfortable beds. What do you do during the day in this remote part of England?
You can walk, fish, ride, play golf, drink in the pure air, or visit Sedbergh, Kirkby
Lonsdale, Kirkby Stephen or Kendal; within easy driving distance are the South
Lakes, Morecambe Bay and Skipton. Then, when you return to Barbon, you will
appreciate what this is all about. You will be a changed person, but I am sure
you will never regret it! Double room and breakfast from £55.00 including VAT.

THE MILL
Mungrisdale, Penrith, Cumbria CA11 0XR

Telephone: 017687 79659

Penrith 10, Keswick 10, London 290, Newcastle-on-Tyne 70

R & R licence; 9 bedrooms (2 ground floor) 2 with shower, 4 private bathrooms; all with TV; full central heating; dinner 7.00 p.m.; diets on request, with a vegetarian choice on offer each evening; baby listening; dogs allowed; snooker, darts and table tennis; sailing, boating and golf nearby; badminton in summer; riding; local fishing; clay pigeon shooting; no credit cards.

There are, to my mind two main advantages to the location of the Mill. Firstly, Mungrisdale is a secluded and little known part of the Lake District and therefore the crowds and traffic of the many holidaymakers are almost non-existent. Secondly, as this picturesque area is on the Eastern edge of the national park, not only is the centre easily accessible but so are such interesting places as the Eden Valley, Hadrian's Wall, the Solway Firth and Carlisle. Even the border regions of Scotland and the Yorkshire Dales are within touring range. Having said this, I am sure that many people would be quite happy to wander no further than a mile or two from this charming hotel, which dates from 1651. The Mill stands at the foot of the fells, set in a pretty garden with a mill leat and waterfall, and inside, it is cosy, cheerful and welcoming. The rooms in the Mill are not large but they are very well furnished and bright with flowers, the bedrooms are pretty and very comfortable, but it is the dining room that really excels. The food is nothing but delicious and beautifully presented, and this is born out by the fact that the restaurant has been awarded an AA Rosette for its cuisine. I can wholeheartedly recommend this quiet family hotel, superbly run by resident proprietors, Richard and Eleanor Quinlan. Dinner, bed and breakfast from £55.00 inclusive. Hotel closed from November till mid February.

THE SWAN HOTEL
Newby Bridge, Nr. Ulverston,
Cumbria LA12 8NB

Telephone: 015395 31681   *Fax: 015395 31917*

**London 261, Manchester 83, Bristol 238, Edinburgh 155,
Newcastle-upon-Tyne 102, Birmingham 159**

F licence; 36 en suite bedrooms including shower, all with TV, radio, tea/coffee making facilities, hairdryer and telephone; central heating; night service; late meals by arrangement; diets; children welcome, baby listening; conferences up to 20; fishing; marina; riding 2 miles; golf 6½ miles; most credit cards accepted.

Set 'twixt river and lake in what must be one of the most superb situations in the Lake District, the Swan has all the facilities that a traveller or holidaymaker could wish for. It has its own lovely marina, shop, fishing in the river and is close to the steam railway at Newby Bridge; all this at the end of Lake Windermere. The hotel was originally a coaching inn but has now been completely modernized to give every convenience. Special autumn breaks are offered and my only regret is that I could not stay longer to explore this lovely part of Cumbria. Room and breakfast from £60.00 single and £90.00 double. The Lonsdale Suite has a king size bed, luxurious drapes and craftsman-built mahogany furniture to luxury standard. Hotel open for 3-day Christmas Holiday break and 1, 2 or 3 day New Year break. 'Swan breaks' any two nights weekends only (Friday and Saturday or Saturday and Sunday) from £94.00 per person, dinner, bed and breakfast in double room with private bath. "Racing at Cartmel" – 2 day stay in May including breakfast and dinner, and an afternoon at the races, to support the "Swan at Newby Bridge Handicap Steeplechase". Spring to autumn "Swan break Super-Plus" – 4 day breaks – dinner, bed and breakfast, mini-cruise and "A Trip Down Memory Lane", from £192.00 per person. November 1995 sees the return of the now, widely acclaimed "Weekend of Gilbert and Sullivan", starring principals past and present in the world of opera. Other terms on request.

SHARROW BAY COUNTRY HOUSE HOTEL
Ullswater, Penrith, Cumbria CA10 2LZ

Telephone: 017684 86301 or 86483   *Fax: 017684 86349*

On the Howtown Road

London 289, Penrith 7, Kendal 33, Keswick 20, Windermere 25

R and R licence; 28 bedrooms; 24 with private bath and/or shower, including 6 cottage suites; TV; radio; antiques; peace; golf locally; lake bathing; boating; riding; fishing; small conference facilities; closed from Dec. 5th–Feb. 24th.

Away from the bustle of the holiday rush, in the most envied position in the Lake District, Francis Coulson M.B.E. and Brian Sack M.B.E. must be congratulated on their 47th year of service to the gourmets of the world, providing the most exquisite food and wines in the most comfortable of atmospheres. Reputed to be the first Country House Hotel in this country and to be approved by the Relais et Chateaux, only 21 being so included in Great Britain, is surely recommendation enough, but speak to anyone who has stayed here and you will hear nothing but superlatives as the owners believe in creating a home from home. The décor is superb, the service impeccable and the overall effect the product of these two brilliant hoteliers. Add to all this the beauty of the Lake and mountains and you have total perfection. I should add there is now a beautiful converted farmhouse called Bank House, about a mile from Sharrow, which has seven superbly furnished bedrooms, all with private bathrooms and lake views. Breakfast is served in the magnificent Refectory dining room, which was converted from the seventeenth century barn. It has a striking Portland stone fireplace and overmantle, which came from Warwick Castle. It also has incredible English silk damask curtains, old English furniture and a specially made carpet, being a copy of that in the Royal Opera House. Lunch and dinner are served at Sharrow Bay. Some of the staff have been with the hotel for over 30 years, and Nigel Lawrence and Nigel Lightburn, who are now directors, will carry on Sharrow Bay's renowned traditions. Tariff on application.

FAYRER GARDEN HOUSE HOTEL
Lyth Valley Road, Bowness-on-Windermere,
Cumbria LA23 3JP

Telephone: 015394 88195   *Fax: 015394 45986*

Bowness 1, Kendal 7, Manchester 76, Newcastle 90, London 280

*R & R licence; 14 en suite bedrooms (3 suitable for the infirm), all with direct
dial telephone and TV; last orders for dinner 8.00 p.m.; special diets; children
welcome; dogs accepted; conferences max. 24; tennis; free use of nearby leisure
centre with swimming pool and squash courts; sailing/boating and riding nearby;
golf 1 mile; shooting/fishing and hot air ballooning by arrangement; open all
year; all credit cards except Diners accepted.*

With superb views over Lake Windermere, yet away from the bustle of the
holidaymakers in Bowness itself, Fayrer Garden House Hotel shares its 5 acres
of grounds with not just its guests, but with deer, squirrels, badgers and the
ubiquitous rabbits. Inside, the beautifully decorated rooms all offer warmth,
comfort, tranquillity and a sense of wellbeing. Iain and Jackie Garside, known
for many years for the excellence of their previous hotel, are now bringing to
bear their skill and expertise to Fayrer Garden. Dining here is an experience.
With the Lake and the fells as a backdrop, the culinary creations, prepared by
Jackie and her team, are delicious and lovingly presented. We, here at *Signpost*,
wish them the success in this new venture, that they previously enjoyed and
so richly deserved. Room and breakfast from £27.50–£45.00, dinner, room and
breakfast from £37.50–£55.00, including VAT.

151

LINTHWAITE HOUSE HOTEL
Crook Road, Bowness-on-Windermere,
Cumbria LA23 3JA

Telephone: 015394 88600   *Fax: 015394 88601*

London 208, Bowness 1, Kendal 7, Manchester 76

R & R licence; 18 en suite bedrooms (5 ground floor rooms), all with direct dial telephone and satellite TV; room service; last orders for dinner 9.00 p.m.; light lounge lunches; special diets; children over 8 years welcome; conferences 20 max; sauna, solarium, spa pool, gymnasium and golf 1 mile; lake bathing; mountain walking and riding 3 miles; sailing/boating and water-skiing 1 mile; golf practice hole par 3; own tarn brown trout; open all year; all major credit cards accepted.

This hotel, situated on the B5284 Bowness to Kendal road, only a mile or so from Bowness, is surely the epitome of what every *Signposter* would like to find. It is set in 14 acres of superbly kept grounds with magnificent views of Lake Windermere and of every major peak in the Lake District. There is a well stocked tarn (in which 5lb trout have been caught) and where one can while away the day with a picnic. The golf practice area is surrounded by lovely woodland walks. Naturally, within a very short distance are all the other amenities that one expects in the area, such as swimming, yachting and tennis. But enough of outside activities! Inside the hotel is immaculate, bright and cheerful and most comfortably furnished. What more can I say, except that the food is superb and that so many of the guests return to Linthwaite again and again. Surely this must speak more eloquently than any words of mine can express. I am sure that any *Signposter* who visits here for the first time will, like others, keep coming back to the atmosphere of peace and tranquillity. Prices on application.

THE MORTAL MAN HOTEL
Troutbeck, Nr. Windermere,
Cumbria LA23 1PL

Telephone: 015394 33193. Visitors 32610   *Fax: 015394 31261*

London 283, Windermere Station 3, Kirkstone Summit 3, Patterdale 9

F licence; 12 en suite bedrooms, all with TV, telephone, trouser press, tea/coffee making facilities; last orders for dinner 9.00 p.m.; bar meals; diets available; dogs welcome; no children under 5 years old; free membership to Leisure Centre including swimming pool, sauna, jacuzzi, squash and gym 3 miles; riding ¼ mile; fishing rights.

Up on the hills on the long rise from Windermere to the summit of the Kirkstone Pass you'll spy a freshly painted, gabled, black and cream house a few hundred yards west. A sign at the entrance to a lane points the way to the Mortal Man, a hotel with a long, romantic and honourable history. It's just the place for a go-as-you-please holiday exploring the fells, lakes and passes. Under the capable management of Annette and Christopher Poulsom the hotel maintains the reputation that it has always enjoyed. As with so many hotels in the area, peace is the main attribute but with the Mortal Man this is accentuated by the fact that it stands on a little-used side road and even in the height of the season one can relax in comfort. Dinner, bed and breakfast from £55.00 single, £110.00 twin. Closed mid-November to mid-February.

THE OLD VICARAGE
COUNTRY HOUSE HOTEL
Witherslack, Cumbria LA11 6RS

Telephone: 015395 52381   *Fax: 015395 52373*

M6 Junction 36 10 mins., Sea 4, Kendal 8, Lake Windermere 6

*R & R licence; 10 en suite bedrooms and 5 in the Orchard House, all with
telephone, colour TV, full central heating; dinner 7.30 p.m. for 8.00 p.m.; diets;
children by arrangement; dogs by arrangement; all weather tennis court for
guests' use; sailing, golf, squash, badminton, riding, shooting, fishing all nearby;
Visa and Mastercard credit cards accepted.*

The Old Vicarage was recommended to me by one of the country's top hoteliers
– and how right he was to do so. For those wishing to visit the Lake District,
to remain in perfect peace and seclusion and yet to sample the art of cooking
and service at their best, then here is the venue in which to do so to perfection.
The hotel is set in a particularly beautiful valley and it offers the finest of food
prepared only from the freshest of ingredients. It is indeed a haven. The
atmosphere is of unhurried simplicity but the thought and energy expended to
achieve this ambience is, I am sure, immeasurable. Mr. and Mrs. Burrington-
Brown and Mr. and Mrs. Reeve have set a standard that many hotels will strive
to match but which few will attain. I look forward to visiting this unique hotel
again, and especially to staying in the "Celebration Suite", one of the new
bedrooms in the Orchard House, with its terraces overlooking unspoilt woodland.
Room and breakfast from £49.00 per person, inclusive of VAT. No service
charges. Open all year.

GEORGIAN HOUSE HOTEL
Manchester Road, Blackrod, Bolton,
Lancashire BL6 5RU

Telephone: 01942 814598　　　　　　　　　*Fax: 01942 813427*

Manchester 22, London 186, Cumbria 110, Liverpool 50, Blackpool 38

*F licence; 101 en suite bedrooms (4 for the disabled), all with direct dial telephone
and TV; room service; baby listening; night service; lift; last orders for dinner
10.00 p.m.; bar meals; diets; children welcome; dogs accepted; conferences 300
max; snooker/billiards; indoor swimming pool; leisure centre; sauna; solarium;
spa pool; gymnasium; dinner dances on Fridays and Saturdays; open all year;
all major credit cards accepted.*

Few hotels today can be described as exciting but this is one of those few that
can offer both excitement and relaxation. It is sophisticated but not pompous,
it is interestingly and well furnished and decorated, it is very comfortable and
it has a list of amenities to keep the most bored of guests occupied. There is a
large billiards room, a swimming pool, gymnasium, jacuzzi and there are sauna
and massage facilities to name but a few. Add to this list 5 conference suites
and a superb restaurant and you have a four star hotel that makes business a
pleasure and holidays in the area a delight. For the former, all modern teaching
aids are available and for the latter, the district has a host of attractions all within
a few miles. Have you been to Camelot or Wigan Pier for example? They are
not to be missed, and the Pennines, Morecambe Bay and even the Lake District
are not far away. For excellent service, food and comfort the Georgian House
Hotel represents all that is best in the area. Room and breakfast (midweek) from
£80.00, double room from £92.00.

MYTTON FOLD FARM HOTEL
Langho, Nr. Blackburn, Lancashire BB6 8AB

Telephone: 01254 240662   *Fax: 01254 248119*

M6 (Junction 31) 11, Blackburn 5½, Clitheroe 5½, Burnley 8

R & R licence; 27 en suite bedrooms (3 ground floor), all with colour TV, telephone and full central heating; last orders 9.30 p.m.; bar meals mid week lunchtimes; diets; children over 7 welcome; no dogs; conferences up to 300; challenging 18 hole golf course; local riding; Access and Visa cards accepted.

Here must be the epitome of family hotels. The proprietors have owned the farm for three generations and the present Mr. and Mrs. Hargreaves are running the hotel with their son David, and twin daughters, Barbara and Carole. The old stables were originally converted and these, together with various extensions, provide a real home from home for any weary traveller. Warm and comfortable furnishings contribute to the relaxing atmosphere and, in the evening, to sit in front of the fire, after a good meal and perhaps a bottle of wine, how good it is to reflect on the success that the family have had. The hotel is useful for the business man, since Preston, Blackburn, Clitheroe and Burnley are all within 10 miles and, for the tourist, Blackpool, The Lake District and the Yorkshire Dales are all easily accessible by car. Of particular interest locally is the Ribble Valley. All these places can be toured from a base at Mytton Fold Farm, only 11 miles from junction 31 on the M6. Prices start at £34.00 single, and £54.00 double. Preferential green fees for residents. Open all year.

CHADWICK HOTEL
South Promenade, Lytham St. Annes,
Lancashire FY8 1NP

Telephone: 01253 720061   *Fax: 01253 714455*

Blackpool 7, Preston 14, Lancaster 30

R & R licence; 72 en suite bedrooms (2 for the disabled) some with four-poster beds, some with spa baths, all with direct dial telephone and TV; room service; baby listening; night service; 24 hour food service; lift; last orders for dinner 8.30 p.m.; bar meals; special diets; children welcome; conferences max. 50; children's adventure soft play room; indoor heated swimming pool; leisure centre; sauna; solarium; spa pool; sea fishing; golf ½ mile; sailing / boating, tennis and squash courts 1 mile; riding 3 miles; open all year; all major credit cards accepted.

I was most impressed with this hotel. It is owned and run by the Corbett family, and every detail has been carefully thought out and provided. The staff are particularly charming and helpful, and they immediately make you feel at home. The décor is bright and airy, and all the rooms are well decorated and comfortable. Here are all the facilities of a large international hotel, but without the pomposity with which one often associates them. There are rooms for the disabled, there is a health club with an indoor, heated swimming pool, spa bath, solarium, and the bedrooms have every convenience including in-house movies and satellite TV. The Chadwick Hotel's newly refurbished restaurant serves excellent food, together with a good wine list. The hotel is situated right on the sea front of the pretty town of Lytham St. Annes, making The Chadwick an ideal venue for the holidaymaker, there are particularly good rates for families with children, or even more so, for the keen golfer as there are many superb courses within a very short distance. Double/twin room and breakfast from £24.00 per person, including VAT.

THE VICTORIA AND ALBERT HOTEL
Water Street, Manchester M3 4JQ
Telephone: 0161 832 1188   *Fax: 0161 834 2484*
Piccadilly Station 1, M62 2, M65 3, Manchester Airport 10, London 201

F licence; 132 en suite bedrooms (2 for the disabled, 17 executive rooms, 4 lounge suites & 6 rooms in the Ladies Wing); all bedrooms have direct dial telephone, tea/coffee making facilities and TV; 24 hour room service; night service; 2 lifts; last orders for dinner 10.30 p.m.; bar meals; special diets; conferences max. 350; snooker/billiards; curio shop; leisure centre; sauna; solarium; gymnasium; indoor heated swimming pool 200 yds; indoor car park; adjacent to Granada Studios Tour; open all year; most major credit cards accepted.

Of the few great international hotels in the north of England, The Victoria and Albert in Manchester city centre, is possibly the newest and certainly the best. Converted from a Victorian warehouse on the River Irwell, no expense has been spared in the design, materials or workmanship of the building, and the same applies to the décor and furnishings. It is a fabulous concept, well executed and it represents the ultimate in comfort. The staff have been chosen from the best in this country and abroad, and the overall result is an hotel of a standard from which all such hotels should be judged. The food, served in the Sherlock Holmes Restaurant and the Café Maigret is superb, and the hushed atmosphere of the hotel fills one with a sense of serenity. For those wishing to hold a meeting or large conference in Manchester, there is a variety of meeting rooms and suites, all with the most modern of visual aid equipment. All the public rooms and bedrooms are named after Granada Television programmes, and this is hardly surprising as the hotel was built by one of the Granada Group companies, and is situated only yards from their famous studios. Also, within a short distance are the Science Museums and G-Mex Centre. Anyone planning to visit this most interesting and exciting city, then The Victoria and Albert Hotel must be the obvious choice. Special weekend rates are offered from £82.00 per night, for a twin/double room including English breakfast and VAT, mid-week from £125.00.

BARGAIN BREAKS

Readers are recommended to telephone the hotels to confirm rates and conditions prior to booking.

THE NORTH WEST

CHESHIRE

ROWTON HALL HOTEL, Chester *page 123*
Special weekend breaks – Friday to Sunday £58.00 per person, per night, which includes accommodation, breakfast and table d'hôte dinner. Single room supplement £10.50 per night.

CUMBRIA

LOWBYER MANOR COUNTRY HOUSE HOTEL, Alston *page 125*
Any 2 nights (excluding Bank Holidays) £82.50 including dinner. Longer breaks on application.

LOVELADY SHIELD COUNTRY HOUSE HOTEL, Nr. Alston *page 126*
Winter breaks from October to December, and Spring Breaks during March, April and May. Any 2 consecutive nights: £99.00 for room with shower, £109.00 for room with bath and £119.00 for room with bath and shower. These prices are per person and include dinner, bed, breakfast and VAT. Additional days pro-rata.

KIRKSTONE FOOT COUNTRY HOUSE HOTEL, Ambleside *page 127*
Special Wine Weekends and low season tariff breaks. Open Christmas and New Year. Prices and further details upon application.

NANNY BROW COUNTRY HOUSE HOTEL & RESTAURANT, Ambleside *page 128*
Bargain breaks available on request.

ROTHAY MANOR HOTEL, Ambleside *page 129*
November–March: Midweek Break, to include dinner, room and breakfast from £136.00 per night for 2 people, Weekend Break from £146.00 per night for 2 people.

WATEREDGE HOTEL, Ambleside *page 130*
3 night Winter and Spring breaks, to include dinner, room, breakfast and VAT. Winter breaks available from 30th October–2nd December 1994, and Spring breaks available from 3rd February–27th April 1995 (excluding Easter). Midweek breaks £138.00 and weekend breaks £150.00. Prices are per person. Winter Breaks available from 29th October–3rd December 1995, tariff on request.

APPLEBY MANOR COUNTRY HOUSE HOTEL, Appleby-in-Westmorland *page 131*
Minimum 2 nights from £49.50 per person nightly, all year, including dinner, room and breakfast, and temporary membership of the leisure club. "Flying Falcons" breaks, 2 nights from £147.00. Try the romance of the "Cloud Nine Experience", champagne, four-poster, flower arrangement, free newspaper from £126.50. "Hangover Breaks", sample 12 single malt whiskies from a range of over seventy, prices from £124.00.

THE PHEASANT INN, Bassenthwaite Lake *page 132*
Winter rates available from November–March.

OVERWATER HALL, Nr. Bassenthwaite Lake, Ireby *page 133*
Bargain Winter Breaks from January to Mid February – 1 night from £34.50. 2 night breaks available from Mid February onwards, from £88.00 per person. All prices include dinner, room and breakfast. Weekly terms available all year round. Open for Christmas and New Year, with a special 3 day package for Christmas.

BARGAIN BREAKS

MARY MOUNT HOTEL, Borrowdale *page 134*
Reduced rates available for winter mid-week and 7 day breaks, from November 1994–March 1995, excluding Bank Holidays. Colour brochure and tariff sent on request.

HARE & HOUNDS COUNTRY INN, Bowland Bridge *page 135*
Midweek Breaks (Sunday–Thursday inclusive): 3 nights half board – £99.00 per person.

TARN END HOUSE HOTEL, Brampton *page 136*
Bargain Breaks are available. Tariff on application.

WHEELGATE COUNTRY HOUSE HOTEL, Coniston *page 137*
Special reduced rates for 3 nights or more. Autumn and Winter breaks also available – please contact hotel for further details.

GRAYTHWAITE MANOR HOTEL, Grange-over-Sands *page 138*
November–March; up to 50% off seasonal tariff. July and August special terms on application. Please write for details.

NETHERWOOD HOTEL, Grange-over-Sands *page 139*
Winter Breaks from 1st November 1994–31st March 1995: 2 nights £100.00– £110.00 and 3 nights £130.00–£140.00. Prices are per person, and include dinner, bed, full English breakfast and VAT. Spring/Summer/Autumn Breaks: 3 nights £174.75–£201.00 per person, and include dinner, bed, full English breakfast and VAT.

AYNSOME MANOR HOTEL, Nr. Grange-over-Sands *page 140*
Special 2, 3 and 7 day rates available throughout the year. £41.00–£45.00 per person, per night, for dinner, bed and breakfast, staying for a minimum of 2 nights. Bonus week (7 nights dinner, bed and breakfast) from £275.00.

THE WORDSWORTH HOTEL, Grasmere *page 141*
1st November–30th March 1995 (excluding Bank Holidays) – Monday to Thursday minimum 2 nights – dinner, bed and breakfast £69.50 per person, per night. Friday, Saturday, Sunday – £77.00 per person, per night. Champagne Breaks, minimum 2 nights including different champagne each night – £92.00 per person, per night.

DALE HEAD HALL LAKESIDE HOTEL, Keswick *page 142*
Logfire Winter breaks available from 7.11.94–15.12.94 and from 2.1.95– 13.4.95: prices from £90.00 for any 2 nights Monday to Friday, and £94.00 for any 2 nights Friday to Sunday inclusive. "Let's Go Break" (Spring / Summer / Autumn 1995) – Monday to Friday – any 3 nights from £46.00 per night. All special breaks are on a dinner, room and breakfast basis per person. Why not ask for their Victorian Christmas and New Year breaks?

LYZZICK HALL HOTEL, Keswick *page 143*
Bargain Breaks available from November–Easter, but hotel closed from mid. Jan.–mid. Feb. Tariff on request.

STAKIS KESWICK LODORE SWISS HOTEL, Keswick *page 144*
For guests staying a minimum of 2 nights, the holiday rate is applicable. The price includes dinner, bed and breakfast, and prices start from £41.00 per person per night. Open all year.

UNDERSCAR MANOR, Nr. Keswick, Applethwaite *page 145*
Details on enquiry at the time.

BARGAIN BREAKS

SCAFELL HOTEL, Nr. Keswick, Borrowdale *page 146*
Midweek Breaks are available from 7th November–23rd December and 13th February–30th March: any 2 consecutive nights Sunday–Thursday inclusive, £67.50 per person, dinner, bed and breakfast. Fell Break Weekends are available from 5th November–18th December, and 11th February–26th March: Friday evening to Sunday lunch, and include all dinners, packed lunches, breakfasts, afternoon tea and Sunday lunch – £99.75.

THE BARBON INN, Nr. Kirkby Lonsdale *page 147*
Breaks of 2 or more days are available. Further details on request.

THE SWAN HOTEL, Newby Bridge *page 149*
Swan Breaks – November 4th to 24th March 1995, 2 nights dinner, bed and breakfast from £94.00 per person. Can be taken Friday/Saturday or Saturday/Sunday. Includes free bottle of "Swan Label" wine, presented on departure. Swan Breaks Super-Plus, from £192.00 per person, for 4 nights, and includes dinner, bed and breakfast, mini cruise and steam train ride down memory lane.

FAYRER GARDEN HOUSE HOTEL, Windermere *page 151*
Winter and Spring Breaks: 2 nights, dinner, room and breakfast in a four-poster room overlooking the Lake, and whirlpool bath – £95.00 per person; 4 nights £155.00 per person with 5th nights accommodation free of charge. Standard rooms also available at reduced rates.

LINTHWAITE HOUSE HOTEL, Windermere *page 152*
Romantic Breaks (minimum 2 nights) – including champagne in room on arrival, heart shaped chocolates, canopied king size double bed with lake view, breakfast and candlelit dinner – tariff on application. Other breaks available throughout the year.

THE MORTAL MAN HOTEL, Nr. Windermere *page 153*
Winter breaks on request.

THE OLD VICARAGE COUNTRY HOUSE HOTEL, Witherslack *page 154*
Bargain Breaks are available all year (excluding Bank Holidays). 2 nights or more from £55.00 per person, per night, including dinner, bed and breakfast.

LANCASHIRE

GEORGIAN HOUSE HOTEL, Bolton *page 155*
Mini Break – Saturday dinner dance, à la carte dinner, accommodation, Sunday lunch and the use of the leisure facilities. Price per person £60.00 including VAT. Maxi Break – Friday and Saturday dinner dances, accommodation on both nights and use of the leisure facilities. Price per person £94.00 including VAT.

MYTTON FOLD FARM HOTEL, Langho *page 156*
Breaks are available for a minimum stay of 2 nights – £150.00 per couple. Price includes dinner on both nights from the table d'hôte menu, room and breakfast. Preferential green fees for residents.

CHADWICK HOTEL, Lytham St. Annes *page 157*
Midweek Mid-Winter Breaks, to include any 2–5 day period except Friday and Saturday, at a rate of £34.20 per person, per night, from our dinner, room and breakfast tariff. These breaks are available from 1st November 1994–1st April 1995, and also include full use of the health facilities.

GREATER MANCHESTER

THE VICTORIA AND ALBERT HOTEL, Manchester *page 158*
Any 2 nights between Friday and Sunday, from £41.00 per person, per night, to include room, breakfast and admission to Granada Studios Tour. Gourmet and Special Interest Weekends are also available – terms upon application.

YORKSHIRE & THE NORTH EAST
SELECTED LOCAL ATTRACTIONS

▮ Historic Houses, Gardens & Parks

CLEVELAND
Burn Valley Gardens, Hartlepool
Fairy Dell, Middlesbrough
Ormesby Hall, Ormesby, Middlesbrough
Ward Jackson Park, Hartlepool

COUNTY DURHAM
Eggleston Hall Gardens, Eggleston
Hardwick Hall Country Park, Stockton-on-Tees
Houghall Gardens, Durham

HUMBERSIDE
Burton Agnes Hall, Driffield
Burton Constable Hall & Country Park, Nr. Hull
Sledmere House, Driffield

NORTHUMBERLAND
Alnwick Castle
Belsay Hall, Castle & Gardens, Belsay
Cragside House & Country Park, Rothbury
Hexham Herbs, Chollerford
Howick Hall Gardens, Alnwick
Hulne Park, Alnwick
Lady Waterford Hall, Berwick-on-Tweed
Meldon Park, Morpeth
Otterburn Hall
Paxton House, Berwick-on-Tweed
Seaton Delaval Hall, Blyth
Shaw Garden Centre, Cramlington
Wallington House Walled Garden & Grounds, Morpeth

TYNE & WEAR
Bessie Surtees House, Newcastle-upon-Tyne
Bolam Lake Country Park, Newcastle-upon-Tyne
Kirkley Hall Gardens, Ponteland, Newcastle-upon-Tyne
Rising Sun Country Park & Countryside Centre, Benton
Saltwell Park, Gateshead

YORKSHIRE
Allerton Park, KInaresborough
Beningbrough Hall, York
Bramham Park, Wetherby
Burnby Hall Gardens, Pocklington
Castle Howard, Coneysthorpe
Constable Burton Hall Gardens, Leyburn
Duncombe Park, Helmsley
East Riddlesden Hall, Keighley
Epworth Old Rectory, Doncaster
Fairfax House, York
Golden Acre Park, Bramhope
Harewood House, Leeds
Harlow Carr Botanical Gardens, Harrogate
Japanese Garden, Horsforth
Kiplin Hall, Richmond
Land Farm Garden, Hebden Bridge
Lotherton Hall, Leeds
Margaret Waudby Oriental Garden, Upper Poppleton
Newburgh Priory, York
Newby Hall Gardens, Ripon
Normanby Hall, Scunthorpe
Nostell Priory, Wakefield
Nunnington Hall, York
Parcevall Hall Gardens, Skipton

YORKSHIRE (continued)
Ripley Castle, Harrogate
Saint Nicholas Gardens, Richmond
Sheffield Botanical Gardens, Sheffield
Sheriff Hutton Park, Nr. York
Stockfield Park, Wetherby
Sutton Park, Nr. York
Temple Newsam House,. Leeds
Thorp Perrow Arboretum, Bedale

▮ Walks & Nature Trails

CLEVELAND
Billingham Beck Valley Country Park

COUNTY DURHAM
Allensford Park, Consett
Blackton Nature Reserve, Teesdale
Derwent Walk, Consett
Durham Coast, Peterlee
Hamsterley Forest, Bishop Auckland

HUMBERSIDE
Elsham Hall Country & Wildlife Park, Brigg
Humber Bridge Country Park, Hessle
Normanby Hall Country Park, Scunthorpe

NORTHUMBERLAND
Allen Banks Woods, Hexham
Bedlington Country Park
Carlisle Park & Castle Wood, Morpeth
Fontburn Nature Reserve
Hareshaw Dene, Bellingham, Hexham
Ingram National Park Visitor Centre, Alnwick
Northumberland Coast, Newton-by-the-Sea, Alnwick
Plessey Woods Country Park
Scotch Gill Wood Local Nature Reserve, Morpeth

TYNE & WEAR
Derwent Walk Country Park, Rowlands Gill
The Leas & Marsden Rock, South Shields
Thornley Woodlands Centre, Rowlands Gill

YORKSHIRE
Anglers Country Park, Wintersett
Barlow Common Nature Reserve, Selby
Bretton Country Park, Wakefield
Bridestones Moor, Pickering
Brimham Rocks, Harrogate
Cannon Hall Country Park, Barnsley
Chevin Forest Park, Otley
Dalby Forest Drive & Visitor Centre, Pickering
Hardcastle Crags, Hebden Bridge
Howstean Gorge, Pateley Bridge
Malham Tarn, Settle
Millington Wood Local Nature Reserve
Marston Moor, Huddersfield
Newmillerdam Country Park, Wakefield
Ogden Water, Halifax
Ravenscar Coastline, Scarborough
Rother Valley Country Park, Sheffield
Sutton Bank Nature Trail – between Helmsley & Thirsk
Ulley Country Park, Sheffield
Worsbrough Country Park, Barnsley

▓ Historical Sites & Museums

CLEVELAND
Guisborough Priory, Guisborough
Gray Art Gallery & Museum, Hartlepool
Guisborough Museum
Saltburn Smugglers Heritage Centre
PSS Wingfield Castle, Hartlepool

COUNTY DURHAM
Barnard Castle
Beamish – The North of England Open Air
    Museum
Durham Cathedral
Durham Castle
Raby Castle, Staindrop

HUMBERSIDE
Burton Agnes Manor House, Driffield
Maister House, Hull
Wilberforce House, Hull

NORTHUMBERLAND
Aydon Castle
Bamburgh Castle
Berwick Castle, Berwick-on-Tweed
Brinkburn Priory, Longframlington
Chesters Roman Fort, Hexham
Chillingham Castle
Dunstanburgh Castle
Edlingham Castle
Etal Castle, Etal, Cornhill-on-Tweed
Grace Darling Museum, Bamburgh
Hadrian's Wall
Hexham Abbey
House of Hardy Museum & Country Store,
    Alnwick
Lindisfarne Castle, Holy Island, Berwick-
    on-Tweed
Marine Life Centre & Fishing Museum,
    Seahouses
Norham Castle, Berwick-on-Tweed
Prudhoe Castle
Warkworth Castle
Wine & Spirit Museum & Victorian Chemist
    Shop, Berwick-on-Tweed

TYNE & WEAR
Castle Keep, Newcastle-upon-Tyne
Hatton Gallery, Newcastle-upon-Tyne
The Laing Art Gallery, Newcastle-upon-Tyne
Newburn Hall Motor Museum, Newcastle-
    upon-Tyne
The Shipley Art Gallery, Gateshead
South Shields Museum, South Shields

YORKSHIRE
Aldborough Roman Town, Nr. Boroughbridge
Assembly Rooms, York
Barden Tower, Bolton Abbey
Barley Hall, York
Beverley Minster, Beverley
Bishops House, Sheffield
Bolling Hall, Bradford
Bolton Castle, Leyburn
Borthwick Institute of Historical Research, York
Bronte Parsonage Museum, Haworth
Captain Cook Memorial Museum, Whitby
Clifford's Tower, York
Dales Countryside Museum, Hawes
Eureka! The Museum for Children, Halifax
Fountains Abbey & Studley Royal, Ripon
Fulneck Moravian Settlement & Museum, Nr.
    Pudsey

YORKSHIRE (continued)
Gainsthorpe Deserted Medieval Village
Georgian Theatre Royal & Museum, Richmond
Jervaulx Abbey, Ripon
Jorvik Viking Centre & Brass Rubbing Centre,
    York
Kirkstall Abbey, Leeds
King's Manor, York
Marmion Tower, Ripon
Mount Grace Priory, Northallerton
National Museum of Photography, Film & Tele-
    vision, Bradford
National Railway Museum, York
Red House, Gomersal
Rievaulx Abbey, Rievaulx
Sion Hill Hall & Birds of Prey Centre, Kirky
    Wiske
Skipton Castle, Skipton
The Old Smithy & Heritage Centre, Owston Ferry
Tetley's Brewery Wharf, Leeds
Treasurer's House, York
York Castle Museum, York
York Story, York
York Minster, York

▓ Entertainment Venues

CLEVELAND
Botanic Centre, Middlesbrough
Cleveland Craft Centre, Middlesbrough
Margrove South Cleveland Heritage Centre,
    Boosbeck, Saltburn-by-the Sea
Stewart Park, Middlesbrough

COUNTY DURHAM
Bowlees Visitor Centre, Middleton-in-Teesdale

HUMBERSIDE
Bondville Miniature Village, Sewerby
Fosse Hill Jet Ski Centre, Driffield
Humberside Ice Arena, Hull
Sewerby Hall, Park & Zoo, Bridlington

NORTHUMBERLAND
Belford Craft Gallery
Tower Knowe Visitor Centre, Kielder Water,
    Hexham

TYNE & WEAR
Bowes Railway Centre, Gateshead
Predator Paintball, Newcastle-upon-Tyne

YORKSHIRE
Catterick Indoor Ski Centre, Catterick Garrison
Flamingo Land Family Funpark & Zoo, Malton
Harrogate Ski Centre, Yorkshire Showground
Hemsworth Water Park & Playworld
Hornsea Pottery Leisure Park & Freeport
    Shopping Village
Kinderland, Scarborough
Lightwater Valley Theme Park, North Stainley
North of England Clay Target Centre, Rufforth
Piece Hall, Halifax
Sheffield Ski Village, Sheffield
The Alan Ayckbourn Theatre in the Round,
    Scarborough
Tockwith (Multi-Drive) Activity Centre,
    Tockwith
Thrybergh Country Park
Turkish Baths, Harrogate
Watersplash World, Scarborough
The World of Holograms, Scarborough

163

YORKSHIRE & THE NORTH EAST
DIARY OF EVENTS 1995

December 31 '94 ALLENDALE BAAL FESTIVAL
Market Square, Allendale, Northumberland.
Villagers parade in costume with burning tar barrels on their
heads to celebrate New Year. Also bonfire.

January 1 to
May 11
HENRY MOORE EXHIBITION
Bretton Country Park, West Bretton, West Yorkshire.

January 20 YORK COIN AND STAMP COLLECTIONS FAIR
York Racecourse, Tadcaster Road, York.
Largest event of this kind outside London.

February 10–25 JORVIK VIKING FESTIVAL
Various venues, York.
Viking themed – combat, feasts, fireworks, torchlit proces-
sion and boatburning, crafts and music.

March 10–12 WORKING DAYS
Abbeydale Industrial Hamlet, Abbeydale Road, South
Sheffield.
Working demonstration of traditional metal crafts plus
home-based crafts.

March 11 CONCERT ROYAL
The Buttercross, Brigg, Humberside.
Commemorates the 300th anniversary of Purcell's death.

*March 23–25 HORSE RACING, THE WILLIAM HILL LINCOLN
FESTIVAL
Doncaster Racecourse, Doncaster, South Yorkshire.

March 25 23RD IAAF/SNICKERS WORLD CROSS COUNTRY
CHAMPIONSHIPS
Maiden Castle, Off A177, Durham City.
Races in junior and senior men's and women's category.
80 nations – the elite of the world's distance runners.

March 25–26 MOTORSPORTS '95
Sheffield Arena, Sheffield, South Yorkshire.

April 1 11TH SPRING SHOW INCLUDING ALPINES
Youth Centre, Grammar School Road, Brigg, Humberside.

April 1 MICKLEGATE SINGERS EASTER CONCERT
Chapter House, York Minster, York.

*April 14–30 EMBASSY WORLD CHAMPIONSHIP SNOOKER
Crucible Theatre, Norfolk Street, Sheffield.

April 15–17 EASTER EXTRAVANGANZA
Beningbrough Hall, Shipton-by-Beningbrough, North
Yorkshire.

April 20–23 SPRING FLOWER SHOW
Valley Gardens, Harrogate, North Yorkshire.

May 16–18	HORSE RACING, THE DANTE MEETING York Racecourse, Tadcaster Road, York.
May 26 to June 11	SWALEDALE FESTIVAL Various venues, Swaledale and Wensleydale, North Yorkshire. Annual rural arts festival with classical, jazz and folk music.
May 29	NORTHUMBERLAND COUNTY SHOW (agricultural) Tynedale Park Rugby Ground, Corbridge, Northumberland.
June 3	ALLENDALE FAIR Market Square, Allendale, Northumberland. County Fair, tug of war, strong man competition and displays.
June 10–11	DURHAM REGATTA River Wear, Durham.
June 16–17	HORSE RACING, THE TIMEFORM CHARITY DAY York Racecourse, Tadcaster Road, York.
June 24 to July 2	FILEY EDWARDIAN FESTIVAL Various venues, Filey, North Yorkshire.
June 25 to July 1	ALNWICK FAIR Alnwick Market Place, Alnwick, Northumberland. Costume re-enactment of a fair dating from the middle ages, with craft stalls, duckings and stage entertainment.
July 7–16	YORK EARLY MUSIC FESTIVAL Various venues, York, North Yorkshire.
July 11–13	GREAT YORKSHIRE SHOW Great Yorkshire Showground, Wetherby Road, Harrogate, North Yorkshire.
July 15–16	DURHAM COUNTY SHOW (agricultural) Clondyke Garden Centre, Lambton Park, Chester-le-Street, Durham.
July 23	BRASS BAND COMPETITION & CONCERT Burton Constable Hall, Nr. Hull, Humberside.
July 27 to August 10	HARROGATE INTERNATIONAL FESTIVAL Various venues, Harrogate, North Yorkshire.
August 8–13	HULL JAZZ FESTIVAL Hull Marina, Hull, Humberside.
August 22–24	HORSE RACING, THE EBOR MEETING York Racecourse, Tadcaster Road, York.
August 31 to September 3	INTERNATIONAL SEA SHANTY FESTIVAL Hull Marina, Hull, Humberside.

September (to be   GREAT NORTH RUN
confirmed)   Official World Half Marathon, Newcastle-upon-Tyne.

September 4–9   SCARBOROUGH OPEN GOLF WEEK
                    North Cliff & South Cliff Courses, also Filey Golf Course,
                    North Yorkshire.

September 6–7   HORSE RACING, ST. LEDGER
                    Doncaster Racecourse, Ledger Way, Doncaster, South
                    Yorkshire.

September 15–16   GREAT AUTUMN FLOWER SHOW
                    Exhibition Hall, Harrogate, North Yorkshire.

October 7–10   YORKSHIRE THREE CHOIRS FESTIVAL
                    Ripon Cathedral, Ripon, North Yorkshire.

*October 20–21   HORSE RACING, RACING POST TROPHY
                    Doncaster Racecourse, Doncaster, South Yorkshire.

*Denotes provisional date

For further information contact:
Yorkshire & Humberside Tourist Board   Northumbria Tourist Board
312 Tadcaster Road   Aykley Heads
York   Durham
YO2 2HF.   DH1 5UX
Tel: 01904 707961   Tel: 0191 384 6905

RAMSIDE HALL HOTEL
Carrville, Durham, County Durham DH1 1TD

Telephone: 0191 386 5282   *Fax: 0191 386 0399*

**Durham 3, A1 (M) 400 metres, Newcastle 15,
Newcastle Airport 20 minutes, Teesside Airport 20 minutes**

F licence; 82 en suite bedrooms (2 for the disabled), all with direct dial telephone and TV; room service; baby listening; night service; lift; last orders for dinner 9.30 p.m.; bar meals; special diets; children welcome; dogs accepted; conferences max. 400; 2 golf courses within 5 miles; open all year; all major credit cards accepted.

Just 400 metres from the A1 (M) – A690 interchange, this sumptuous hotel has grown from a restaurant complex with a few rooms, to the international standard hotel that it is today. There are few country house hotels that can match the luxury of its bedrooms, and still with a range of restaurants, guests can choose the style of dining that they prefer. There is a grill room, a carvery and a full restaurant. Each serves a large selection of excellent dishes, superbly presented and cooked. There is naturally, a list of wines to suit all tastes and pockets. Added to this, is a variety of conference facilities for the businessman, ranging from the Ballroom and Foyer seating 400 theatre style, to a syndicate room for 10 delegates. For those on holiday, the city of Durham is nearby, and the North Pennines and North Yorkshire Moors are only a short distance away. There is no doubt that for convenience of access with the motorway complex and with the Teesside and Newcastle Airports being so close, this hotel must be top of every businessman's list for the area and a must for the tourist. Of course, you could just pamper yourself on a gourmet break for which a number of package deals are available. Room and breakfast from £82.00 single, £98.00 double, including VAT.

ROYAL COUNTY HOTEL
Old Elvet, Durham, County Durham DH1 3JN

Telephone: 0191 386 6821   *Fax: 0191 386 0704*

Newcastle 15, Edinburgh 115, London 265

F licence; 150 en suite bedrooms (1 for the disabled), all with direct dial telephone and TV; room service; baby listening; night service; 3 lifts; last orders for dinner (Mon–Sat) 10.15 p.m.; diets; children welcome; dogs accepted; conferences 140 max; Brasserie; indoor heated swimming pool; leisure centre; sauna; solarium; steam room; spa pool; gymnasium; open all year; all major credit cards accepted.

The historic city of Durham is surely the ideal location for the holidaymaker from which to explore the delightful north eastern corner of England. The beautiful scenery of the counties of Durham, Yorkshire, Northumberland and even Cumbria, are all within easy reach, and the city itself is a must on any tourists itinery. For the businessman, Durham also makes an ideal centre for meetings and conferences, as the industrial areas of the north east are all easily accessible by road or rail. Situated right in the heart of Durham, on the very banks of the River Wear, is this gem of an hotel. Originally a coaching inn, but now extended and modernised, The Royal County offers everything that the discerning guest could hope for. The comfort is superb, the service excellent but discreet, and the ambience, warm and friendly. There is a restaurant offering the most delicious food from well thought out menus, and a Brasserie for more informal meals. After indulging in all this luxury, the hotel has a super leisure centre to suit all moods, with an indoor heated swimming pool, gymnasium, sauna and solarium. I cannot recommend the Royal County too highly – it is a hedonists delight! Room and breakfast from £96.00 single, £124.00 double/twin, weekly rates on application. Swallow Breakaway Packages are available, please see the Bargain Break section for further details.

THE WATERFRONT HOTEL
Dagger Lane, Old Town, Kingston Upon Hull,
Humberside HU1 2LS

Telephone: 01482 227222   *Fax: 01482 227222*

Beverley 9, York 35, Manchester 100

F licence; 30 en suite bedrooms, all with direct dial telephone and TV; room service; night service; last orders for dinner 10.00 p.m.; bar meals; special diets; dogs accepted by arrangement; conferences max. 100; night club; sailing / boating 150 yds; sea bathing nearby; several golf courses within 5 miles; all credit cards except Diners accepted.

This extraordinary hotel has been created from a Victorian warehouse, and in the process of this conversion, it has been awarded many national and international accolades. Not surprisingly, the atmosphere here is unusual, but this does not detract in any way from the comfort of the guests. Every detail has been well thought out, and the décor is warm and naturally different. There are various bars and restaurants, together with a nightclub, so wherever you choose to wine and dine, you are sure to be agreeably surprised. For the businessman, there are conference facilities with all the latest equipment, and for the holidaymaker, there is, within walking distance, the waterfront with its marina. Not far away is the Humber Bridge, and further afield are the east coast resorts of Bridlington and Scarborough. York and Harrogate are easily reached on a day trip through the lovely Yorkshire countryside. For those looking for something different in an hotel, without sacrificing the comfort that we now expect, The Waterfront is an experience well worth trying. Room from £45.00 including VAT.

WAREN HOUSE HOTEL
Waren Mill, Bamburgh, Northumberland NE70 7EE

Telephone: 01668 214581   *Fax: 01668 214484*

Berwick 14, Alnwick 14, Newcastle 45, London 350

F licence; 7 en suite bedrooms (all no smoking), with telephone and colour TV; last orders 8.30 p.m.; special diets; no children; croquet lawn; tennis court; sea-bathing; riding; bird-watching; local sailing/boating; 7 golf courses within 12 miles; shooting/fishing by arrangement; all major credit cards accepted.

The North-East coast offers few hotels of distinction, but Waren House is one of those which can boast exceptional quality. After battling with the traffic on the A1, a sign points you to Waren Mill. Follow 2 miles of peaceful back roads and signposts will direct you up the tree lined drive to the house. Having been quietly shown to your room where sherry awaits you, perhaps before doing anything else, you will complete the unwinding by enjoying a hot tub in a superb bathroom. Throughout the hotel the furnishings, mostly beautiful antiques, and the immaculate and well chosen décor, exude a warm and friendly atmosphere. But this is not all. Waren House is a haven for the gastronome. Delicious repasts prepared from the freshest of ingredients are tastefully presented and a most thoughtfully chosen wine list is provided with the largest selection of half bottles I have ever seen. Discreet service completes the air of peace and well-being and Anita and Peter Laverack, the owners, are to be congratulated on the ways they constantly find to improve this delightful hotel. I should add, that a visit to this area is more than worthwhile, not only to stay at Waren House, but to visit such castles as Bamburgh, Alnwick, Dunstanburgh and Warkworth. For the ornithologist, there is a wealth of bird life at Budle Bay and the Farn Islands Bird Sanctuaries and, of interest to the tourist, Lindisfarne and the Cheviot Hills are but a short distance away. Room and breakfast from £52.00 per person, double occupancy and two suites are also available. No smoking except in the library. RAC 3 Star, ETB 4 Crown Highly Commended. Open all year.

APPLETON HALL HOTEL
Appleton-le-Moors, N. Yorkshire YO6 6TF

Telephone: 01751 417227 / 417452   *Fax: 01751 417540*

London 232, York 33, Whitby 26, Scarborough 24, Thirsk 24, Malton 15

R and R licence; 10 en suite bedrooms, including 2 suites and a four-poster, all with TV; full central heating; lift; meals to 8.30 p.m.; diets; dogs welcome; golf 1½ miles, riding 3 miles, fishing by arrangement; Mastercard, Amex, Visa credit cards accepted.

If you are looking for peace and tranquillity away from the usual tourist routes, then here at Appleton Hall is the hotel for which you have been searching. The Hall is an English country house which has been converted to form a most comfortable hotel with all its bedrooms en suite. There are magnificent views, especially from the elegant lounge with its comfortable furniture and log fire. As the days grow longer and warmer, afternoon tea is served on the terrace. The Hall is situated at the end of the picturesque and historic village of Appleton-le-Moors. Inside, there is a cosy bar serving over 80 brands of whisky, apart from the normal range of drinks. Mrs. Davies uses the freshest of ingredients, and produces a delicious range of English dishes which are available throughout the day and evening. One day is hardly enough time to enjoy this hotel and its lovely surroundings, and special breaks are available for those wishing to stay longer. Dinner, bed and breakfast from £45.00, £2.50 supplement per person for suites or four-poster room. Open all year round.

171

ROSE AND CROWN HOTEL
Bainbridge, Wensleydale, North Yorkshire DL8 3EE

Telephone: 01969 650225   *Fax: 01969 650735*

London 250, Leeds 55, York 60, Newcastle 70

F licence; 12 en suite bedrooms, all with colour TV and full central heating; last orders 9.30 p.m.; bar meals, diets; children welcome; dogs allowed; day conferences up to 100; private functions; pool table; fishing from hotel; Mastercard and Visa cards accepted.

For *Signpost* readers who have had enough of the grand hotel and are looking for a simpler venue from which to explore either Yorkshire, Lancashire or Cumbria, then the Rose and Crown offers the best of alternatives. Situated overlooking the green and village of Bainbridge in some of the loveliest of English countryside, it surely is in a prime position for a small hotel. Originally built in 1445, the hotel is now run by the Collins family and the personal touch is always evident. The furnishings and décor are warm and comfortable, including log fires and original beamed ceilings. The food, all of which is home made, is prepared from local produce wherever possible, and this is reflected by the number of regional dishes on the menu. The Rose and Crown makes a super base from which to immerse oneself in the immediate surroundings or to tour a vast area containing all that is best in the North of England. Open all year. Room and breakfast start at £28.00 per person in winter, to £31.00 in summer, dinner, bed and breakfast from £37.00, and weekly rates for dinner, bed and breakfast on application.

OAKWOOD HALL HOTEL
Bingley, West Yorkshire BD16 4AW

Telephone: 01274 564123/563569   *Fax: 01274 561477*

Bradford 6, Keighley 4, Leeds 15, London 206

F licence; 20 en suite bedrooms (4 ground floor), all with telephone, col. TV, full central heating; night porter; meals to 9.30 p.m.; diets; children welcome; conferences up to 50; Mastercard, Amex, Visa, Diners credit cards accepted.

Situated on the outskirts of the market town of Bingley, in wooded surroundings, Oakwood Hall is a large Victorian listed building which has been most tastefully and comfortably decorated and furnished to provide all that the tourist or business person expects of a modern hotel, without detracting from the splendour that our forebears admired. A full à la carte menu of English and Continental cuisine is available, as are bar meals. It is perhaps superfluous to say that the food is exceptional, as is witnessed by the fact that many people from a wide area choose either to dine here or to hold private functions. The restaurant is open for lunches every day except Saturday. The hotel is as much a perfect venue from which to conduct a business visit as it is an excellent centre from which to tour this lovely part of Yorkshire. Leeds, Bradford, Halifax and Harrogate are only a short drive from the hotel and within walking distance are the delights of the Aire Valley. The Leeds–Liverpool canal with the famous Bingley Five Rise Locks is a must for any tourist. Ilkley Moor, the Brontë country and the superb scenery around Skipton are also within easy motoring distance. Room rates – from £45.00 single, £80.00 double, inclusive of full English breakfast and VAT. Open all year, except for one week at Christmas.

DEVONSHIRE ARMS
COUNTRY HOUSE HOTEL
Bolton Abbey, Skipton, North Yorkshire BD23 6AJ
Telephone: 01756 710441   Telex: 51218   Fax: 01756 710564
Leeds 20, York 40, Ilkley 6, Harrogate 20

F licence; 40 en suite bedrooms (18 ground floor), all with telephone, TV; night service; last orders 10.00 p.m.; bar meals; diets; children welcome; baby listening; dogs accepted; conferences max. 150; golf nearby; riding, helicopter tours & tailor-made team building activity events can be arranged; classic car motoring; shooting; fishing; leisure health & beauty therapy centre.

The Devonshire at Bolton Abbey, for many years renowned as one of the best hotels in Yorkshire, is a contrast in styles. On the one hand there is the original coaching inn with the warmth and atmosphere of days gone by, and on the other, is the new extension with all the light and space created by a modern building. The superb furnishings and décor have been most tastefully chosen by the Duchess of Devonshire herself, using many paintings and antiques from her home at Chatsworth. Seven of the bedrooms have four-poster beds made by the craftsmen at Chatsworth Carpenters, and six rooms have been designated non-smoking. However, this is no old-fashioned hotel, for the modern conveniences are discreetly at hand and the service is impeccable, earning it the coveted Yorkshire and Humberside Tourist Board "Hotel of the Year Award", for the past 3 years. The food, acclaimed by all in the county, is delicious, well presented and served by willing and attentive staff. It need hardly be added that the hotel is situated in one of the most enviable of positions. Set in the heart of Wharfedale, it is close to Bolton Abbey, and is within easy motoring distance of Yorkshire's many other attractions. Here is the ideal venue for a business meeting or conference, and, as with most things, The Devonshire can cater for these, providing all the visual aids, secretarial services, telex. etc. necessary. To sum up, this is a charming, stylish hotel, thoroughly modern in its approach to comfort and efficiency. Room and breakfast from £95.00 single, £125.00 double. Open all year. All major credit cards accepted.

THE BALMORAL HOTEL AND
HENRY'S RESTAURANT
Franklin Mount, Harrogate, N. Yorks. HG1 5EJ

Telephone: 01423 508208   *Fax: 01423 530652*

London 200, York 20, Yorkshire Dales 15, Leeds/Bradford Airport 18

R & R licence; 20 en suite bedrooms (9 four poster rooms), all with direct dial telephone and TV; room service; baby listening; limited night service; last orders for dinner 9.00 p.m. for 9.30 p.m.; diets; children welcome; dogs accepted; conferences (boardroom) 20 max (theatre style) 30 max; solarium; indoor heated swimming pool and leisure facilities 100 yards away; 4 golf courses and riding stables nearby; tennis by arrangement; open all year; major credit cards accepted.

What a delightful surprise it was to discover this superb hotel. It is situated in its own award winning gardens, away from the centre of town and yet it is within walking distance of all the amenities that Harrogate provides. I will not, however, dwell on Harrogate itself with its conference centre, shops and wonderful surrounding countryside, for it is the hotel which is so unusual. The Balmoral is beautifully furnished, mostly with antiques and tastefully decorated to create a warm, luxurious and welcoming atmosphere. The bedrooms are all individual, many having four poster beds and again, are extremely comfortable with thoughtfully chosen décor. Everything that you could possibly need is provided and to stay in one of these rooms is an experience in luxury. The food here is not only imaginative but is prepared from the finest ingredients, cooked to perfection and served by friendly and attentive staff. If we gave such awards, this hotel would certainly be my "discovery of the year". Room and breakfast from £67.00 single, £90.00 double and weekly rates on application. Short breaks are also available throughout the year. E.T.B. 4 Crowns Highly Commended.

GRANTS HOTEL
Swan Road, Harrogate, North Yorkshire HG1 2SS

Telephone: 01423 560666   *Fax: 01423 502550*

A1 10, M1 10, Leeds 15, M62 15, Manchester 70

F licence; 42 en suite bedrooms (1 for the disabled), all with direct dial telephone and TV; room service; baby listening; night porter; lift; last orders for dinner 9.30 p.m.; bar meals; special diets; children welcome; dogs accepted; conferences max. 70; golf and tennis ½ mile; riding 3 miles; open all year; all major credit cards accepted.

I will not dwell on the delights of Harrogate and the beautiful county of Yorkshire, other than to say that there can be nowhere in England with so much to do and see, in either town or country, within so short a walking or driving distance. To me, one of the greatest attractions is Grants Hotel. It is rapidly gaining a well deserved reputation as one of the best small town house hotels in the country. From the first warm welcome to the final departure, the efficient and courteous staff ensure that a stay here is a memorable one. The beautifully decorated rooms exude an air of luxury, and the bedrooms are superbly comfortable, with all the touches that make life so easy these days in a top class establishment. The Chimney Pots Restaurant, also building a name for itself over a wide area, is excellent and the food is varied, interesting and delicious. The running of the hotel is orchestrated by Peter and Pam Grant, who are to be congratulated on the many accolades and awards that they receive. The hotel is ideally situated for shopping, conferences, touring and so on, but it is also particularly suitable for short breaks either of a quiet nature or of a more sporting type. Grants is affiliated to "The Academy" Health and Leisure Centre, with swimming pool, gym, dance studio, squash courts, indoor and outdoor tennis and spa treatment salon. Room and breakfast from £49.50, Super Value Breaks available.

THE WHITE HOUSE HOTEL
10 Park Parade, Harrogate, N. Yorkshire HG1 5AH

Telephone: 01423 501388   *Fax: 01423 527973*

Yorkshire Dales 15, York 16, Leeds 16, London 200

R & R licence; 10 en suite bedrooms, all with direct dial telephone and TV; room service; baby listening; last orders for dinner 9.00 p.m.; bar meals at lunchtime; special diets; children welcome; no dogs; conferences max. 50; several golf courses nearby; open all year; Visa, Amex and Diners credit cards accepted.

When visiting Harrogate either on business or as a tourist, there are few hotels that can match the personal service, comfort, tranquillity and cuisine that The White House offers. The House, built in 1836 as a venetian villa for the Mayor of Harrogate, faces 200 acres of delightful parkland, and is thus, far removed from the pandemonium of the town centre which is only a 10 minute walk away. Inside, the rooms are fabulously decorated and furnished, and yet have a "lived in" feel that immediately puts you at ease. A great deal of thought has been expended to ensure that guests want for nothing, and the owner, Jennie Forster, together with her staff, are always on hand to help with advice on the locality. The food here is interesting, often unusual and simply delicious. This is indeed the epitome of a country house hotel, within easy walking distance of the centre of this delightful floral town, and within a short drive of all that the superb county of Yorkshire is famous. Single room and breakfast from £70.00, dinner, room and breakfast from £88.00, including VAT.

STONE HOUSE HOTEL
Sedbusk, Nr. Hawes, Wensleydale,
N. Yorkshire DL8 3PT

Telephone: 01969 667571   *Fax: 01969 667720*

Harrogate 49, Leeds 57, York 65, Newcastle 74, Edinburgh 157, London 250

R & R licence; 18 bedrooms (5 ground floor), 17 en suite; all with direct dial telephone and TV; baby listening; last orders for dinner 8.00 p.m.; special diets; children welcome; dogs accepted; conferences max. 36; games room; snooker/ billiards; croquet; grass tennis court; bird watching; shooting/fishing locally; sailing/boating 5 miles; riding 10 miles; golf 17 miles; horse racing at Catterick, Ripon and Thirsk; hotel closed in January; all major credit cards accepted.

A country house hotel should ideally provide warmth and comfort, personal service, excellent food and outstanding surroundings. Here, at the Stone House Hotel, you are cosseted by all this and much more. The owners, the Taplin family, take a great interest in the welfare and comfort of their guests. They share their interest in such things as a collection of Dinky models and antiques, and they willingly guide people on what to do in the vicinity. The Taplin's ensure that the food is of the highest quality, and the wines well chosen. All this is provided in a lovely building, built at the beginning of the century, situated high up in a secluded position with spectacular views of the Pennines. For readers wishing to "get away from it all", and yet who want to experience all that is best in the Yorkshire Dales, this must be, not only one of the finest venues, but also represents the best value for money. Room and breakfast from £25.50 per person, and dinner, room and breakfast from £41.00 per person, including VAT. A 5% discount is available for stays of 3–6 nights and a 10% discount for a 7 night stay. These must be on a dinner, room and breakfast basis.

FEVERSHAM ARMS HOTEL
Helmsley, North Yorkshire YO6 5AG

Telephone: 01439 770766   *Fax: 01439 770346*

York 20, Teeside Airport 35

F licence; 18 en suite bedrooms (6 ground floor), some four poster, all with radio, telephone, TV, full central heating; last orders 9.30 p.m.; diets; children welcome; baby listening; dogs welcome; conferences up to 30 (18 residential); games room; swimming pool; tennis court and gardens in hotel's grounds; riding and golf nearby; Visa, Amex, Mastercard and Diners Club cards accepted.

Originally an old coaching inn, this friendly and comfortable hotel imbues in its guests a sense of warmth and well being. The bedrooms are well appointed with every modern convenience, including hair drier, safe, trouser press, tea/coffee making facilities and television with satellite channels. The reception rooms are equally relaxing and comfortable. The acclaimed restaurant specialises in game and seafood, but there is a vast menu which caters for all tastes. The cooking is excellent, the presentation admirable, and the award winning wine list is incredible, with the largest collection of Spanish wines that I have seen in the U.K. There is also a bar menu, which would put many an hotel's restaurant menu to shame, and on a hot day, to dine either sitting on the patio or by the superb swimming pool, is my idea of heaven. I feel that most guests will loathe to leave the Feversham Arms, but if they must, then Helmsley is an excellent centre for many sporting activities and for exploring the North York Moors National Park. Room and breakfast from £55.00 single, £70.00 twin or double, and four-poster or suite £80.00. Bargain breaks available all year round. Open all year.

THE PHEASANT
Harome, Helmsley, N. Yorkshire YO6 5JG

Telephone: 01439 771241

Helmsley 3, York 22, London 220, Scarborough 28, Leeds 48, Edinburgh 160

R & R licence; 14 en suite bedrooms (1 ground floor), all with telephone, colour TV, tea/coffee making facilities; full central heating; last orders 8.00 p.m.; bar meals (lunch); diets; children over 14 welcome; dogs by arrangement; conferences max. 12; own heated indoor swimming pool; golf, tennis, riding, fishing all nearby; credit cards not accepted.

The Pheasant was recommended to me by another hotelier of note in Yorkshire and how right he was to guide me to it. Set in a pretty village, overlooking the village pond, it has been imaginatively created from a group of buildings on two sides of a courtyard. Inside, the log fires, the antiques and the numerous beams lend an air of warmth and comfort to the tastefully decorated rooms. Old fashioned in atmosphere the hotel might be, but the best of all the modern conveniences are also there where needed. The bedrooms, for example, all have colour television, telephone, tea/coffee making facilities, etc. Mrs 'Tricia Binks provides the most delicious food and many of the ingredients come from the hotel's own large garden and paddock. Holly Cottage is also available – this is a charming, thatched 16th century cottage just 350 yards from the hotel, with two double bedrooms and two sitting rooms, all attractively furnished to the same high standard as the hotel. It is serviced by the hotel staff and meals are taken in the hotel. A quiet and peaceful haven with a delightful atmosphere. Having said all this, The Pheasant makes an ideal base from which to explore this most beautiful part of England, where there is so much to see and do. Dinner, room and breakfast from £51.50 (early season), £57.50–£59.95 (high season) including VAT. Closed January and February.

RYEDALE LODGE
Nunnington, Nr. Helmsley,
North Yorkshire YO6 5XB

Telephone: 01439 748246

Helmsley 5, York 20, East coast 30, London 230, Edinburgh 160

R licence; 7 en suite bedrooms (1 ground floor), all with colour TV, telephone and full central heating; last orders 9.30 p.m.; diets; children welcome, baby listening; no dogs; conferences up to 20; fishing; golf and riding 5 miles; shooting by arrangement; Visa and Access cards accepted.

What a delightful find! In what used to be a country railway station, Jon and Janet Laird have created a superb little hotel. Where trains once ran, you can now stroll and listen to the evening bird song and the distant lowing of cattle. It is an idyllic setting. However, Ryedale Lodge is exceptional not only for its situation, but for its comfort; inside, every room is tastefully and beautifully furnished, and an air of warmth and serenity pervades throughout. As the reader can no doubt deduce, I find this hotel particularly inviting, but it is for its food that I shall be most tempted to return. Not only is Janet Laird a good cook, but she chooses the finest and freshest ingredients to produce the most varied and imaginative menu. The results are stupendous! I look forward eagerly to visiting this hotel again and again. If you look at a map of Yorkshire, Nunnington is almost in the middle and as such Ryedale is truly the centre of all that is best in this lovely and historic county. Hotel closed for three weeks in January only. Room and breakfast from £41.50, weekly rates from £330.00 per person.

181

GEORGE AND DRAGON HOTEL
17 Market Place, Kirkbymoorside,
North Yorkshire YO6 6AA

Telephone/Fax: 01751 433334

A1 – Thirsk 20, York 30, Scarborough 28

F licence; 19 en suite bedrooms, all with direct dial telephone, TV and hospitality tray; room service; last orders for dinner 9.00 p.m.; bar meals; special diets; dogs accepted; conferences max. 25; golf and shooting nearby; open all year; Mastercard, Amex and Visa credit cards accepted.

For those who enjoy the ambience of a coaching inn with the comforts of a modern hotel, and for those who want good food and wine, then here is the ideal hotel. Guests wishing to explore the North Yorkshire Moors, the many famous homes, abbeys and castles of the area, then this is the best venue from which to do so. The George and Dragon is situated in the centre of the small town of Kirkbymoorside, and thus virtually all of North Yorkshire is within easy drive of the hotel. York, Harrogate and the east coast are practical day trips, whilst Pickering and Helmsley are only minutes away. The hotel itself is still very much the inn of yesteryear in atmosphere, but it has all the comforts that we now expect. All the rooms are furnished in keeping with the building, and oak beams complete the picture. Above all, the food is excellent and there is a well chosen wine list to complement the menu. There is only one problem. The temptation to stay in the hotel or to venture out only into the immediate locality, tends to make plans to visit further afield go away. Room and breakfast from £44.00 single, £34.00 double/twin per person, dinner, room and breakfast from £44.50 including VAT.

LASTINGHAM GRANGE HOTEL
Lastingham, Nr. Kirkbymoorside, Yorkshire YO6 6TH

Telephone: 01751 417345 or 417402

London 232, Malton 15, Scarborough 24, Thirsk 24, Whitby 26, York 33

R and R licence; 12 en suite bedrooms, 4 with bath, 8 with bath and shower, all with telephone, trouser press, hair drier; children welcome, baby listening in all rooms; drying room; diets; golf 5 miles; riding 1 mile.

You can discover this delightfully situated, elegant country house by leaving the A170 at Kirkbymoorside and making for Hutton-le-Hole. The Grange is stone-walled and built round a courtyard. It is set within 10 acres of well-kept gardens and fields, on the edge of the moors, in the historic village of Lastingham, a peaceful backwater in the heart of the National Park. Lastingham Grange is owned and personally run by Mr. and Mrs. Dennis Wood. The atmosphere, even during the height of the season, is unhurried and peaceful, the south-facing terrace providing a pleasant setting in which to relax and enjoy the beautiful rose garden, noted for the variety and rarity of its many flowering shrubs and trees. The spacious and homely lounge, with its open fire, and the comfortable bedrooms with their impressive views, are all tastefully furnished. The food is excellent – speedily and cheerfully served. Room and breakfast from £59.00 single. Short breaks available. Open March to the beginning of December.

MONK FRYSTON HALL
Monk Fryston, Nr. Leeds,
North Yorkshire LS25 5DU

Telephone: 01977 682369   *Fax: 01977 683544*

York 18, Harrogate 25, Selby 7, A1 2

F licence; 28 bedrooms (6 ground floor) all with private bathroom, radio, telephone and TV; central heating; late meals to 9.30 p.m.; diets; children welcome, baby listening; dogs welcome; conferences up to 16 residential, day conferences up to 50; credit cards accepted.

This is surely the epitome of a country house hotel. In a superb house, with a history going back to the Middle Ages, you can enjoy every modern comfort and convenience whilst wining and dining in a style reminiscent of those former times. The richly panelled rooms are lit by stone mullioned windows and, in winter, are warmed by open fires creating a glowing ambience of well being. Outside, with the splendid stone elevations of the house as a backdrop, you can stroll by the lake or on the terraces of the gardens, both formal and informal. If motoring up the A1, visiting the races at either Doncaster or York, holding a small conference or simply touring in this lovely area, then Monk Fryston makes an excellent place to stay and indulge oneself. Room and breakfast from £64.00–£72.00 (single) £90.00–£99.00 (double), service and VAT included. Weekend break, dinner, bed and breakfast (2 nights) £108.00–£112.00 per person. Includes Bank Holidays except Christmas and New Year. Open all year.

EAST AYTON LODGE
COUNTRY HOTEL & RESTAURANT
Moor Lane, East Ayton, Nr. Scarborough, N. Yorkshire YO13 9EW

Telephone: 01723 864227   *Fax: 01723 862680*

Scarborough 3, Whitby 24, York 36, Leeds 65

F licence; 17 en suite bedrooms (3 for the disabled), all with direct dial telephone and TV; room service; baby listening; night service; last orders for dinner 9.00 p.m.; bar meals; special diets; children welcome; dogs accepted; conferences max. 100; shooting/fishing nearby; golf and tennis 3 miles; riding 5 miles; open all year; all major credit cards accepted.

The North Yorkshire Moors are, to me and to others, one of the most beautiful parts of Britain, and a visit to them is essential for any lover of the countryside. Where better then, than to stay at an hotel on the edge of these moors, with its own 3 acres of gardens in which to relax. With both sea and river fishing close by, lovely walks in the Forge Valley, and the whole of historic Yorkshire all around East Ayton Lodge, it is an ideal centre for a holiday. Having relaxed, after what can often be a strenuous day of exploring, dinner can be chosen from either the comprehensive table d'hôte, or the interesting à la carte menus, and enjoyed in the large, comfortable dining room. There is a well chosen wine list from which to indulge yourself, and finally the inviting bedrooms beckon one to a well-earned rest. It should, perhaps, be mentioned that the hotel offers conference facilities to companies who are looking for a peaceful setting, and an "out of town" venue. Room and breakfast from £27.50, dinner, room and breakfast from £37.50, including VAT.

THE JUDGES LODGING HOTEL
9 Lendal, York, North Yorkshire YO1 2AQ

Telephone: 01904 638733   *Fax: 01904 679947*

Leeds 24, Manchester 72, Edinburgh 192, London 209

F licence; 12 en suite bedrooms (2 with spa baths), all with direct dial telephone and TV; room service; baby listening; night service; last orders for dinner 9.30 p.m.; bar meals; special diets; children welcome; dogs by arrangement; conferences max. 20; sailing/boating 200 yards; 4 major golf courses within 5 miles; open all year; all major credit cards accepted.

Imagine yourself in York in the early 18th century. You are arriving at your grand house in the city centre. There is a glow from the windows and the servants await you. Now, retaining that ambience in your mind, transport yourself to the present day; add the comforts that we have all come to expect, and you will begin to sense the flavour of a stay at The Judges Lodging. The house has been impeccably kept to its original plan and atmosphere, and yet it has been cleverly transformed into a small, warm and intimate hotel. The furnishings and décor are beautifully in keeping with the building. There is a lovely candlelit restaurant serving delicious food, and a wine list to suit all palates. Now, when you visit York, you cannot only see all the historical sites such as the Minster, the Jorvik Viking Centre and the National Railway Museum, but you can stay in one of the most historic houses in the city. It is an experience in itself, and it can set the scene for exploring the many other houses and abbeys with which Yorkshire abounds and the wild and exciting Yorkshire Moors. Room and breakfast from £65.00 single, £85.00 double, including VAT.

ALDWARK MANOR GOLF HOTEL
Aldwark, Alne, Nr. York, North Yorkshire YO6 2NF

Telephone: 01347 838146/7   *Fax: 01347 838867*

York 12½

F licence; 17 en suite bedrooms (1 for the partially disabled), all with direct dial telephone and TV; 24 hour room service; baby listening; night service; last orders for dinner 9.30 p.m.; bar meals; special diets; children welcome; conferences max. 80; 18 hole golf course; fishing; riding and shooting by arrangement; open all year; all major credit cards accepted.

Aldwark Manor is a large country house that has been transformed into a friendly hotel amidst its own magnificent 18 hole golf course. The course actually spans the River Ure, and a bridge has recently been built especially to enable players to cross. The Manor itself has just been renovated to provide every possible convenience and comfort for its guests. This is no "posh" or "stuffy" hotel, but a warm and friendly venue in which to wine and dine, to explore the varied countryside for which this part of Yorkshire is noted, or simply to play golf on the superb and interesting golf course. The food here is excellent, and can be accompanied by a bottle from the intelligently chosen wine list. Aldwark Manor offers many "bargains" such as golfing breaks and romantic breaks, the latter including a four-poster bed, candlelit dinner, champagne and flowers. This is a great place to stay for the sports enthusiast, the bon viveur, or for those simply looking for a relaxing holiday. Room and breakfast from £55.00 including VAT.

BARGAIN BREAKS

Readers are recommended to telephone the hotels to confirm rates and conditions prior to booking.

YORKSHIRE AND THE NORTH EAST

COUNTY DURHAM

RAMSIDE HALL HOTEL, Durham   *page 167*
Weekend Breaks including free entry to Beamish Museum – 3 nights for the price of 2. Also available are Celebration Packages including champagne and flowers, and Christmas Packages. There is no charge for children under 16 in the above bargain breaks. Tariff on application.

ROYAL COUNTY HOTEL, Durham   *page 168*
Swallow Breakaway Packages – 2 nights, half board plus one lunch on the day of your choice. Prices on application.

HUMBERSIDE

THE WATERFRONT HOTEL, Hull   *page 169*
Weekend Breaks are available – tariffs on application. Champagne Breaks to include champagne, dinner, bed and breakfast, for 2 nights or more, from £39.00 per person, per night.

NORTHUMBERLAND

WAREN HOUSE HOTEL & RESTAURANT, Bamburgh   *page 170*
Bargain breaks available – tariff on application. Free upgrade from standard to superior, or superior to suite, subject to availability on check-in.

YORKSHIRE

APPLETON HALL HOTEL, Appleton-le-Moors   *page 171*
Winter and Autumn breaks available for 2 or more days. Full brochure and tariff available on request. Open for Christmas and New Year special festive breaks.

ROSE & CROWN HOTEL, Bainbridge   *page 172*
"Let's Go Breaks" available all year round, excluding Bank Holidays; 2 nights dinner, bed and breakfast with private facilities – prices on application.

OAKWOOD HALL HOTEL, Bingley   *page 173*
Reduced rates are offered at the weekend: Friday, Saturday and Sunday to include full English breakfast and VAT – from £40.00 single, £65.00 double.

DEVONSHIRE ARMS COUNTRY HOUSE HOTEL, Bolton Abbey *page 174*
The Devonshire offers Romantic Breaks, Small Luxury Breaks and a range of other special breaks including golfing, fishing, clay pigeon shooting, helicopter tours and classic car motoring excursions; tariff on application.

THE BALMORAL HOTEL & HENRY'S RESTAURANT,
Harrogate   *page 175*
Special weekend breaks including dinner, accommodation, breakfast, service and VAT. Celebration Breaks including champagne on arrival, posy of flowers, choice from the Celebration Menu, Bucks Fizz and Smoked Salmon breakfast, with four-poster room available. Prices on application.

GRANTS HOTEL, Harrogate   *page 176*
At off-peak times, we offer "2 nights for the price of 1", which means that the total cost for 2 people for 2 nights bed and breakfast is from £125.00. Super Value Break rates from £45.00 per person, per night, on a dinner, bed and breakfast basis.

BARGAIN BREAKS

THE WHITE HOUSE HOTEL, Harrogate *page 177*
Double rooms from £80.00 per night for 2 people when staying a minimum of 2 nights, to include a Saturday or Sunday and taking dinner on at least one night. Offer not available during Trade Shows.

STONE HOUSE HOTEL, Nr. Hawes *page 178*
"Let's Go Breaks" for a minimum stay of 2 nights: October 1994–April 1995 from £35.00 per person, per night for dinner, bed and breakfast, and October 1995–April 1996 from £37.00. Offer excludes Christmas, New Year and Easter.

FEVERSHAM ARMS HOTEL, Helmsley *page 179*
Any 2 nights including full English breakfast, 4 course dinner by candlelight, free tennis and swimming in our sports complex, golf and riding nearby at reduced rates. Prices inclusive of VAT from: Winter – £40.00, Spring – £46.00, Summer – £49.00, all per person, per night, double occupancy. Four poster with de-luxe bath add £5.00 per person, per night.

THE PHEASANT, Harome, Helmsley *page 180*
Tariff £51.50 from 1st November–mid May 1995, thereafter £57.50 per day.

RYEDALE LODGE, Nr. Helmsley *page 181*
2 consecutive nights stay between 1st October 1994 and 31st May 1995, including room, breakfast and dinner for £128.00 per person. Summer 2 day break between 1st June 1995 and 30th September 1995, £134.00. 3 nights or more – tariff on application.

GEORGE AND DRAGON HOTEL, Kirkbymoorside *page 182*
2 nights, dinner, bed and breakfast – £89.00 per person, based on 2 people sharing a twin/double room. Golf Midweek Breaks – 2 days free golf and 2 nights dinner, bed and breakfast – £115.00 per person.

LASTINGHAM GRANGE HOTEL, Lastingham *page 183*
Dinner, bed and breakfast from £76.95 for 2 days or more, and dinner, bed and breakfast from £69.75 for 1 week or more. Prices are per person, per night.

MONK FRYSTON HALL, Monk Fryston *page 184*
Weekend breaks until 27th March 1995 – £108.00 per person for 2 nights, £162.00 per person for 3 nights.

EAST AYTON LODGE COUNTRY HOTEL & RESTAURANT,
Nr. Scarborough *page 185*
Midweek or Weekend Breaks from £75.00 per person for 2 nights accommodation, dinner and breakfast, or 3 nights from £110.00 per person. Theatre Breaks including tickets for the Alan Ayckbourn Theatre in the Round from £75.00 per person all inclusive. Christmas Breaks from £210.00 per person for 3 nights, or 4 nights from £250.00 per person. New Year from £100.00 per person for 2 nights, including gala dinner on New Year's Eve.

THE JUDGES LODGING HOTEL, York *page 186*
Bargain breaks are available from November–Easter. Tariff on application.

ALDWARK MANOR GOLF HOTEL, Nr. York, Alne *page 187*
Any 2 nights, dinner, bed and breakfast – £105.00 per person. Any 2 nights, dinner, bed and breakfast plus 3 rounds of golf – £135.00 per person.

WALES
SELECTED LOCAL ATTRACTIONS

◼ Historic Houses, Gardens & Parks

CLWYD
Chirk Castle, Bodelwyddan
Bodrhyddan Hall, Rhuddlan
Bodnant Garden, Tal-y-Cafn
Erddig Hall, Wrexham
Eiria Park, Colwyn Leisure Centre

DYFED
Manor House Wildlife & Leisure Park, Tenby
Tudor Merchant's House, Quay Hill, Tenby

GWYNEDD
Bryn Bras Castle, Llanrug, Nr. Llanberis
Parc Glynllifon, Nr. Caernarfon
Plas Newydd, Llanfairpwll, Anglesey

GWENT
Bryn Bach Park, Tredegar
Caldicot Castle & Country Park, Nr. Newport
Tredegar House, Newport

GLAMORGAN
Castell Coch, Tongwynlais, Cardiff
Cosmeston Lakes Country Park & Medieval
  Village
Dyffryn House & Gardens, St. Nicholas, Nr.
  Cardiff
Llanerch Vineyard, Pendoylan
Margam Park, Port Talbot

◼ Walks & Nature Trails

CLWYD
Greenfield Valley Heritage Park, Holywell
Llyn Brenig Visitor Centre, Corwen
Logger Heads Country Park, Nr. Mold
Ty Mawr Country Park, Cefn Mawr, Nr.
  Wrexham

DYFED
Bwlch Nant Yr Arian Forest Visitor Centre,
  Ponterwyd
Gelli Aur Country Park, Llandeilo   .
Llysyfran Reservoir & Country Park, Nr.
  Haverfordwest
Pembrey Country Park, Pembrey .

GWYNEDD
Bryntirion Open Farm, Dwyran, Anglesey
Coed-y-Brenin Forest Park & Visitor Centre,
  Ganllwyd, Dolgellau
The Greenwood Centre, Port Dinorwic
Parc Padarn, Llanberis
South Stack Cliffs Reserve & Ellins Tower
  Information Centre, Holyhead
Tyn Llan Crafts & Farm Museum, Nr.
  Porthmadog
'Y Stablau', Gwydyr Forest Park, Llanrwst

GWENT
Festival Park, Ebbw Vale
Llandegfedd Reservoir, Pontypool

POWYS
Brecon Beacons Mountain Centre, Nr. Libanus
Gigrin Farm & Nature Trail, Rhayader
Lake Vyrnwy RSPB Reserve & Information
  Centre
Ynys-Hir Reserve & Visitor Centre, Machynlleth

GLAMORGAN
Afan Forest Park & Countryside Centre, Port
  Talbot
Bryngarw Country Park, Nr. Bridgend
Garwnant Visitor Centre, Cwm Taf, Merthyr
  Tydfil
Gnoll Country Park, Neath

◼ Historical Sites & Museums

CLWYD
Bodelwyddan Castle
Denbigh Castle
Flint Castle & Town Walls
Valle Crucis Abbey, Llangollen
Rhuddlan Castle, Nr. Rhyl

DYFED
Castell Henllys Iron Age Hillfort, Crymych
Carreg Cennen Castle, Trapp, Nr. Llandeilo
Museum of the Welsh Woollen Industry,
  Llandysul
Castle Museum & Art Gallery, Haverfordwest
Kidwelly Castle
Manorbier Castle, Nr. Tenby
Milford Haven Museum, The Docks, Milford
  Haven
Picton Castle, Haverfordwest
Pembroke Castle
St. Davids Bishop's Palace

GWYNEDD
Beaumaris Castle
Caernarfon Castle
Conwy Castle
Cymer Abbey, Dolgellau
Dolwyddelan Castle
Dolbadarn Castle
Harlech Castle
Llanfair Slate Caverns, Nr. Harlech
The Lloyd George Museum, Llanystumdwy,
  Criccieth
Penrhyn Castle, Bangor

GWENT
Chepstow Castle, Chepstow
The Nelson Museum & Local History Centre
Penhow Castle, Nr. Newport
Raglan Castle
Tintern Abbey, Tintern

POWYS
Powys Castle & Museum, Welshpool
Tretower Court & Castle, Crickhowell

GLAMORGAN
Aberdulair Falls – Vale of Neath, Neath
Caerphilly Castle
Cardiff Castle
Castell Coch, Cardiff
Cefn Coed Colliery Museum, Crynant, Neath
National Museum of Wales, Cardiff
Welsh Folk Museum, Cardiff

◼ Entertainment Venues

CLWYD
Afonwen Craft & Antique Centre, Nr. Mold
Llyn Brenig Visitor Centre, Cerrigydrudion

DYFED

The Llywernog Silver-Lead Miles, Nr. Aberystwyth
Oakwood Park (Theme Park), Narberth

GWYNEDD

Alice in Wonderland Visitor Centre, Llandudno
Anglesey Bird World, Dwyran
Anglesey Sea Zoo, Brynsiencyn
Butlins Starcoast World, Pwllheli
James Pringle Weavers of LlanfairP.G.
Sygun Copper Mine, Beddgelert
Penmachno Woollen Mill, Nr. Betws-y-Coed
Felin Isaf Water Mill, Glan Conwy
Ffestiniog Railway, Porthmadog
Maes Artro Tourist Village, Llanbedr
Portmeirion Village, Nr. Porthmadog

GWYNEDD (continued)

Snowdon Mountain Railway, Llanberis
Trefriw Woollen Mills, Trefriw
Welsh Gold, Dolgellau
Welsh Highland Railway, Porthmadog

POWYS

Welshpool & Llanfair Light Railway
Welsh Whisky Visitor Centre, Brecon

GLAMORGAN

Dan-yr-Ogof Showcaves, Abercraf
Margam Park, Port Talbot
Penscynor Wildlife Park, Cilfrew, Nr. Neath
Rhondda Heritage Park

WALES
DIARY OF EVENTS 1995

January 1   BBC NATIONAL ORCHESTRA OF WALES NEW YEAR CONCERT
St. David's Hall, Cardiff.

February 18   INTERNATIONAL RUGBY UNION, WALES v ENGLAND
Cardiff Arms Park, Cardiff.

March 18   INTERNATIONAL RUGBY UNION, WALES v IRELAND
Cardiff Arms Park, Cardiff.

April 29 to
May 6   LANDSKER WALKING FESTIVAL
Around Narberth, Pembrokeshire (Dyfed).
Week of guided walks with evening entertainment.

*April 30 to
May 2   THE GREAT LLANDUDNO EXTRAVAGANZA
The Promenade and other areas, Llandudno, Gwynedd.
Street theatre, fairs, parades and Victorian dress.

May 6–8   ALL OUR YESTERDAYS STEAM GALA
Ffestiniog Railway, Porthmadog, Gwynedd.
Steam Gala with military flavour, visiting locomotives from England and France.

May 12–14   MIDWALES MAY FESTIVAL
Newtown, Powys.

May 27–28   CRAFTS IN ACTION FESTIVAL
St. Donats Castle, South Glamorgan.

May 27 to
June 3   ST. DAVIDS CATHEDRAL FESTIVAL
St. Davids, Dyfed.
Week long festival of the best classical music.

June 17–23	THREE PEAKS YACHT RACE – BARMOUTH TO FORT WILLIAM The Quay, Barmouth, Gwynedd.
June 17–26	CRICCIETH FESTIVAL OF MUSIC AND THE ARTS Various venues, Criccieth, Gwynedd.
July 4–9	LLANGOLLEN INTERNATIONAL MUSICAL EISTEDDFOD The Pavilion, Llangollen, Clwyd.
July 14–16	THE 5TH INTERNATIONAL POTTERS FESTIVAL Arts Centre, Penglais Hill, Aberystwyth, Dyfed. Worldwide festival held every 2 years.
July 24–27	ROYAL WELSH SHOW Royal Welsh Showground, Llenelwedd, Builth Wells. Wales' Premier Agricultural Show.
July 24–30	CONWY FESTIVAL Streets around Conwy, Gwynedd. Street festival of entertainment, arts and crafts.
August 5–12	ROYAL NATIONAL EISTEDDFOD OF WALES Bro Colwyn, Hendre Fawr, Abergele, Clwyd.
August 10–11	UNITED COUNTIES SHOW The Showground, The Mount, Queen Street, Carmarthen, Dyfed.
August 11–13	BRECON JAZZ FESTIVAL Various venues, Brecon, Powys.
September 7–15	BARMOUTH ARTS FESTIVAL IN CONJUNCTION WITH THE NATIONAL TRUST CENTENARY Dragon Theatre, Barmouth, Gwynedd.
September 14–16	INTERNATIONAL SHEEPDOG TRIALS 1995 Pentreffynnon and Plas Ucha, Whitford, Holywell, Clwyd.
October 14–22	LLANDUDNO OCTOBER FESTIVAL A festival of voice, international stars of music, theatre and comedy.

*Denotes provisional date

For further information contact:
Wales Tourist Board
Brunel House
2 Fitzalan Road
Cardiff CF2 1UY.
Tel: 01222 499909

TYDDYN LLAN COUNTRY HOUSE HOTEL AND RESTAURANT
Llandrillo, Nr. Corwen, Clwyd LL21 0ST

Telephone: 01490 440264   *Fax: 01490 440414*

Bala 8, Llangollen 15, Corwen 4½

R & R licence; 10 bedrooms all with en suite bathrooms; direct dial telephone; room and night service; baby listening; last orders for dinner 9.30 p.m.; bar meals; special diets; children welcome; dogs allowed (but not in public rooms); small conferences; private 1½ mile stretch for fishing; shooting can be arranged; riding, sailing & boating nearby; golf in Bala and Llangollen; hotel closed February; Access and Visa accepted.

This elegant Georgian country house hotel is situated peacefully on the outskirts of Llandrillo village near Corwen. Tyddyn Llan is a superb hotel efficiently and pleasantly run by the owners, Peter and Bridget Kindred, and nothing is too much trouble for them in adding to the comfort of their guests. Peter's flair for design is very evident, his style and originality make use of many antiques, period furniture and interesting objets d'art. Bedrooms are all very individual, having en suite facilities, and lovely views of the Berwyn Mountains. Croquet may be played in the gardens, and there is an attractive water garden. The hotel has its own private fishing on 4 miles of the River Dee. Bala Lake is close by and enthusiasts can enjoy wind surfing, sailing and canoeing. Riding, golf, guided walks and pony trekking can easily be arranged. There are facilities too, for small executive conferences. Bridget personally supervises the tempting, modern cuisine which is beautifully cooked and presented. I cannot praise the meals I had too highly, the wine list too, is superlative. I know that you will love visiting this hotel as much as I do. Room and breakfast from £44.00 per night, or weekly from £430.00, also including dinner.

TREFEDDIAN HOTEL
Aberdovey, Gwynedd LL35 0SB

Telephone: 01654 767213

London 215, Birmingham 111, Manchester 110, Dolgellau 24, Barmouth 34, Harlech 45, Machynlleth 11, Talyllyn & Cader Idris 14

F licence; 46 en suite bedrooms, all with colour TV; lift; drying room; children welcome; baby listening; dogs welcome by arrangement but not in public rooms; games room, with snooker table, pool table, table tennis; indoor heated swimming pool and solarium; putting green; tennis court; golf; sea bathing; boating; fishing nearby; garage.

The Trefeddian Hotel stands in its own grounds, away from the main road, and is one mile from the middle of Aberdovey, a town with many attractions and which is becoming a centre where everyone, particularly the young, can pursue many outdoor activities. For example, supervision and special instruction can be arranged for sailing, to mention one of the sports available. The Directors, Mr. and Mrs. John Cave and Mr. Peter Cave, are responsible for the running of this first class family hotel, which has all the amenities that are part of a splendid holiday. The lounges are spacious, relaxing and peaceful and have recently been beautifully refurbished. The bedrooms, with views of Cardigan Bay, are comfortable and elegantly decorated. The menus offer a good choice of interesting and nicely presented dishes, complemented by a well chosen wine list. The Trefeddian is in the immediate vicinity of a four mile stretch of sandy beach and overlooks the golf course with the ever changing view of the sea beyond. The courtesy and efficiency of the staff create a happy atmosphere. Dinner, bed and breakfast from £40.00 per person, inclusive of VAT. Weekly terms, mini breaks, reductions for children, all shown on tariff sent, with brochure, on application. Open 10th March to 2nd January 1996 (including Christmas and New Year), but office always open.

BRON EIFION COUNTRY HOUSE HOTEL
Criccieth, Gwynedd LL52 0SA

Telephone: 01766 522385   *Fax: 01766 522003*

London 245, Porthmadog 5, Betws-y-Coed 30, Caernarvon 17, Pwllheli 9

*R & R licence; 19 bedrooms (1 ground floor) all en suite; all with direct dial
telephone, col. TV, tea/coffee making facilities, trouser press and hairdryer;
meals till 9.00 p.m.; diets; vegetarian dishes always available; children welcome;
dogs by arrangement; boardroom conferences and meetings; functions and
receptions; golf, tennis, sea and river bathing, fishing and riding all nearby.*

Bron Eifion Country House Hotel is situated half a mile out of Criccieth on the
A497 road to Pwllheli, and is well signposted. It is set in five acres of beautiful,
tranquil gardens, with woodlands and lakes beyond. The climate here is mild
and pleasant, and the beauty spots of Snowdonia and the Lleyn Peninsula are
within easy reach. The owners, Alan and Carole Thompson, are to be congratulated on constantly up-grading and refurbishing the hotel to a very high standard.
All fixtures and fittings are most luxurious, wallpapers are charming Victorian
copies, and much thought has gone into every aspect of the hotel. Bedrooms
are of a good size, de luxe and very well appointed. Overlooking the garden is
the attractive restaurant which has an excellent reputation for good food and
sensibly priced wine. Meals are imaginatively presented using only the freshest
ingredients. Drinks or coffee may be enjoyed in the panelled, galleried hall, or
in clement weather, on the verandah. Comfortable surroundings and good food
at reasonable charges can be found at the Bron Eifion, I highly recommend it.
Room and breakfast from £45.00 single, £37.00 twin per person. Dinner, room
and breakfast from £45.00 per person inclusive of VAT. Weekend, Traditional
Christmas and New Year breaks available. Open all year.

BONTDDU HALL HOTEL
Bontddu, Nr. Dolgellau,
Gwynedd LL40 2SU

Telephone: 01341 430661   *Fax: 01341 430284*

**Barmouth 5, Dolgellau 5, Aberystwyth 35, Caernarfon 50,
Birmingham 110, London 235**

F licence; 20 en suite bedrooms, all with telephone, colour TV, clock radio, hairdryer, tea/coffee making facilities; central heating; night service to midnight; late meals to 9.30 p.m.; diets; children welcome; dogs welcome; sea bathing, golf and riding all 5 miles; gold mine nearby; Access, Amex, Visa credit cards accepted.

Bontddu Hall, wonderfully situated in 14 acres of landscaped grounds, overlooks fine views of the Mawddach Estuary and famous Cader Idris range of mountains. The unspoilt charm of this attractive Victorian mansion has always made it a favourite of mine, and the owners Margaretta and Michael Ball, know what is good. You will enjoy excellent food from an interesting country house evening dinner menu, dishes are varied and nicely served. Salmon and lobster are a speciality when available. In the Garden Restaurant an appetizing lunch is served and a Special Carvery lunch on Sundays. The furniture, pictures, colour schemes and flowers are all reminiscent of a country house and the hotel has been completely refurbished. All rooms are very comfortable and the ''Princess of Wales'' Bar extends a warm welcome. Nearly all bedrooms are with estuary and mountain views. In the Lodge, above the main drive are some additional rooms with balconies and exceptional views. I can only recommend a visit, and you will want to come again and again. Room and breakfast from £62.50 (single), £90.00 (double/twin), inclusive of VAT. Weekly demi-pension £399.50 per person; terms for four-poster suites on application. Open Easter to October.

THE EMPIRE HOTEL
Church Walks, Llandudno, Gwynedd LL30 2HE

Telephone: 01492 860555   *Fax: 01492 860791*

London 250, Chester 48, Betws-y-Coed 18, Manchester Airport 80

F licence; 51 en suite bedrooms (7 suites), all with direct dial telephone and TV; room service; baby listening; night service; 2 lifts; last orders 9.30 p.m.; bar meals; special diets; children welcome; conferences max. 40; indoor and outdoor heated swimming pools; sauna; spa pool; sea bathing; leisure centre ½ mile; hotel closed at Christmas; all major credit cards accepted.

The Empire Hotel and "No. 72" are centrally situated close to the Promenade and the excellent shopping facilities of Llandudno. Both these are personally owned and managed by Len and Elizabeth Maddocks, who always give you a warm welcome and ensure a memorable holiday. The facilities at The Empire are excellent and include outdoor and indoor swimming pools, a children's paddling pool, sauna, whirlpool and steam room. A beauty therapist is available for massage and beauty treatments. There are two restaurants to suit every taste, a cocktail bar and dancing every Saturday night, with an earlier cocktail party. The bedrooms are extremely well appointed and include satellite TV and video player (with a large library of videos). All rooms, in both The Empire and "No. 72", have antique furniture, silk drapes, marble floored Victorian-style bathrooms, jacuzzi baths and every conceivable luxury. "No. 72" is an attractive Victorian town house, which offers discerning guests something really special. The eight bedrooms are luxuriously fitted with the original cast iron beds (fully renovated and very comfortable!), which are dressed with fluffy pillows, duvets and French linen. Wall hangings complete the exquisite décor of this house. Room and breakfast from £45.00 single, £75.00 double and weekly from £255.00 per person.

WARPOOL COURT HOTEL
St. Davids, Pembrokeshire SA62 6BN

Telephone: 01437 720300   *Fax: 01437 720676*

London 264, Birmingham 177, Severn Bridge 130, Carmarthen 46, Fishguard 16, Haverfordwest 16

F licence; 25 en suite bedrooms all with telephone, colour TV with satellite movies, baby listening, tea/coffee making facilities; family rooms; full central heating; meals to 9.15 p.m.; diets; children welcome; dogs accepted; leisure facilities: table tennis, gymnasium and sauna, pool table, heated covered swimming pool (April to October); all weather tennis court; 9 hole golf course nearby (2 miles); sea bathing; sandy beaches; lovely walks; major credit cards accepted.

The Warpool Court is sited in a wonderful position overlooking the wild Atlantic and within a few minutes' walk of the famous St. David's Cathedral. This splendid country house hotel, with its unique collection of antique tiles, has been recommended by *Signpost* for a long time. It is owned by Peter Trier and through his expertise you can be assured of good food, gracious living and a warm welcome from him and his staff. The colour schemes are soft and restful and the staff cheerful and efficient. The hotel has a high reputation for good food and a fine selection of well chosen wines. Four course table d'hôte menus are excellent and whenever possible local produce is used. Salmon is smoked on the premises, crab and lobster are caught at the nearby village of Solva – these are supported by an interesting vegetarian menu. The lounge bar provides a relaxed atmosphere for diners, and the residents' lounge ensures peace and comfort. There are numerous outdoor activities available, the most popular being walking, bird watching and surfing. Room and breakfast from £60.00 (single), £90.00 (twin) inclusive of VAT. Other terms on application including 'Country House Breaks'. Full Christmas and New Year packages. Open February to December inclusive.

GLIFFAES COUNTRY HOUSE HOTEL
Crickhowell, Powys NP8 1RH

Telephone: 01874 730371   *Fax: 01874 730463*

London 153, Crickhowell 3½, Abergavenny 9½, Brecon 10½

F licence; 22 en suite bedrooms all with self dial telephone, colour TV, tea/coffee making facilities and baby listening; children welcome; dogs (but not in hotel); late meals by arrangement; diets; TV room; small conferences up to 25; receptions welcome; salmon and trout fishing; tennis; putting; croquet; full size billiards table in traditional surroundings; golf, riding, hang gliding, sailing and boating all nearby; Amex, Access, Diners and Visa accepted.

Gliffaes provides spacious comfort in the true country house tradition. It stands in 29 acres of parkland and well kept gardens with flowering shrubs and trees which are amongst the rarest and most beautiful to be found in this country. The hotel is situated in the lovely valley of the River Usk, midway between the Brecon Beacons and the Black Mountains, and yet only one mile off the main A40 road. Gliffaes Country House Hotel has been family owned since 1948, and is now under the personal care of Nick and Peta Brabner, two wonderful and experienced people who are doing a great job. They are supported by Nick's mother, Jane Brabner who with her husband Major S. G. Brabner created a home that has an atmosphere of friendliness, informality and high standards. Care is taken to maintain the best of country house cooking. My excellent dinner, chosen from the table d'hôte menu, showed imagination and was well served by the efficient staff (an à la carte menu is also available). There is a good selection of wines. The well-appointed bedrooms, all with their own bathroom or shower, are individual in décor and furnishings. The downstairs rooms are elegantly furnished and comfortable and delicious home-made afternoon teas are thoroughly recommended. Most rooms command views of the surrounding hills and the river running through the wooded valley. The Lodge has now been converted into an annexe, equipped for self catering to a degree. It has a family room and two double bedrooms. Fishing for salmon and trout is provided for on the 2½ miles of the Usk, owned by the hotel and reserved primarily for guests. Room and breakfast from £33.50 to £49.00 per person including service and VAT. Short stay and weekly rates on application. (Closed 5th January to 25th February).

BODFACH HALL COUNTRY HOUSE HOTEL
Llanfyllin, Powys SY22 5HS

Telephone: 01691 648272   *Fax: 01691 648272*

**London 3–3½ hrs, Leeds 3–3½ hrs, Liverpool 1½ hrs,
West Midlands 1½ hrs**

*F licence; 9 en suite bedrooms, all with direct dial telephone and TV; room
service; last orders for dinner 8.45 p.m.; bar meals; special diets; children
welcome; dogs accepted; leisure centre, golf and tennis nearby; open all year;
all major credit cards accepted.*

Bodfach Hall Country House Hotel can be found at the end of the A490 just ¼
mile off the Oswestry to Lake Vyrnwy Road. Four acres of mature and sheltered
gardens contain many interesting trees and shrubs. Parts of the house date back
to the 17th century, although there has been a building on the site since the 12th
century. There are many fine stained glass windows, and all periods of the
building are sympathetically interwoven in this lovely old house. The morning
room, where breakfast is served, has a spectacular painted relief ceiling, and the
drawing room, an 18th century moulded ceiling and fine marble fireplaces. There
is a sun room with terrace and a large lounge bar. Most bedrooms have wonderful views and all are en suite, with either bath or shower. The dining room is
oak panelled, and a four course table d'hôte dinner is offered, as well as a choice
of à la carte and vegetarian dishes. The interesting wine list is reasonably priced.
There is plenty to see and do – walking, climbing, sketching, and there are
three golf courses to choose from, as well as tennis courts and a sports centre
in nearby Llanfyllin. The Gray family feel that peace and comfort are important
for their guests, and this, they easily achieve. Room and breakfast is sensibly
priced from £34.00 per person.

BARGAIN BREAKS

Readers are recommended to telephone the hotels to confirm rates and conditions prior to booking.

WALES

CLWYD

TYDDYN LLAN COUNTRY HOUSE HOTEL & RESTAURANT, Llandrillo *page 193*
Midweek and Weekend Breaks from £60.00–£67.50 per person, for 2 people sharing, and is inclusive of 4 course dinner, full cooked breakfast and VAT. Special Winter Break prices on request.

GWYNEDD

TREFEDDIAN HOTEL, Aberdyfi *page 194*
Two day mini breaks from £38.00 per night, inclusive of dinner, bed and breakfast and VAT. Golfing breaks, please ask for details. Reduced rates for children.

BRON EIFION COUNTRY HOUSE HOTEL, Criccieth *page 195*
Breaks available all year. Telephone for extra special rates. November–March, Christmas and New Year breaks.

BONTDDU HALL HOTEL, Nr. Dolgellau *page 196*
Any 2 consecutive nights, half board £120.00 per person inclusive of service and VAT, excluding Bank Holidays. Extra nights pro rata. Please specify Bargain Breaks at time of enquiry.

THE EMPIRE HOTEL, Llandudno *page 197*
Bargain breaks are available throughout the year. 2 nights from £85.00 per person, dinner, bed and breakfast, based on 2 people sharing twin/double room.

DYFED

WARPOOL COURT HOTEL, St. David's *page 198*
2 nights (out of season) – dinner, bed and breakfast from £57.00 per person, per night sharing a double room and 7 nights (out of season) from £51.00 per person, per night.

POWYS

GLIFFAES COUNTRY HOUSE HOTEL, Crickhowell *page 199*
Short stay and weekly rates on application.

BODFACH HALL COUNTRY HOUSE HOTEL, Llanfyllin *page 200*
Bargain breaks are available all week: 2 to 6 nights, dinner, bed and breakfast from £42.50 per person, per night. Weekly terms: dinner, bed and breakfast from £280.00 per person.

SOUTHERN SCOTLAND
SELECTED LOCAL ATTRACTIONS

■ Historic Houses, Gardens & Parks

BORDERS
Bowhill, 3m W of Selkirk
Dawyck Botanic Garden, Stobo
Floors Castle, Kelso
Kailzie Gardens, 2m E of Peebles
Manderston, 2m E of Duns
Mellerstain House, 7m NW of Kelso
Melrose Abbey
Mertoun Gardens, St. Boswells
Priorwood Garden, Melrose
Thirlestane Castle, Lauder
Traquair House, 8m E of Peebles

DUMFRIES & GALLOWAY
Drumlanrig Castle & Country Park, 3m N of Thornhill
Galloway House Gardens, Garlieston
Maxwelton House, 13m NE of Dumfries
Meadowsweet Herb Garden, Castle Kennedy, Stranraer
Threave Garden, 1m W of Castle Douglas

LOTHIAN
Dalmeny House, By South Queensferry
The Georgian House, Charlotte Sq., Edinburgh
Gladstone's Land, Royal Mile, Edinburgh
House of the Binns, 15m W of Edinburgh
Hopetoun House, W of South Queensferry
Inveresk Lodge Garden, 6m E of Edinburgh
Malleny Garden, Balerno, W of Edinburgh
Royal Botanic Gardens, Edinburgh
Suntrap (Garden) Gogarbank, 6m W of Edinburgh

■ Walks & Nature Trails

BORDERS
Jedforest Deer & Farm Park, Camptown
Pease Dean, Nr. Cockburnspath

DUMFRIES & GALLOWAY
Caerlaverock National Nature Reserve, South of Dumfries

LOTHIAN
Cammon Estate, NE off Queensferry Road, Edinburgh
John Muir Country Park, Dunbar

■ Historical Sites & Museums

BORDERS
Dryburgh Abbey, 5m SE of Melrose
Robert Smail's Printing Works, Innerleithen
Hermitage Castle 5m NE of Newcastleton
Jedburgh Abbey

BORDERS (continued)
Jim Clark Memorial Trophy Room, Duns
Melrose Abbey
Smailholm Tower, 6m W of Kelso

DUMFRIES & GALLOWAY
Burns House, Dumfries
Caerlaverock Castle, 8m SE of Dumfries
Carlyle's Birthplace, Ecclefechan
Dumfries Museum & Camera Obscura, Dumfries
Maclellan's Castle, Kirkcudbright
Mill on the Fleet Heritage Centre, Gatehouse of Fleet
New Abbey Cornmill, 8m S of Dumfries
Sweetheart Abbey, New Abbey
Threave Castle, 3m W of Castle Douglas

LOTHIAN
Craigmillar Castle, 2.5m SE of Edinburgh
Dirleton Castle & Garden, 7m W of North Berwick
Edinburgh Castle
Linlithgow Palace
Palace of Holyrood House, Edinburgh
Preton Mill & Phantassie Doocot, 23m E of Edinburgh
Tantallon Castle, 3m E of North Berwick
The Heritage of Golf, Gullane

■ Entertainment Venues

BORDERS
Borders Wool Centre, Nr. Galashiels
Peter Anderson of Scotland Cashmere Woollen Mill & Museum, Galashiels
St. Abb's Head, 2m N of Coldingham

DUMFRIES & GALLOWAY
Old Blacksmith's Shop Centre, Gretna Green
Robert Burns Centre, Dumfries

LOTHIAN
Edinburgh, Camera Obscura, Castlehill
Edinburgh Clan Tartan Centre, Leith
Edinburgh, Crabbie's Historic Winery Tour, Great Junction Street
Edinburgh Crystal Visitor Centre, Penicuik
Edinburgh, Kinloch Anderson Heritage Room, Leith
National Gallery of Scotland, The Mound, Edinburgh
The Scottish Whisky Heritage Centre, Royal Mile, Edinburgh

SOUTHERN SCOTLAND
DIARY OF EVENTS 1995

March 12	BERWICKSHIRE CROSS – COUNTRY TEAM EVENT Duns Castle, Borders.
March 19	BUCCLEUCH HUNT CROSS-COUNTRY TEAM EVENT Floors Castle, Kelso.
March 25	BUCCLEUCH HUNT POINT-TO-POINT Friars Haugh, Kelso.
April 20–22	HORSE RACING: THE SCOTTISH GRAND NATIONAL MEETING Ayr Racecourse, Ayr, Strathclyde.
April 28–30	GIRVAN FOLK FESTIVAL Girvan, Dumfries & Galloway.
May 1–31	RIVER TWEED FESTIVAL Throughout the Borders.
May 28	PIPE BAND, FLOORS CASTLE Kelso.
May 28	LOCH FYNE OYSTERS SEA FOOD FAIR Clachan, Nr. Cairnsow.
June 10	DUMFRIES GUID NYCHBURRIS FESTIVAL WEEK Various activities, Dumfries.
June 16	SELKIRK COMMON RIDING Selkirk, Borders.
June 19–24	PEEBLES BELTANE FESTIVAL Peebles, Borders.
July 8	JEDBURGH BORDER GAMES Jedburgh, Borders.
July 15–17	HORSE RACING: THE GLASGOW FAIR MEETING Ayr Racecourse, Ayr, Strathclyde.
July 16	PIPE BAND, FLOORS CASTLE Kelso.
July 16–22	KELSO CIVIC WEEK Kelso.
July 28–29	BORDERS UNION SHOW Kelso.
July 29 to August 6	PORT WILLIAM CARNIVAL WEEK Port William, Dumfries & Galloway.
August 12	PEEBLES AGRICULTURAL SHOW Peebles, Borders.
August 20	DUMFRIES & GALLOWAY HORSE SHOW Castle Douglas.
August 27	MASSED PIPE BANDS, FLOORS CASTLE Kelso.
September 14–16	HORSE RACING: THE WESTON MEETING Ayr Racecourse, Ayr – The Gold Cup on the 16th.

For further details contact:

The Scottish Tourist Board, 23 Ravelston Terrace, Edinburgh EH4 3EU.
Tel: 0131 332 2433

KELSO   BORDERS

SUNLAWS HOUSE HOTEL
Kelso, Roxburghshire TD5 8JZ

Telephone: 01573 450331   *Fax: 01573 450611*

Edinburgh 50, Newcastle 60, Berwick 24, Jedburgh 9, Kelso 3, Hawick 20

*F licence; 22 en suite bedrooms (9 on ground floor), all with radio, direct dial
telephone, satellite TV; full central heating; night service; meals to 9.30 p.m.;
diets; children welcome; baby listening; dogs welcome; conferences up to 20;
tennis; riding; shooting; fishing; new health and beauty salon; golf 3 miles; major
credit cards accepted.*

Sunlaws House is owned by the Duke of Roxburghe who lives at the impressive
Floors Castle (well worth a visit in itself) and who supervised its conversion into
an hotel, and continues to take a keen interest in the success of this once family
house. The hotel is situated 3 miles south west of Kelso through Heiton on the
A698 turning right with a signposted lane. Fishing on its own beat of the river
Teviot and shooting in the Roxburghe Estates are both very popular. Leaflets
on fishing breaks and shooting breaks are available. Hearty breakfasts are the
order of the day and I certainly enjoyed one during my stay. Emphasis is on
Scottish cooking and there is a good selection of wines – some of the older
wines coming, no doubt, from His Grace's cellar. Accommodation is of a high
standard, as you would expect, the bedrooms being comfortable and relaxing.
The conservatory, where I enjoyed a pre-dinner drink, is delightful and bar
lunches and afternoon teas can be served here. The Roxburghe Suite is available
for private parties or conferences. Mr. David Webster ably manages this small
country house hotel of character. Open all year. Tariff on application.

CRINGLETIE HOUSE HOTEL
Peebles, Borders EH45 8PL

Telephone: 01721 730233   *Fax: 01721 730244*

Edinburgh 20, Glasgow 50, London 360, Galashiels 19, Lanark 28

F licence; 13 en suite bedrooms all with telephone, remote control colour TV; lift to 1st and 2nd floors only; children welcome; comfortable residents' lounge and also non-smoking lounge; dogs permitted, but not in public rooms, or left unaccompanied in bedrooms; golf 3 miles; tennis; riding 3 miles; putting; croquet; fishing by permit on Tweed; Mastercard, Visa credit cards accepted.

I have been visiting this fine turreted hotel for 20 years and each year on my return I notice certain improvements. Bedrooms, over the years for instance, have been re-arranged, individually styled and attractively decorated. One aspect that does not change is the cooking. Aileen Maguire is in charge of the kitchen and she prepares consistently good, well presented dishes at, what I consider to be, very good value and this also applies to the varied selection of wines. The walled kitchen garden, well stocked with vegetables and fruit, provides the kitchen with the freshest possible produce. Not surprisingly the restaurant has won wide acclaim. Cringletie was designed by David Bryce the well known Scottish architect and built in 1861. The hotel stands in 28 acres of well kept gardens and woodlands with marvellous views overlooking the Eddleston valley and is situated 2 miles north of Peebles on the A703 Edinburgh to Peebles road. As Edinburgh is only half an hour's drive away, this hotel is ideal for some shopping in that lovely city or for touring the Border country where you can witness some spectacular scenery. You will be well cared for by the Maguire family during your stay. Room and breakfast from £52.50 single, double as single £65.00 and £98.00 for 2 people in double/twin room. Dinner £24.50, Sunday lunch £15.00 and weekday lunch from £5.50. Closed 2nd January to 10th March 1995 inclusive, open for Christmas and New Year. Enquire about 2 day Spring/ Autumn breaks.

COMLONGON CASTLE
COUNTRY HOUSE HOTEL
Clarencefield, Dumfries,
Dumfries and Galloway DG1 4NA

Telephone: 01387 870283 *Fax: 01387 870266*

Annan 6, Dumfries 10, Gretna 11, M6/M74 12, Carlisle 25, Edinburgh 85

R & R licence; 11 en suite bedrooms (including 2 honeymoon suites with Jacuzzi baths), all with direct dial telephone and TV; room service; baby listening; last orders for dinner 8.00 p.m.; special diets; children welcome; riding; 3, 18 hole golf courses within 10 miles; shooting and fishing by arrangement; hotel closed from January–14th February; Mastercard and Visa credit cards accepted.

Comlongon Castle is set in fifty acres of beautiful grounds with lawns, ornamental ponds and superb walks leading down to the very shore of the Solway Firth. Many people still go to nearby Gretna to marry, but few realise that here at the castle, just 11 miles from Gretna, they can get married with all the pomp and ceremony of banquet and piper, and then stay on for their honeymoon. The bridal suites are superb with four-poster beds and Jacuzzis. What more romantic a setting can there be? For historians the castle is an ideal venue from which to explore the Border country, and for the natural historian, the grounds are kept as a nature reserve featuring an abundance of flowers, wild animals including otters, and the many birds for which this area is famous. Before a delicious five course dinner is served in the evening, guests of a strong disposition can enjoy a tour of the haunted keep! Comlongon Castle is away from the crowded tourist areas, and yet is within easy driving distance of all that is best in the western borders. Room and breakfast from £85.00 (double), £43.00 (single), dinner from £23.00 including VAT.

MOFFAT HOUSE HOTEL

High Street, Moffat, Dumfries and Galloway DG10 9HL

Telephone: 01683 20039   *Fax: 01683 21288*

A74 (M) 1, Carlisle 40, Edinburgh 55, Perth 110, Oban 140, Birmingham 240

F licence; 20 en suite bedrooms (including 1 deluxe with four-poster bed and 3 rooms for the partially disabled), all with telephone, TV and hospitality tray; baby listening; last orders for dinner 8.45 p.m.; bar meals; special diets with an extensive vegetarian selection; children welcome; dogs accepted in bedrooms only; conferences max. 20; good hill walking; leisure centre nearby; golf 1 mile; tennis ½ mile; riding 2 miles; major credit cards accepted; open all year.

Moffat is one of those delightful small towns which lures travellers by its charm and environs. It has won both the 'Best Kept Village in Scotland' and the 'Scotland In Bloom' awards and is surrounded by some of the best hill walking country and beautiful scenery in southern Scotland. Set in the very heart of the town, Moffat House is an Adam building which has been skilfully converted into a most comfortable hotel, within 2½ acres of landscaped gardens. The public rooms are warm and inviting and the bedrooms are immaculately decorated, comfortably furnished and have all the amenities that we now expect of a good modern hotel. The owners, the Reid family, have been here for twenty years, and in that time, they have constantly improved it, so that it is without doubt, the best hotel for miles around. It is only minutes from the A74 (M) and yet it nestles in relatively unknown and beautiful countryside. For anyone wishing to take a holiday in this lovely area or, indeed, for someone wanting to take a break between England and Edinburgh, or Glasgow and beyond, Moffat House is the ideal choice. Room and breakfast from £52.00 single, £75.00 double. Dinner, room and breakfast from £56.50 per person, including VAT. Winter Breaks are also available.

KIRROUGHTREE HOTEL
Newton Stewart, Dumfries and Galloway DG8 6AN

Telephone: 01671 402141 · *Fax: 01671 402425*

Newton Stewart 1, Stranraer 25, Dumfries 53, Glasgow 82, Carlisle 86, Edinburgh 101

F licence; 17 en suite bedrooms, all with direct dial telephone and TV; room and night service; last orders for dinner 9.30 p.m.; special diets; children over 10 welcome; dogs accepted in 5 rooms only; conferences max. 30; pitch and putt; croquet; grass tennis court; golf ½ mile; shooting/fishing 2 miles; sea bathing and riding 15 miles; leisure centre 18 miles; hotel closed Jan. and Feb.; Visa and Mastercard credit cards accepted.

The Kirroughtree Hotel, from its eight acre hillside location above Newton Stewart, enjoys glorious views of the Galloway countryside, making it an ideal touring centre. All the bedrooms in the former 1719 mansion, have been refurbished to a very high level, and the renowned culinary standards have been enhanced since the purchase by the McMillan family. Awards now include two AA rosettes, Taste of Scotland Special Merit and all 3 RAC Merit Awards. The two elegant dining rooms – the red and the blue one – are both an oasis of comfort and pleasantly professional service, with the soothing tones of the drawing room's grand piano in the background. What particularly impressed me, was the way guests were always welcomed at the entrance; one of many "personal touches" in evidence, even to a short-stay guest. For golfers, there is free golf on the new and exciting Cally Golf Course at Gatehouse, where quiet, relaxing golf is guaranteed. Concession rates are also available at other fine local courses. The less energetic guests can enjoy pitch and putt, lawn tennis and croquet in Kirroughtree's grounds. Close to the hotel, salmon and trout fishing, rough shooting and deer stalking can be arranged in season. Room and breakfast from £100.00 per person, sharing a twin/double room, including VAT.

CORSEMALZIE HOUSE HOTEL
Port William, Nr. Newton Stewart,
Dumfries and Galloway DG8 9RL

Telephone: 01988 860254   *Fax: 01988 860213*

Stranraer 23, Glasgow 94, Dumfries 64, Newton Stewart 13, Port William 6

F licence; 14 bedrooms, 13 with bath and shower (1 with shower), all with radio, telephone and TV; meals to 9.15 p.m.; diets; children welcome; baby listening; dogs accepted; conferences; dancing in winter; own shooting and fishing (salmon, trout and coarse); croquet and putting; sailing, boating, golf, badminton, tennis and sea bathing 6 miles; riding 8 miles; sea angling 7 miles; squash 23 miles.

What a perfect spot in which to spend a holiday, in the depths of the Galloway countryside with facilities from the hotel which include shooting, fishing, riding, tennis, bird watching and hill walking. Local membership is available at two golf courses. The hotel, rather off the beaten track, has been skilfully converted into a very fine and comfortable country house hotel and it has managed to retain the grace and atmosphere of a private mansion. All the public rooms have character and quality and are attractively decorated. The cocktail bar is intimate where people meet to discuss the day's adventures. The dining room offers a relatively small menu, never a bad thing, which has been carefully thought out, and I saw the well stocked larder where fresh produce is the order of the day. The bedrooms are pleasantly decorated with all the necessary modern equipment. The resident proprietors, Mr. and Mrs. Peter McDougall, ensure that you will have an enjoyable stay and receive courteous service. There is a definite appeal for sportsmen as well as guests in search of countrified peace and good living in a lovely setting. Room and breakfast from £31.50–£39.00 (single), £58.00 (double). Closed mid-January to end February.

BARON'S CRAIG HOTEL
Rockcliffe, By Dalbeattie,
Dumfries and Galloway DG5 4QF

Telephone: 01556 630225   *Fax: 01556 630328*

Edinburgh 94, Glasgow 94, London 353, Dalbeattie 7

*F licence; 22 en suite bedrooms (5 ground floor), all with colour TV, direct dial
telephone; children welcome; cold late meals on request; drying room; dogs
accepted; golf, riding, sea bathing, boating, windsurfing, fishing all nearby.*

Here is an "off the beaten track" country house hotel, standing in twelve acres
of mainly wooded ground with views overlooking the Solway Firth. In spring,
it is bright with bulbs, rhododendrons and azaleas. There is a definite charm to
this peaceful, scenic part of Scotland where life moves along at an easy pace.
At Baron's Craig, you can either enjoy complete seclusion, or make use of the
local amenities such as safe bathing, boating, fishing and golf. The proprietor,
Mr. Capaccioli, together with Mrs. Hastings, are always on hand to give you
their personal attention, and their staff are willing and friendly. The attractive
dining room, with panoramic views, offers good food, together with a sensible
wine list. The furnishings throughout the hotel are of the highest standards, and
the public rooms are spacious and comfortable, and include many antiques. To
find the Baron's Craig Hotel, take the A75 from Dumfries, quickly turning left
on to the 710. Follow this road around the coast, and turn left for Rockcliffe after
Lochend. Room and breakfast from £45.00–£57.00 single, £38.00–£49.00 per
person, double, including VAT. Closed from the end of October to Easter.

TRIGONY HOUSE HOTEL
Thornhill, Dumfriesshire DG3 5EZ

Telephone: 01848 331211

Dumfries 11, Carlisle 43, Ayr 46, Glasgow 63, Edinburgh 64

F licence; 8 en suite bedrooms, all with direct dial telephone and TV; last orders for dinner 8.30 p.m.; bar meals; special diets; children over 10 welcome; no dogs; golf, shooting and fishing locally; open all year; Visa and Mastercard credit cards accepted.

A tranquil woodland garden surrounds Trigony House, yet it is close enough to the A76 to have easy access to the Solway coast, the M6 south and the M74/A74 north. There is also a picturesque route north west to Ayr and the Ayrshire coast. The hotel, originally a hunting lodge, has been tastefully refurbished and redecorated. The original entrance hall and staircase woodwork are very well preserved, and complement the fine furnishings and warm welcome. Good food is tremendously important to the proprietors, the Kerr family, whose cuisine, where possible, features only the best of local produce, carefully prepared to provide a true "Taste of Scotland". The menus in the evening are enhanced by a wine list of superior vintages at sensible prices. Lunchtime bar meals offer an imaginative variety of dishes cooked to order, and in winter (and even sometimes in Scotland's summer), within sight of a roaring log fire. Drumlanrig Castle and Country Park, home of the Duke and Duchess of Buccleuch and Queensberry, and Maxwelton House in Moniaive, the birthplace of Annie Laurie named in the famous ballad, are within five and eight miles of Trigony. Close to the hotel are some of the best salmon and trout beats on the River Nith, and should you wish to enjoy the fishing, arrangements can be made. There are a variety of other sporting opportunities in the area, including game shooting and a selection of good golf courses. Scottish Tourist Board 3 Crown Highly Commended. Dinner, room and breakfast from £53.00 single, £89.00 double, including VAT.

BARGAIN BREAKS

Readers are recommended to telephone the hotels to confirm rates and conditions prior to booking.

SOUTHERN SCOTLAND

BORDERS

SUNLAWS HOUSE HOTEL, Kelso *page 204*
Special themed and just plain relaxing 2 day breaks are available from January–May. Tariff on application.

CRINGLETIE HOUSE HOTEL, Peebles *page 205*
Bargain breaks available from Saturday 11th March 1995–Friday 5th May 1995 and from Sunday 22nd October 1995–Thursday 21st December 1995. Any 2 or more nights including dinner, bed and breakfast – £57.50 per person, per night.

DUMFRIES AND GALLOWAY

COMLONGON CASTLE COUNTRY HOUSE HOTEL, Dumfries *page 206*
Short breaks are available – prices on application.

MOFFAT HOUSE HOTEL, Moffat *page 207*
3 day, dinner, bed and breakfast breaks from £150.00 per person; 2 day, dinner, bed and breakfast breaks from £105.00 per person. Golfing breaks are also available.

KIRROUGHTREE HOTEL, Newton Stewart *page 208*
Midweek/Weekend Breaks are offered throughout the year (except January and February). This corner of Scotland has one of the mildest climates in the country and so our "Special Over 60's, Out of Season Breaks", i.e. March, November and December are particularly attractive. Rates from £39.00 per person, for dinner, bed and breakfast, for a minimum of 3 days. Other terms on application.

CORSEMALZIE HOUSE HOTEL, Port William *page 209*
Bargain breaks from £39.00 per person, per night for dinner, bed and breakfast for stays of 3 nights or more.

BARON'S CRAIG HOTEL, Rockcliffe, by Dalbeattie *page 210*
Bargain breaks on application.

TRIGONY HOUSE HOTEL, Thornhill *page 211*
Spring Breaks from March to June. Minimum of 2 nights, dinner, room and breakfast from £77.50 per night double, and £47.25 per night single.

CENTRAL SCOTLAND
SELECTED LOCAL ATTRACTIONS

Historic Houses, Gardens & Parks

CENTRAL
Culcreuch Castle & Country Park, Fintry

FIFE
Balcaskie House & Gardens, 2m W of
    Pittenweem
Cambo Gardens, 1m S of Kingsbarns
Earlshall Castle & Gardens, 1m E of Leuchars
Falkland Palace & Gardens, 11m N of Kirkaldy
Hill of Tarvit Mansionhouse & Garden, 2m S of
    Cupar
Kellie Castle & Garden, 3m N of Pittenweem
Sir Douglas Bader Garden for the Disabled, Duffus
    Park, Cupar

STRATHCLYDE
Ardanaiseig Gardens, 22m E of Oban
Arduaine Garden, 20m S of Oban
Barguillean Garden, 3m W of Taynuilt
Brodick Castle, Garden & Country Park, Isle of
    Arran
Culzean Castle & Country Park, 4m W of
    Maybole
Dean Castle & Country Park, Kilmarnock
Greenbank Garden, Clarkston, Glasgow

TAYSIDE
Bell's Cherrybank Gardens, Perth
Blair Castle, 7m NNW of Pitlochry
Branklyn Garden, Perth
Cluny House Gardens, 3½m from Aberfeldy
Edzell Castle & Garden, 6m N of Brechin
Duntrune Demonstration Garden, Dundee
House of Dun, 3m W of Montrose
Magginch Castle Gardens, 10m E of Perth
Scone Palace, 2m NE of Perth

Walks & Nature Trails

CENTRAL
Gartmorn Dam Country Park & Nature Reserve,
    By Sauchie

FIFE
Scottish Deer Centre, 3m W of Cupar

STRATHCLYDE
King's Cave, shore, 2m N of Blackwaterfoot
Lauder Forest Walks, 3m S of Strachur,
    Glenbranter
Muirshiel Country Park, 9m SW of Paisley
Puck's Glen, 5m W of Dunoon

TAYSIDE
Monikie Country Park, 10m N of Dundee
Queen's View Centre, Loch Tummel, 6m NW of
    Pitlochry
St. Cyrus National Nature Reserve, Nether
    Warburton

Historical Sites & Museums

CENTRAL
Blackness Castle, 4m NE of Linlithgow
Castle Campbell, Dollar Glan, 10m W of Stirling
Doune Castle, 8m S of Callander
Inchmahome Priory, Lake of Menteith
National Wallace Monument, 1½m NNE of
    Stirling
Stirling Castle

FIFE
Aberdour Castle
Balgonie Castle, By Markinch
Inchcolm Abbey (via ferry from South
    Queensferry)
St. Andrews Cathedral
St. Andrews Castle

STRATHCLYDE
Bachelor's Club (re. Robert Burns), Tarbolton
Bonawe Iron Works, Nr. Taynuilt
Dumbarton Castle
Doon Valley Heritage, 2m S of Patna
Gladstone Court Museum, Biggar
The Hill House, Helensburgh
John Buchan Centre, 6m E of Biggar
Burns Cottage & Museum, 2m S of Ayr
Coats Observatory, Paisley
David Livingstone Centre, Blantyre
Inveraray Castle & Gardens
Kilmory Castle Gardens, Lochgilphead
Rothesay Castle, Isle of Bute
Souter Johnnie's Cottage, Kirkoswald
The Tenement House, Garnethill, Glasgow
Weaver's Cottage, Kilbarchan, 12m SW of
    Glasgow

TAYSIDE
Angus Folk Museum, Glamis
Arbroath Abbey
Atholl Country Collection, Blair Atholl
Barrie's Birthplace, Kirriemuir
Black Watch Regimental Museum, Balhousie
    Castle, Perth
Glamis Castle, 5m SW of Forfar
Killiecrankie Visitor Centre, 3m N of Pitlochry
Loch Leven Castle, via Ferry from Kinross

Entertainment Venues

CENTRAL
Bannockburn Heritage Centre, 2m S of Stirling
Blair Drummond Safari & Leisure Park
Rob Roy & Trossachs Visitor Centre, Callander
Village Glass, Bridge of Allan

FIFE
Deep Sea World, North Queensferry

STRATHCLYDE
Ardnamurchan Natural History & Visitor Centre,
    Nr. Glenborrowdale
Antartex Village, Balloch
Balloch Castle Country Park, at south end of Loch
    Lomond
The Burrell Collection, Glasgow
Glenbarr Abbey Visitor Centre, 12m NW of
    Campbeltown
Glenfinart Deer Farm, Ardentinny
Inverawe Smokery, Bridge of Awe
Kelburn Country Centre, between Largs & Fairlie
The Time Capsule, Monklands, Coatbridge

TAYSIDE
Beatrix Potter Garden & Exhibition, Brinham
Caithness Glass (Perth), Inveralmond
Crieff Visitor's Centre
Dundee, Discovery Point

CENTRAL SCOTLAND
DIARY OF EVENTS 1995

February 4	SCOTLAND *v.* IRELAND RUGBY UNION Murrayfield, Edinburgh.
March 4	SCOTLAND *v.* WALES RUGBY UNION Murrayfield, Edinburgh.
March 31 to April 17	EDINBURGH INTERNATIONAL SCIENCE FESTIVAL Edinburgh.
April 28 to May 20	MAYFEST Glasgow.
May 22–28	1995 SCOTTISH INTERNATIONAL CHILDREN'S FESTIVAL Edinburgh.
May 28	BLAIR ATHOLL HIGHLAND GAMES Blair Atholl, Nr. Pitlochry.
May 29	SHORE CARNIVAL Shores of Holy Loch and Loch Long.
June 10	KILMORE & KILBRIDGE HIGHLAND GAMES Oban, Stratchclyde.
June 22–25	ROYAL HIGHLAND SHOW Ingleston, Edinburgh.
June 25	CORONATION PAGEANT Scone Palace, By Perth, Tayside.
June 30 to July 9	GLASGOW INTERNATIONAL JAZZ FESTIVAL Glasgow.
July 12–15	BELL'S SCOTTISH OPEN GOLF Gleneagles Hotel, Tayside.
July 15–18	CUTTY SARK TALL SHIPS RACE Port of Leith, Edinburgh.
July 20–23	1995 – 124th OPEN GOLF CHAMPIONSHIP Royal and Ancient Golf Club, St. Andrews.
July 28	WEST COAST WEST HIGHLAND YACHTING WEEK By Oban.
August 4–26	EDINBURGH MILITARY TATTOO Edinburgh Castle.
August 12	WORLD PIPE BAND CHAMPIONSHIP Glasgow.
August 12–27	DRAMBUIE EDINBURGH FILM FESTIVAL Edinburgh.
August 13 to September 2	EDINBURGH INTERNATIONAL FESTIVAL & FESTIVAL FRINGE Various locations, Edinburgh.
August 24	ARGYLLSHIRE HIGHLAND GATHERING Oban.
August 25	COWAL HIGHLAND GATHERING Dunoon, Strathclyde.
September 3	HIGHLAND GAMES Blairgowrie, Tayside.
September 16	RAF BATTLE OF BRITAIN INTERNATIONAL AIRSHOW Leuchars, Fife.

For further information contact:
The Scottish Tourist Board, 23 Ravelston Terrace, Edinburgh EH4 3EU.
Tel: 0131 332 2433

ALLT-CHAORAIN HOUSE HOTEL
Crianlarich, Perthshire FK20 8RU

Telephone: 01838 300283   *Fax: 01838 300238*

Oban 42, Stirling 47, Glasgow 50, Fort William 51, Perth 56, Edinburgh 88

Res. licence; 8 en suite bedrooms (4 ground floor), all with direct dial telephone and TV; dinner served at 7.00 p.m.; special diets; smokers restricted to sun lounge; dogs accepted; croquet lawn; golf and tennis 14 miles; sailing and boating nearby; shooting and fishing by arrangement; hotel closed during the winter; credit cards accepted.

"Welcome to my home" says Roger McDonald. His home Allt-Chaorain, is a compact and comfortable house noted for the warmth of its welcome and hospitality. Set high, it has level gardens and outstanding views of the surrounding mountains. Guests enjoy a "house party" atmosphere, helping themselves from the honesty bar and dining together in the evening. The table d'hôte menu changes daily, usually offering a choice of dishes for the main course. The accent is on good home cooking with generous helpings and plenty of fresh vegetables. After enjoying dinner it is pleasant to sit in the sunroom and watch the evening light on the mountains, or, if the evening is chill, to enjoy the log fire burning in the lounge. For walkers, this is a particularly good spot with the West Highland Way and the Munroes easily accessible, and for tourists, the network of quiet roads conjoining at Crianlarich make it a natural centre. Allt-Chaorain is just west of Crianlarich on the A82 before Tyndrum. Room and breakfast from £30.00, dinner, room and breakfast from £45.00, including VAT.

CULCREUCH CASTLE
Fintry, Loch Lomond, Stirlingshire, Scotland G63 0LW

Telephone: 01360 860228/860555   *Fax: 01360 860556*

**Stirling 17, Glasgow Airport 25, Perth 48, Aberfoyle 17,
Edinburgh Airport 42, Fort William 93**

F licence; 8 en suite bedrooms, all with direct dial telephone and TV; room service; baby listening; limited night service; last orders for dinner 8.30 p.m.; Dungeons Steak Bar; bar meals; special diets; children welcome; conferences max. 75; squash courts and indoor bowling close by; boating; shooting / fishing; golf and riding 10 miles; self-catering holiday lodges; open all year; all major credit cards accepted.

Tucked away in rural peace lies the village of Fintry, and over the river, in acres of parkland, stands Culcreuch Castle, dating from 1296. It is run in a friendly and informal manner by the Haslam family, and its antique furnishings and peaceful atmosphere reflect a country home. There are eight comfortable and individual bedrooms, some within 6 foot walls, some offering four-poster beds, one with antique, Chinese wallpaper, and one family suite. You can choose from the varied, table d'hôte menus over a drink in the drawing room or in the cellar bar, where you can enjoy the company of local folk. In the intimate, panelled dining room, you will be served meals of excellent quality, which are complemented by wines from a cellar of some 32 bins. The Castle is sheltered by the Campsie Fells, and has extended views over wooded countryside to distant hills. This central location puts the hotel close to Edinburgh and Glasgow and much of Scotland's dramatic scenery. Within the parkland, are eight log chalets, two of them serviced, and six self-catering. Fintry is 17 miles west of Stirling where the B818 and the B822 meet. Room and breakfast from £35.00 per person, weekly from £360.00 including dinner by candlelight.

THE LAKE HOTEL
Port of Menteith, Perthshire FK8 3RA

Telephone: 01877 385258   *Fax: 01877 385671*

Glasgow 30, Edinburgh 40, Stirling 18, Oban 84, Perth 50

F licence; 12 bedrooms, all with en suite bathroom, telephone and TV; room service; last orders for dinner 9.00 p.m.; bistro for lunches; special diets; children over 10 welcome; dogs by arrangement; golf, riding, shooting and fishing all nearby; hotel open all year; Visa and Mastercard welcome.

The Lake Hotel stands on the shore of the Lake of Menteith, with the most romantic of views spread before it. Owned and supervised by Mr. and Mrs. Leroy who also own The Manor House at Oban, you can expect high standards of hospitality, service, cuisine, comfort and house-keeping. The hotel has recently been renovated and refurbished throughout, with a sympathetic eye to the age and style of the building. The bedrooms are comfortable and attractive, with two suites (bedroom, dressing room and large bathroom) overlooking the lake. There is a smart cocktail lounge which leads to the lakeside conservatory restaurant. The mood created here by the view, quiet music – often a live pianist – and discreet service, is just right for the appreciation of the dishes from the well planned menu of Head Chef, Stuart Morrison. He uses fresh local fish, meat and game, with vegetables, salads and fruits as they come into season, with delicious results. His breakfasts, too, are something rather special. Drinks and coffee are served in the lounge which has plenty of books and magazines to enjoy. There is also The Bistro and bar which serves light meals during the day. From Stirling, take the A84 shortly picking up the A873. After Ruskie, take the A81, and the hotel is ¼ mile on the left hand side. Dinner, room and breakfast per person from £46.00 (low season) £75.00 high season inc. VAT. Weekly from £259.00 low season and £434.00 high season. 4 Crown Highly Commended.

ARDEONAIG HOTEL
South Loch Tay, Killin, Perthshire FK21 8SU

Telephone: 01567 820400   *Fax: 01567 820282*

Perth 50, Stirling 50

F licence; 16 en suite bedrooms (5 ground floor), all with tea/coffee making facilities; last orders for dinner 9.00 p.m.; bar meals; special diets; dogs accepted; conferences max. 16; public telephone box in hotel; 9 hole golf course; own harbour and boats; shooting/fishing; riding nearby; limited service in the winter; only Switch credit card accepted.

The Ardeonaig Hotel is non other than a pure haven for the visitor and sportsman alike. It is situated amongst the breathtaking scenery of this beautiful part of Scotland, amongst meadows and trees, where you will find the hotel's 9 hole golf course laid out beside Loch Tay. Within a 25 minute drive, there are more golf courses at Killin, Kenmore and Aberfeldy. This secluded 17th century inn has its own salmon fishing rights on the Loch, where the hotel's boats are moored in a small harbour, and a rod room and drying room is available. Guests can also fish for salmon on the River Tay, and excellent stalking can be arranged. The most hospitable owners, Eileen and Alan Malone, were finalists in the "'Scottish Field' – Morrisons' Bowmore Restaurant of the Year 1993", and are continuing to build a fine reputation for both the food and wine in their restaurant. The tasty Scottish cuisine is created from the freshest of local produce, and is complemented by a good selection of international wines. The Ardeonaig boasts a cheery bar, which offers some of the best Scottish malts, a cosy sitting room, and a second floor library with wonderful views over Loch Tay and the hills of Ben Lawers. This delightful area is wonderful walking country, and has outstanding scenery with quiet roads for the discerning tourist. I can recommend a stay at the Ardeonaig either for the sporting facilities on hand, or purely for a spate of peace and relaxation. Room and breakfast from £39.50, dinner, room and breakfast from £57.50. Prices include VAT.

CROMLIX HOUSE
Kinbuck, By Dunblane, Nr. Stirling, Perthshire FK15 9JT

Telephone: 01786 822125   *Fax: 01786 825450*

**Stirling 8, Perth 27, Glasgow 30, Edinburgh Airport 30,
Glasgow Airport 38, Edinburgh 34**

R & R licence; 14 en suite bedrooms (including 8 spacious suites), all with direct dial telephone and TV; room service; baby listening; limited night service; last orders for dinner 8.30 p.m.; light lunches; special diets; children welcome; dogs allowed in bedrooms only; conferences max. 40; croquet; 3 trout lochs; 3,000 acre estate; tennis; riding and shooting by arrangement; golf 5 miles; own chapel for weddings; open all year; all major credit cards accepted.

Five minutes off the A9, in its own 3,000 acre estate, the calm and serenity of Cromlix House is a different world, with rolling parkland, an abundance of wildlife, miles of walks, and three trout lochs. The row of wellies at the front door and lack of a "reception", sets the feeling of entering David and Ailsa Assenti's home. It is immediately relaxing, welcoming and obviously well loved. An imposing exterior belies a wonderful interior, full of history, antique furniture, blazing log fires in all six public rooms (including the dining rooms), and a large conservatory – glorious for summer breakfast and afternoon tea. Masses of fresh flowers together with a charming private chapel, make Cromlix the ultimate venue for an intimate wedding of 40 people. All the bedrooms, including the eight spacious suites are individual. No other house of this size can offer such a range of suites. Each is luxuriously furnished with care, and appointed with many personal and thoughtful extras. Half of the large bathrooms are original Edwardian, with huge baths, generous toiletries and bathrobes. Dining at Cromlix is an experience not to be missed. Award winning cuisine is prepared with care and imagination, whilst all of the staff are helpful, attentive and quietly professional. Nothing is too much of a problem. On reflection, it is the lack of pretention, coupled with attention to detail, which lifts Cromlix into a class of its own. Room and breakfast from £65.00 (suites £75.00), dinner, room and breakfast from £100.00. Prices include VAT.

LOCH MELFORT HOTEL
Arduaine, by Oban, Argyll PA34 4XG

Telephone: 01852 200233 *Fax: 01852 200214*

Oban 19, Lochgilphead 18, Glasgow 99, Fort William 67, Perth 111

F licence; 26 en suite bedrooms (10 on ground floor) all with sea view, telephone, radio and TV; tea/coffee making facilities; baby listening; meals to 9.00 p.m.; informal light lunches in Chart Room Bar, packed lunches, afternoon tea, lunch parties in the dining room on request; special diets; children welcome; dogs accepted in Cedar Wing; sailing; boating and sea bathing; fishing; clay pigeon shooting; riding nearby; Visa and Master Card accepted.

The Loch Melfort Hotel is situated just off the scenic coast road (A816) midway between Oban and Crinan, and has magnificent views over to the islands of Jura, Shuna and Scarba. The staff are efficient and attentive under the direction of resident owners, Rosalind and Philip Lewis. The public rooms are comfortable, with soft, restful colour schemes, and there is a choice of bedrooms either in the Cedar Wing with balcony or patio, or in the main house, which includes two luxury rooms, one with a king-size bed and sofa beds, useful for children. The award-winning cuisine is prepared by Philip Lewis, who uses predominantly fresh produce, often featuring local sea food, lamb and Aberdeen Angus beef. Those with a sweet tooth will enjoy the home-made desserts, and I am told that the Sunday evening seafood buffet is very good. The popular ''Chart Room Bar'' serves lunches and suppers, offering some interesting dishes, together with the more traditional fare. The hotel stands in its own grounds, next to the well known Arduaine Gardens which are open all year, and owned by the National Trust for Scotland. In this part of the west coast you will find craggy hills and soft wooded glens, and exploring by foot or car is rewarding. If you like the ocean, then boats run from Oban to the many islands off the coast including Mull. If you are looking for relaxation, or enjoy outdoor pursuits and the fresh air, then I can highly recommend the Loch Melfort Hotel. Room and breakfast from £47.50. Hotel closed from January 4th–March 1st, and is open over Christmas and New Year.

THE BUSBY HOTEL

Field Road, Clarkston, Glasgow, Strathclyde G76 8RX

Telephone: 0141 644 2661   *Fax: 0141 644 4417*

M74 3, Hamilton 3, Glasgow City Centre 4, Glasgow Airport 8, Ayr 20

R & R licence; 32 en suite bedrooms, all with direct dial telephone and TV; 24 hour room service; baby listening; lift; last orders for dinner 9.30 p.m.; bar meals from noon–9.00 p.m.; special diets; children welcome; dogs accepted by arrangement; conferences max. 200; plenty of golf, tennis, riding, shooting and fishing in the area; open all year; all major credit cards accepted.

Despite being on the edge of Scotland's largest commercial area, the privately owned Busby Hotel is located in a tree-lined avenue, beside the River Cart, to the south of Glasgow, close to the new town of East Kilbride. The hotel is only ten minutes from the M74 (linked to the M8 and M73), and twenty minutes from Glasgow's International Airport. With the railway station only two minutes away, and frequent trains to Glasgow Central and East Kilbride, the hotel's extensive parking facilities are ideal if you wish the "train to take the strain". Many first class golf courses are close to the hotel, with the principal Ayrshire courses just 30 or 40 minutes away, and tee reservations can be arranged by the hotel. The area around The Busby is rich in attractions, chief of which must be the Burrell Collection in nearby Pollok Park. All the comfortable bedrooms in the hotel are en suite and have recently been refurbished. The highly acclaimed cuisine served in the Bridge Restaurant, can be chosen from either of the comprehensive à la carte or table d'hôte menus. For less formal eating, meals are served in the lounge bar from noon to 9.00 p.m. Small meeting and large conference rooms are available for up to 200 delegates. A warm welcome always awaits you from the owners, Mr. and Mrs. Watson and their caring and efficient staff. Room and breakfast from £37.50 midweek, £30.00 at the weekend, and dinner, room and breakfast from £55.00 midweek and £38.00 at the weekend. All prices include VAT.

THE MANOR HOUSE
Gallanach Road, Oban, Argyll PA34 4LS

Telephone: 01631 62087   *Fax: 01631 63053*

**Edinburgh 123, Dundee 116, Glasgow 96, Inverness 118,
Fort William 50, London 489**

F licence; 11 en suite bedrooms, all with telephone, colour TV and full central heating; bar lunches; diets; dogs allowed; sea bathing; sailing and boating ½ mile; indoor heated swimming pool, sauna and solarium, golf, each within 2 mile radius; helipad; closed during January; Mastercard and Visa cards accepted.

For peace and quiet within walking distance of the bustle of Oban, I recommend the elegant little Manor House Hotel. Built beside the sea on the tip of the bay, it enjoys unrivalled views over the harbour, the adjacent islands and the mountains beyond. The hotel is owned and supervised by Mr. and Mrs. J. Leroy who also own The Lake Hotel at Port of Menteith, along with their managers, Mr. and Mrs. Patrick Freytag. You can expect hospitality, service, comfort, good food and a very high standard of housekeeping. The house is furnished in keeping with its dignity and age, it offers pretty, well appointed bedrooms, an elegant drawing room and parlour and a well furnished cocktail bar with large windows overlooking the bay, making it a pleasant spot for an apéritif or a bar lunch. The dining room, which has an excellent reputation locally, is styled in pink, and glows with silver and candlelight. Chef Patrick Freytag offers a tempting menu composed of Scottish and continental cuisine, specializing in dishes made from abundant local fish and game in season. Oban is well placed for exploring the scenic West Coast, but for me, its chief delight is the opportunity to take to the sea, either on the car ferry to Mull or on the smaller craft visiting other islands and places of interest. If fishing is your wish you could hardly be better situated. Dinner, room and breakfast per person from £42.00 (low season) £66.00 high season inc. VAT. Weekly from £259.00 (low season) and £399.00 (high season). An S.T.B. 4 Crown Highly Commended hotel, with an AA Rosette for food.

THE CREGGANS INN
Strachur, Argyll PA27 8BX

Telephone: 01369 86279   *Fax: 01369 86637*

Inveraray 19, Dunoon 19, Glasgow 59, Oban 69, Campbeltown 85, Edinburgh 101

F licence; 19 bedrooms (1 for the disabled), 18 en suite and 1 with private bathroom, all with telephone and TV; room service until 11.30 p.m.; baby listening; last orders for dinner 9.00 p.m.; bar meals; special diets; children welcome; dogs accepted; conferences max. 85; pool table; sailing/boating; washing/drying facilities; sea bathing, shooting, fishing and tennis nearby; riding 10 miles; golf 15 miles; open all year; all major credit cards accepted.

More than 400 years ago, Mary Queen of Scots landed at Creggans on her way through the Highlands. An inn with a tradition of hospitality, homely comfort and individual attention, The Creggans stands on a headland looking over Loch Fyne, to tremendous prospects of hill and sea. Sir Fitzroy MacLean, whose family has owned this delightful hotel since 1957, explained, "we have spent many years striving for excellence, and it is in that spirit that we are continuing to develop our facilities so we can be certain of providing the best for discerning guests". The latest developments are the installation of yacht moorings to allow guests to arrive at the hotel from Loch Fyne, and helicopter tours from the Inn. Inveraray Castle, home of the Clan Campbell, is 19 miles away, and you can also visit Inveraray Jail, Scotland's "living 19th century prison". The Inn is an ideal base for holidays such as sailing, fishing, golfing, walking and touring, or just relaxing in front of an open fire. The Creggans has a well deserved reputation for excellent food; not surprising as Lady MacLean, who still supervises the kitchen, is the author of several famous cookery books. The hotel's 12 seater mini bus is at your disposal for daily charter, with Jimmy as an expert driver and teller of local stories, only the truth in his stories is not guaranteed! A warm welcome awaits you at The Creggans Inn by the General Manager, Jean-Pierre Puech. Room and breakfast from £55.00, dinner room and breakfast from £72.00 including VAT.

STONEFIELD CASTLE HOTEL
Tarbert, Loch Fyne, Argyll PA29 6YJ
Telephone: 01880 820836   *Fax: 01880 820929*
**Lochgilphead 12, Inveraray 38, Campbeltown 38, Oban 51,
Glasgow 95, London 500**

F licence; 33 bedrooms (32 en suite), all with direct dial telephone and TV; room service; lift; bar meals from 12.15 p.m. to 2.00 p.m. and last orders for dinner 9.00 p.m.; special diets; children welcome; dogs accepted; conferences max. 100; snooker/billiards; outdoor heated swimming pool; sauna; solarium; sea bathing; sailing/boating; clay shooting, golf, riding nearby; fishing; open all year; all major credit cards accepted.

Here is something unusual in the way of a holiday setting. Tastefully converted from a 19th century castle, once the home of the Campbells and overlooking Loch Fyne, Stonefield Castle is charmingly situated on a peninsula separating the Isles of Islay and Jura from Arran. It has panoramic views over the sea and its gardens are known for some of the finest rhododendrons in Britain, azaleas and other exotic shrubs that flourish in the mild west coast climate. Inside the castle, the rooms are spacious and comfortable. There is a large panelled cocktail bar, lounge-hall, library and drawing room. All the bedrooms are comfortably furnished, with those in the older part of the house being in traditional style, whilst a newer wing has rooms of a more contemporary style. There are also several luxurious master bedrooms. The dining room, which enjoys stunning views, offers interesting table d'hôte menus, using local produce where possible. The accompanying wine list satisfies every taste and pocket. A snooker room and sauna suite is located within the hotel, and there is an outdoor heated swimming pool, well sited to maximise the views over the gardens and sea. Most traditional outdoor pursuits are available nearby and ferry trips to Arran, Gigha (gardens to see), Islay, Mull and Iona, together with the Mull of Kintyre are all within reach. The hotel sign is on the left of the A83 about 9 miles from Lochgilphead travelling south. Dinner, bed and breakfast from £45.00–£75.00 per person, per night, depending on type of room and season.

GREEN PARK HOTEL
Pitlochry, Tayside PH16 5JY

Telephone: 01796 473248   *Fax: 01796 473520*

**Edinburgh 68, Glasgow 83, Braemar 41, Inverness 69, Kingussie 45,
Kinloch Rannoch 21, Perth 28**

*F licence; 37 en suite bedrooms (10 on ground floor), all with telephone,
tea/coffee making facilities, colour TV; children welcome; conferences; chess;
cards; table tennis; bar billiards; 9 hole putting; swings; sailing and surfing on
the loch; pony trekking, golf and fishing by arrangement.*

After a long journey, it is a delight to stay in the Green Park Hotel with its breathtaking panoramic views of Loch Faskally and the surrounding green hills. The
hotel is accessible by both car and British Rail Bargain Travel. You can be sure
of a warm welcome from the staff, and this attitude pervades throughout. There
are bright and spacious lounges, and the Sun Lounge overlooks the loch. The
equally attractive bedrooms are comfortable and well equipped as you would
expect in such a well run hotel. Bar lunches and bar dinners are available daily
from 12–2.00 p.m. and 6–8.30 p.m., and on Saturday, by popular demand,
there is the hors d'oeuvres table. A popular feature is the cold buffet served for
Sunday dinner. Guests attending the Pitlochry Festival Theatre will appreciate
meals being served from 6.30 p.m., with the restaurant closing at 8.30 p.m. With
Pitlochry centre only 5 minutes' walk away, you can find a variety of pastimes
to make your holiday complete. Bed and breakfast from £40.00, inclusive of VAT.
Bargain Breaks available and Curling Weekends in October. Closed from the
end of October to the end of March, but the office is open for enquiries.

THE LOG CABIN HOTEL
Kirkmichael, Nr. Pitlochry, Perthshire PH10 7NB

Telephone: 01250 881288   *Fax: 01250 881402*

Pitlochry 12, Edinburgh 70, Glasgow 85, Blairgowrie 12

F licence; 13 en suite bedrooms, all with radios; TV available; central heating; meals till 9 p.m.; bar meals available lunchtime; supper in the evening; diets; rooms suitable for the disabled; children welcome; dogs welcome; fishing; craft shop; photo stalking; own stocked trout loch, salmon fishing by arrangement; shooting includes blackcock, grouse and use of clay trap; riding by arrangement and pony trekking; stalking by prior arrangement; private tuition for clay shooting and fishing; golf: 40 courses within 2 hrs.

For the sportsman and the lover of the great outdoors, the Log Cabin Hotel is a warm and comfortable base. It is simple, informal, and hosted in a very friendly manner by Daphne Kirk and Alan Finch. Such comforts as the blazing log fire in the bar, a wide choice of malt whiskies, a good meal and a well stocked cellar, are the perfect remedy to round off a tiring day. The cabin-style bedrooms are warm and cosy, and all have en suite facilities. The restaurant has lovely views, and it is not unusual to see deer wandering past, as you enjoy the good Scottish fare served here. Numerous outdoor pursuits are on offer to guests, for example, riding over the surrounding heather clad hills (no tarmac to contend with here), field sports on the hotel's moors and loch or on local estates, stalking with your camera escorted by a keeper, or touring along quiet, scenic roads, passing many interesting sights. Set nine hundred feet above sea level amid heather and pine, and close to Glenshee, the hotel offers excellent skiing packages for people of all abilities, and mention should also be made of the New Year Festivities, of which an early booking is advisable. Dinner, bed and breakfast from £39.95 per person, and bed and breakfast from £25.00 including VAT. Reductions are offered for children up to 12, other terms on application including Winter, Spring, Christmas and New Year breaks.

DALMUNZIE HOUSE HOTEL
Spittal O'Glenshee, Blairgowrie, Perthshire PH10 7QG

Telephone: 01250 885224   *Fax: 01250 885225*

Perth 35, Dundee 37, Braemar 15, Blairgowrie 20

F licence; 18 bedrooms (1 for the disabled, 16 en suite); lift; last orders for dinner 8.30 p.m.; light bar lunches; special diets on request; children welcome; dogs accepted; conferences max. 20; games room; bar billiards; 9 hole golf course; tennis; shooting/fishing (trout/salmon, own rainbow trout stocked loch); skiing in Glenshee; riding 15 miles; closed in November and December; Mastercard and Visa accepted.

If you are looking for perfect peace and quiet or for a sporting holiday, this impressive country house, hidden away in the hills, is an excellent venue. Dalmunzie has been in the Winton family for many years, and is now looked after by Simon and Alexandra Winton, whose care and attention result in a well run house, personal service, and a happy atmosphere. The sitting rooms, cosy cocktail bar and spacious bedrooms are all in excellent decorative order, well furnished and comfortable, and log fires and central heating ensure warmth in every season. Good old fashioned service is available for your requirements – tea trays are still brought to your room! In the dining room, the varied table d'hôte dishes are well cooked and feature traditional Scottish fare, which is accompanied by a carefully chosen wine list. This family owned sporting estate can organise almost any shooting holiday, whilst other field sports, trout fishing, walking and climbing also await you here. Dalmunzie have their own 9 hole golf course available for guests. Nearby Glenshee offers well organised skiing for all abilities, and for those wishing to explore on wheels, there are quiet roads and much to see. Room and breakfast from £35.00 per person, weekly rates from £350.00 per person, full board. During the ski season, dinner, bed and breakfast from £39.00–£45.00.

BARGAIN BREAKS

Readers are recommended to telephone the hotels to confirm rates and conditions prior to booking.

CENTRAL SCOTLAND

CENTRAL

ALLT-CHAORAIN HOUSE HOTEL, Crianlarich   *page 215*
Savings of 5% for 2–3 nights, 7½% for 4–5 nights and 10% for 6–7 nights. All stays must include dinner, bed and breakfast.

CULCREUCH CASTLE, Loch Lomond, Fintry   *page 216*
Bargain breaks available from November–March, excluding the Christmas and New Year period: any 2 nights, to include candlelit dinner, room and breakfast £100.00 per person. Family lodges within the Castle grounds are available as hotel bedrooms (serviced) or for self-catering. Colour brochures and tariffs on application. For other breaks throughout the year, prices on application.

THE LAKE HOTEL, Port of Menteith   *page 217*
Low season – £44.00 per person, per night for 2 nights including dinner, bed and breakfast. High season – £70.00 per person for 2 nights including dinner, bed and breakfast.

ARDEONAIG HOTEL, South Loch Tay   *page 218*
Reductions for stays of 3 nights or more. Salmon fishing breaks throughout the fishing season. Prices on application.

CROMLIX HOUSE, Nr. Stirling   *page 219*
Minimum of 2 nights including full breakfast and 4 or 5 course dinner, canapes, coffee and petit fours. Rooms from £65.00 (£70.00 at the weekend), spacious luxury suites with private sitting room from £80.00 (£85.00 at the weekend). Prices are per person, per night, based on two people sharing a double room, available from Dec.–May and Oct.–Dec. Please apply for details on breaks between June and September. Christmas and New Year house parties – minimum 3 days from £350.00.

STRATHCLYDE

LOCH MELFORT HOTEL, Arduaine, by Oban   *page 220*
From £44.00 (during March and November) dinner, bed and breakfast – £55.00, minimum stay of 2 nights. Christmas and New Year – special 3 day holiday rates available.

THE BUSBY HOTEL, Glasgow   *page 221*
Dinner, room and breakfast in a twin/double room from £38.00 per person, per night, £50.00 single per person, per night, for a minimum stay of 2 nights. Special offers for Christmas, Hogmanay and Easter. Flexi-Breaks available all year.

THE MANOR HOUSE, Oban   *page 222*
£42.00 per person, per night for 2 nights in low season; £62.00 per person, per night for 2 nights in high season. Prices include dinner, bed and breakfast and free entry to indoor heated swimming pool, sauna, solarium and golf club.

BARGAIN BREAKS

THE CREGGANS INN, Strachur   *page* 223
Special Winter Breaks are available from 1st October 1994–31st May 1995,
except Christmas, New Year and Easter. Price is £65.50 per person, for 2 nights,
on the basis of 2 people sharing a room, and includes dinner, bed and breakfast.
We place the greatest emphasis on food, using fresh seafood from Loch Fyne and
game from the Argyll hills. Our breakfasts are memorable, with a particularly
Scottish flavour.

STONEFIELD CASTLE HOTEL, Tarbert   *page* 224
Bargain breaks available – price on application.

TAYSIDE

GREEN PARK HOTEL, Pitlochry   *page* 225
Spring Breaks and Autumn Breaks available from £37.00 per person, per night,
with Curling Weekends in October – prices on application.

THE LOG CABIN HOTEL, Kirkmichael, Nr. Pitlochry   *page* 226
3 days breaks or more, including dinner, room and breakfast available all year.
Special New Year packages, midweek and winter shooting packages, and skiing
breaks – please phone or write for details.

DALMUNZIE HOUSE HOTEL, Spittal O'Glenshee   *page* 227
Friendly country house hotel, sitting on 6,000 acre sporting estate, with 9 hole
golf course, tennis, shooting and fishing, and skiing only 5 miles away. From
Jan.–April: 2 nights from £78.00 and 5 nights from £180.00. From April–Oct.:
3 nights from £151.00. Prices are per person, for dinner, bed and breakfast.

THE HIGHLANDS & SCOTTISH ISLANDS
SELECTED LOCAL ATTRACTIONS

Historic Houses, Gardens & Parks

GRAMPIAN

Castle Fraser & Garden, 4m N of Dunecht
Crathes Castle & Garden, Nr. Banchory
Cruickshank Botanic Gardens, Aberdeen University
Damside Garden Herbs, Benholm by Johnshaven
Drum Castle & Garden, By Banchory
Duff House, Banff
Duthie Park & Winter Gardens, Aberdeen
Fasque, Fettercain
Fyvie Castle
Haddo House, Tarves
James Cocker & Sons, Rosegrowers, Aberdeen
Leith Hall & Garden, Kennethmont, Huntly
Monymusk Walled Garden
Pitmedden Garden & Museum of Farming by Ellon

HIGHLAND

The Achiltibuie Hydroponicum
Balmacara Estate & Lochalsh Woodland Garden, Kyle of Lochalsh
Brodie Castle, 4m W of Forres
Dunrobin Castle, Gardens & Museum, Golspie
Inverewe Garden, by Poolewe
Oldwick Castle, Wick

ISLE OF MULL

Torosay Castle & Gardens, 1½m SSE of Craignure

ISLE OF SKYE

Dunvegan Castle

Walks & Nature Trails

GRAMPIAN

Aden Country Park, Mintlaw
Braeloine Visitor Centre, Glan Tanar, By Aboyne
Bullers of Buchan, Cruden Bay
Forview Nature Reserve, Newburgh

HIGHLAND

Abriachan Garden Nursery Walk, Loch Ness
Aultfearn Local Walk Kiltarlity
Falls of Foyers Woodland Walks
Farigaig Forest Trails
Glen Affric Forest Walks
Plodda Falls Scenic Walk
Reelig Forest Walks, W of Inverness

ISLE OF MULL

Carsaig Arches, on shore 3m W of Carsaig

ISLE OF SKYE

Dalabil Glen, between Tarskavaig and Ostair
Forestry Walk – between Ardvasar and Aird of Sleat
The Trotternish Ridge

Historical Sites & Museums

GRAMPIAN

Aberdeen Maritime Museum – Provost Ross's House
Ballindalloch Castle, Ballindalloch
Balmoral Castle, Crathie
Braemar Highland Heritage Centre, Braemar
Brodie Castle, Forres
Castle Fraser, Nr. Inverurie
Dallas Dhu Distillery, Forres
Colgarff Castle, Strathdon

GRAMPIAN (continued)

Crathie Church, Crathie
Elgin Cathedral
Kings College Chapel & Visitor Centre, Aberdeen
Provost Skene's House, Aberdeen
St. Machar's Cathedral, Old Aberdeen

HIGHLAND

Cawdor Castle, 5m S of Nairn
Culloden Battlefield, 5m E of Inverness
Dornoch Cathedral
Durness Visitor Centre
Eilean Donan Castle, 9m E of Kyle of Lochalsh
Fort George, 10m W of Nairn
Glen Coe Visitor Centre, 17m S of Fort William
Glenfinnan Monument, Lochaber, 18m W of Fort William
High Miller's Cottage, Cromarty, 22m NE of Inverness
Leckmelm Shrubbery & Arboretum, Nr. Ullapool
Lochinver Visitor Centre
Urquhart Castle on Loch Ness, Nr. Drumnadrochit

ISLE OF MULL

Duart Castle, on E point of Mull
The Old Byrem, Dervaig

ISLE OF SKYE

Colbost Folk Museum
Giant MacAskill Museum, Dunvegan
Piping Centre, Borreraig
Skye Museum of Island Life, Kilmuir

Entertainment Venues

GRAMPIAN

Alford Valley Railway, Alford
Castle Grant, Grantown-on-Spey
Fowlsheugh R.S.P.B. Seabird Colony
Glenshee Ski Centre, Cairnwell, By Braemar
Honeyneuk Bird Park, Nr. Macduff
Loch Muick & Lochnagar Wildlife Reserve, By Ballater
Loch of Strathbeg R.S.P.B. Reserve, Crimond
North East Falconry Centre, Cairnie, By Huntley
Peterhead Fish Market
Royal Lochnagar Distillery, Crathie
St. Cyrus National Nature Reserve, By Montrose
Speyside Heather Centre, Grantown
Storybook Glen, Maryculter
The Malt Whisky Trail, Speyside
Ugie Fish House, Peterhead

HIGHLAND

Aviemore Centre
Dulsie Bridge
Glen Ord Distillery, Muir of Ord
Highland Folk Museum, Kingussie
Loch Ness Centre, Drumnadrochit
Made in Scotland Exhibition of Crafts, Beauly
Rothiemurchas Estate, Nr. Aviemore
Strathspey Steam Railway, Nr. Aviemore
Torridon Countryside Centre, 9m SW of Kinlochewe

ISLE OF MULL

Isle of Mull Wine Company, Bunessan
Mull Railway, Craignure
Mull Little Theatre, Dervaig
Tobermory Distillery Visitor Centre

ISLE OF SKYE

The Clan Donald Visitor Centre at Armadale Castle
Talisker Distillery, Loch Harport
Skye Oysters, Loch Harport

THE HIGHLANDS AND SCOTTISH ISLANDS
DIARY OF EVENTS 1995

January 21	SPILLERS BONIO SIBERIAN HUSKEY CLUB RALLY Glenmore Forest Park, Nr. Aviemore, Highland.
March 20–24	ISLE OF MULL DRAMA FESTIVAL Aros Hall, Tobermory.
April 15	CULLODEN COMMEMORATION SERVICE Culloden, Nr. Inverness, Highland.
April 28–30	ISLE OF MULL MUSIC FESTIVAL Tobermory.
June 9–10	SKYELIVE Various events, Isle of Skye.
June 10–23	SKYE AND LOCHALSH FEIS Isle of Skye.
June 11	KILDRUMMY CASTLE RALLY Kildrummy, By Alford, Grampian.
June 30 to July 2	HIGHLAND TRADITIONAL MUSIC FESTIVAL Dingwall, Highland.
July 3	NATIONAL ARCHERY TOURNAMENT Armadale, Sleat, Isle of Skye.
July 15	ELGIN HIGHLAND GAMES Elgin, Grampian.
July 22	INVERNESS HIGHLAND GAMES Inverness.
July 24–29	SKYE FOLK FESTIVAL Portree, Isle of Skye.
July 24–29	INVERNESS TATTOO Inverness.
August 2	SKYE HIGHLAND GAMES Portree, Isle of Skye.
August 3	158th BLACK ISLE SHOW Muir of Ord, Highland.
August 10	SALEN SHOW Glenaros, Isle of Mull.
September 2	BRAEMAR ROYAL HIGHLAND GATHERING Braemar, Grampian.
October 13–15	2300 CLUB CAR RALLY Tobermory, Isle of Mull.
October 13–20	ROYAL NATIONAL MOD 1995 Golspie, Highland.

For further details contact the nearest Tourist Information Centre or:
The Scottish Tourist Board
23 Ravelston Terrace
Edinburgh EH4 3EU
Tel: 0131 332 2433

THE MARCLIFFE AT PITFODELS
North Deeside Road, Aberdeen, Grampian AB1 9YA
Telephone: 01224 861000 *Fax: 01224 868860*
Balmoral Castle 53, St. Andrews 82, Edinburgh 106, Glasgow 146

F licence; 42 en suite bedrooms (1 for the disabled), all with telephone & TV; room service; baby listening; night service; lift; last orders for dinner 10.00 p.m.; special diets; children welcome; conferences max. 400; games room; snooker/ billiards; golf 1 mile; riding 2 miles; tennis & squash 3 miles; shooting/fishing by arrangement; all major credit cards accepted.

Here is an hotel of exceptional quality, owned and run by Stewart and Sheila Spence, whose hospitality is renowned. Set in eight acres of woodland garden, it is but a few minutes from the centre of Aberdeen and within 15 minutes of two golf courses, and some of Scotland's finest scenery. The personal service and the ambience is that of a country house, whilst offering discreet and flexible arrangements for entertaining and business meetings. Five foot double king size or Zip Link twin beds are provided in all the spacious bedrooms, where you will find added extras such as towelling bathrobes, hairdryers and refrigerated mini bars. The luxurious suites are graciously adorned with period furniture, flowers, fruit, and again, many other creature comforts. There are two restaurants; The Conservatory, which serves the most delicious lunches and dinners, and the more formal Invery Room, where in addition to the outstanding cuisine, one may draw on a cellar of 300 wines. Both restaurants maintain the highest levels of presentation and quality. The Marcliffe is an ideal base for touring the nearby attractions such as art galleries and museums, and both castle and distillery tours are available. For the sportsman, shooting, salmon fishing, stalking and golf at Royal Aberdeen can all be arranged by the hotel. The Marcliffe is situated on the A93 between Cults and the city centre, and it is where you will experience first class standards in every aspect. Room and breakfast from £70.00, dinner, room and breakfast from £95.00. Prices include VAT. A member of Small Luxury Hotels of the World. Open all year.

DARROCH LEARG HOTEL
Ballater, Royal Deeside, Aberdeenshire AB35 5UX
Telephone: 013397 55443   *Fax: 013397 55443*
Aberdeen 42, Braemar 17, Perth 68, London 519

R & R licence; 20 en suite bedrooms, 1 ground floor, with direct dial telephone, col. TV, tea/coffee facilities, full central heating, trouser press & hair dryer; diets; children welcome, baby listening; dogs accepted; conferences 20 max.; golf, tennis, riding, fishing & walking nearby; Mastercard and Visa accepted.

The Darroch Learg Hotel stands on the wooded slopes of the Craigendarroch. It has panoramic views over the golf course, the Balmoral Estates and the surrounding forests and mountains. A listed granite built country house, it has been restored and run as an hotel by the Franks family since 1961. The many regular guests testify to the friendly hospitality, comfortable and well appointed rooms and the excellent food. Drinks are served either in the drawing room or in the comfortable smoking room. The dining room has a conservatory extension – a delightful place to dine whilst enjoying the view. Head Chef, Robert Macpherson and his team, use the finest Scotch beef, lamb and seafood, to create their imaginative menus. The restaurant has been awarded two AA Rosettes and is recommended by the Taste of Scotland. All the bedrooms are attractive and well equipped, and many have wonderful views towards the Grampian Mountains. Five of the bedrooms are in Oakhall, another listed building with grounds adjoining Darroch Learg. The hotel is an ideal venue for a golfing holiday – the Ballater course is minutes away, and there are five other courses within a 17 mile radius. Rich with river and woodland, Royal Deeside is a delight for walking, rambling or travelling by car; there is a diversity of scenery within easy reach. Many of the castles, gardens and distilleries in the area are open to visitors. The Darroch Learg is on the right hand side of the A93 to Braemar, at the western end of Ballater. Room and breakfast from £37.00 per person and dinner, room and breakfast from £58.00 per person. The hotel, which is closed in January, has been awarded "4 Crowns Highly Commended" by the Scottish Tourist Board and is a Scotland's Commended Hotel.

MANSEFIELD HOUSE HOTEL
Mayne Road, Elgin, Morayshire IV30 1NY

Telephone: 01343 540883 *Fax: 01343 552491*

Glasgow 180, Aberdeen 67, Inverness 39, Perth 134

F licence; 17 en suite bedrooms, all with direct dial telephone and TV; room service; baby listening; night service; lift; last orders during weekdays 9.30 p.m.; weekends 10.30 p.m.; special diets; children welcome; guide dogs only accepted; conferences max. 25; sauna; tennis; gymnasium; swimming pool, sailing and boating 5 miles; several golf courses nearby; riding, shooting and fishing can be arranged; open all year; all major credit cards accepted.

Mansefield House is a gracious Georgian town house that has been skilfully converted into an hotel of distinction. You will find friendly hospitality and service throughout this family owned hotel, along with high standards of house keeping, and notable cuisine. The restaurant has been awarded a Rosette for its food, and such delicacies as fresh lobster, scallops and prawns, feature on the menus. Antique and traditional furnishings and fabrics enhance both the well appointed public rooms and the bedrooms, which are spacious, comfortable and well equipped. The small town of Elgin is well situated for a touring holiday and the hotel can arrange golf on any of the nearby golf courses, or fishing on the River Spey. To find the hotel, entering Elgin from the south, take the bypass at the roundabout at the end of the town, straight on to reach a mini roundabout, and the hotel is on the right hand side. Single room and breakfast from £55.00, double from £90.00. Scottish Tourist Board 4 Crown Highly Commended.

AULTBEA HOTEL
Aultbea, Ross-shire IV22 2HX

Telephone: 01445 731201   *Fax: 01445 731214*

Ullapool 45, Inverness 77

F licence; 8 en suite bedrooms, all with direct dial telephone and TV; room service; baby listening; last orders for dinner 9.00 p.m.; bar meals; special diets; children welcome; dogs accepted; pool table; sea bathing; sailing/boating (own rough slipway); open all year; credit cards accepted.

This friendly hotel is personally run by owners Peter and Avril Nieto. Situated on the shore of Loch Ewe, the Aultbea Hotel has two restaurants, one aptly named the Waterside Bistro, the other, The Zetland. The Bistro serves snacks and grills throughout the day, and the restaurant offers a choice of à la carte and table d'hôte menus, including the popular carving trolley. Full use is made of locally caught fish, Scottish beef, lamb and venison, and home-made bread is baked daily. There is an excellent choice on the wine list, which is complemented by a good selection of liqueurs, whilst the cocktail bar serves draught beers and offers some 40 malts. On summer days, there are tables to sit at on the patio, where you can enjoy a drink or a meal and soak up the glorious scenery. The well-equipped bedrooms are pleasant, with the emphasis on quality beds, the larger rooms having extra wide ones. For residents, there is a comfortable sitting room, and the hotel is clean and bright throughout. Nearby are sandy beaches, famous gardens and wonderful mountains, making the area good for walking and climbing, as well as for touring. Fishing is available on several lochs, and sea fishing can be arranged. The Aultbea Hotel can be found just off the A832 scenic coastal road. Room and breakfast from £32.50.

DALRACHNEY LODGE HOTEL
Carrbridge, Inverness-shire PH23 3AT

Telephone: 01479 841252   *Fax: 01479 841382*

Inverness 23, Perth 65, Aberdeen 100, Glasgow 2½ hours, Edinburgh 2½ hours

F licence; 11 en suite bedrooms, all with direct dial telephone and TV; room service; last orders for dinner 9.00 p.m.; bar meals; special diets; children welcome; dogs accepted; golf 100 yards; indoor swimming pool and sauna ½ mile; shooting/fishing by arrangement; open all year; all major credit cards accepted.

Dalrachney Lodge Hotel was originally built in 1845 as a hunting lodge. Its somewhat plain exterior, conceals a warm and gracious hotel, run with professional skill by Grant and Helen Swanney. Log fires and comfortable furnishings, together with good old-fashioned service, create a very relaxing atmosphere throughout this hotel. The attractive, airy bedrooms, are individually adorned, most having wonderful views over the 16 acre grounds, and families are well provided for. The dining room offers a nice touch of formality, together with excellent food, chosen from either the table d'hôte or à la carte menus. Each dish can be complemented by a wine from the well balanced list. More informal meals can be enjoyed in the bar, where a considerable collection of malt whisky demands some attention. The area has wonderful scenery and quiet country roads, yet is only 1 mile from the A9 trunk route. For walkers, climbers and sightseers, the ski lifts at the Lecht and Cairngorm, operate throughout the summer. Carrbridge's 9 hole golf course is next to the hotel, and there are a further dozen courses within easy reach. The hotel has ½ mile of the River Dulnain, and can arrange fishing and shooting, and nearby, Aviemore offers attractions for the young at heart. Scottish Tourist Board 4 Crown Highly Commended. Room and breakfast for two people from £60.00, dinner, room and breakfast for two people from £100.00. Prices include VAT.

CAPE WRATH HOTEL
Durness, Sutherland IV27 4SW

Telephone: 01971 511212

Fax: 01971 511313

Durness 2¼, Inverness 102

F licence; 10 en suite bedrooms (1 for the disabled); room service; baby listening by arrangement; last orders for dinner 7.30 p.m.; special diets by prior arrangement; children welcome; dogs accepted; sea bathing; own shooting/fishing; golf 2 miles; hotel closed during the winter; all major credit cards accepted.

Many areas offer the visitor a glimpse of a past way of life, but all too often a busy holiday season can alter things. Not so here, in the farthest reaches of Scotland, where distance guards its peace, and the mountains stand sentinel. Come here for the scenery, the colours, the shapes, the vastness of it. The golden beaches, the craggy coastline, the mountains, lochs and moors, all on an unimaginable scale. Come for the sport, the fishing, the shooting and the "talking". Come and meet the local folk and enjoy the "crack" in the bar in the evening. Come to relax and enjoy the simple creature comforts, the kind hospitality and good food and wines at the Cape Wrath Hotel. Come too, to explore its byways, to know its history, to be part of it, and to take away with you, unique memories of a different world and a peace that is unsurpassed.

237

CULDUTHEL LODGE
14, Culduthel Road, Inverness IV2 4AG

Telephone/Fax: 01463 240089

**Edinburgh 158, Aberdeen 108, Glasgow 170, Loch Ness 7,
Inverness Airport 7, West Coast 1 hour**

Res. licence; 12 en suite bedrooms, all with direct dial telephone, cassette/CD player, umbrella and TV; last orders for dinner 8.00 p.m.; vegetarian diets; dogs accepted; tennis ½ mile; golf 1 mile; shooting and fishing ½ mile, by arrangement; riding 10 miles; open all year; Visa and Mastercard accepted.

This beautifully appointed small hotel is owned and run by David and Marion Bonsor, who provide a welcoming atmosphere, high standards of housekeeping and good food. Set in a quiet residential area, a ten minute walk from the centre of Inverness, it is an ideal location for a spot of shopping, theatre going, sightseeing, touring and golf. Inverness is compact and a few minutes' drive will take you out into a variety of stunning countryside. However you spend your day, it is pleasant to return to the homely atmosphere created at Culduthel Lodge and to sample Marion Bonsor's delicious, freshly cooked food. Her table d'hôte menu changes daily, using the best of local produce and in season, vegetables from the garden. There is also a small, carefully chosen wine list. This comfortable hotel has restful colour schemes throughout, and antique and reproduction furnishings complement the Georgian house. A bowl of fruit, decanter of sherry and flowers in your room as a welcome, and a complimentary newspaper in the mornings, all add to the relaxing ambience of this hotel. Once in Inverness, follow the road system round and pick up the sign for Culduthel. This will take you into Culduthel Road and you will see the hotel on the right hand side. Room and breakfast from £33.00 per person, dinner, bed and breakfast from £49.00.

THE HOLLY TREE HOTEL
Kentallen, By Appin, Argyll PA38 4BY

Telephone: 01631 740292

Fax: 01631 740345

Fort William 18, Oban 30, Inverness 65, Glasgow 100

F licence; 11 en suite bedrooms (2 for the disabled), all with direct dial telephone and TV; room service; last orders for dinner 9.30 p.m.; bar meals; special diets by prior arrangement; children welcome; dogs accepted; conferences max. 30; sailing and boating nearby; riding, shooting and fishing 15 miles; leisure centre, tennis and golf 18 miles; open all year; Mastercard and Visa credit cards accepted.

The Holly Tree is a delightful little hotel that started life as a country railway station. Standing on the shore of Loch Linnhe, all of the hotel's rooms enjoy lovely views over water and mountain. The pretty en suite bedrooms are spacious and comfortable, and exude an air of relaxation. On my last visit, the hotel had just been taken over by Mr. and Mrs. Harvie, who are keen to enhance its reputation for good food, by concentrating on the abundant supplies of fresh fish and local game. To dine whilst watching the evening light fading over the mountains, is an unforgettable experience. Kentallen is an excellent base from which to explore the west coast and its mountainous interior. Glencoe is nearby, and the ferry at Onich gives access to the beautiful Ardnamurchan Peninsula. The Holly Tree is on the A828 a few miles south of Ballachulish. The hotel is open all year with a limited service during the winter months. Room and breakfast from £37.50 per person, and dinner, room and breakfast from £59.00 per person. Prices are inclusive of VAT.

LOCHALSH HOTEL
Kyle Of Lochalsh, Highland IV40 8AF

Telephone: 01599 4202
From Dec. '94   534202

Fax: 01599 4881
534881

Plockton 5, Achnasheen 40, Inverness 86, Glasgow 194, Edinburgh 207

F licence; 40 en suite bedrooms, all with direct dial telephone and TV; room service; baby listening; night service; lift; last orders for dinner 9.30 p.m.; light lunches; special diets; children welcome; dogs accepted; conferences max. 40; shooting/fishing; hotel closed during Christmas week; all major credit cards accepted.

Built in the days of rail travel, the Lochalsh Hotel retains an aura of the 30's, enhanced by the high standards of service and hospitality dispensed by Mr. Woodtli, the General Manager, and his staff. It is still possible to arrive in Lochalsh by rail, and the busy ferry still plies back and forth across the narrow Kyle to the Isle of Skye. The view from the grounds and most of the windows in the hotel, is one of the most beautiful in Britain. The Lochalsh is warm, comfortable and well ordered, with soft decorative schemes. The bedrooms are spacious and well equipped, and the bar in the cocktail lounge offers, amongst a variety of drinks, a wide selection of malts. In the dining room, there is a good choice of dishes available from the menu, all of which are beautifully presented and efficiently served, local seafood is a speciality. Lochalsh is an ideal centre for exploring the wild beauty of the west coast. Two hours will see you into Inverness after a delightful drive via Loch Ness, and few can resist the lure of Skye. To locate the hotel, simply follow the signs for the ferry. Room and breakfast from £65.00 single, and £85.00 double for 2 people.

INVER LODGE HOTEL
Lochinver, Sutherland IV27 4LU

Telephone: 01571 844496   *Fax: 01571 844395*

London 630, Edinburgh 254, Glasgow 266, Inverness 95, Lairg 47, Ullapool 37

F licence; 20 en suite bedrooms, all with direct dial telephone, mini bar, colour TV, trouser press, tea/coffee making facilities and hairdryer; room service; last orders for dinner 9.00 p.m.; bar meals; special diets; children welcome; dogs accepted; snooker/billiards; sauna; solarium; sea trips; shooting/fishing; hotel closed during the winter; credit cards accepted.

Inver Lodge was commissioned and built to a very high specification in 1988, on a site chosen for the superb views of Lochinver Harbour and the islands dreaming off-shore. The hotel offers its guests traditional highland hospitality, coupled with every modern convenience and luxury. The cuisine, under the expert eye of John Robertson, offers a well presented table d'hôte dinner from £27.00, with a wine list to complement the menus. The bedrooms are warm and elegant, and equipped to the highest standards, including a trouser press concealed within the wardrobe, and a tea tray tucked away in a neat drawer. You will find a bowl of fruit and some shortbread awaiting you, and should you require something more substantial, room service offers anything from a snack to a steak! Best of all, the bedrooms overlook the sea, with the only exceptions being the Suilven and Canisp rooms, which have windows facing the mountains and sea. To enjoy even more stunning views, climb the path behind the hotel and stand by the cairn. In three directions, as far as the eye can see, there are mountains of every shape and size, and on the fourth side, the craggy coastline. You can enjoy fishing for salmon and trout on one of the rivers where the hotel has fishing rights, or on one of the many lochs. A sea trip to Handa Island is to be recommended. The A387 delivers you to Loch Inver, and Inver Lodge is half way down the village on the left. Room and breakfast from £65.00 single, double £110.00.

241

EDDRACHILLES HOTEL
Badcall Bay, Scourie, Sutherland IV27 4TH

Telephone: 01971 502080   *Fax: 01971 502477*

Ullapool 40, Thurso 95, Inverness 98, Glasgow 266

F licence; 11 en suite bedrooms (4 on ground floor), all with direct dial telephone and TV; last orders for dinner 8.00 p.m.; bar lunches available; special diets by arrangement; children of 3 years and over welcome; sailing/boating; fishing; hotel closed Nov.–Feb. inclusive; Mastercard and Visa credit cards accepted.

The Eddrachilles commands a fine position, overlooking the sea with mountains behind it. Inside, the hotel is clean, bright and comfortable, with many of the windows having a sea view, thanks to the foresight of Mr. and Mrs. Alasdair Wood, who have restored and extended this old building, and are kind and hospitable hosts. The logistics of providing food and drink in these remote parts, makes the discovery of an à la carte and table d'hôte menu, together with an interesting wine list, a pleasant surprise. The emphasis is on home cooking, using fresh and seasonal ingredients. Hill lamb, venison and seafood are the local delicacies. The north of Scotland is unique; its remote and untouched beauty cannot be described in a few words. You can explore it from quiet, single-track roads, or, for the more energetic, there are numerous scenic walks and climbs. Nearby Handa Island, is famous as a bird sanctuary, and boat trips across the short stretch of water can be made from Tarbert. When returning to Eddrachilles after a tiring day of exploration, you can always be assured of warmth, comfort and good food. To find the hotel from Ullapool, take the A835 which joins the A837 and eventually the A894. Badcall Bay is on the left just before you reach Scourie. Room and breakfast from £31.00, dinner, room and breakfast from £41.50. Prices include VAT.

KILLIECHRONAN HOUSE
Aros, Isle Of Mull, Argyll PA72 6JU

Telephone: 01680 300403   *Fax: 01680 300463*

Salen 2, Craignure 14, Tobermory 15, Iona 35

R & R licence; 6 en suite bedrooms, all with direct dial telephone and radio; last orders for dinner 8.00 p.m.; special diets; dogs accepted; sea bathing; sailing/ boating; pony trekking; shooting/fishing; stalking by arrangement; golf 5 miles; hotel closed during the winter except for Christmas and Hogmanay; Mastercard and Visa credit cards accepted.

What more picturesque and quiet rural setting than at the head of Loch na Keal, on the west side of Mull? When I was there, a stag was leisurely cropping the grass in the garden, not the least worried at me photographing him. Killiechronan House is part of the beautiful 5000 acre Killiechronan Estate, with its own fishing and pony trekking facilities, and arrangements for stalking can easily be made. There are five miles of coastline along the north side of the Loch, and, of course, miles of seldom used, single track roads. The hotel is easily accessible from the mainland, as it is only 14 miles from the ferry terminal at Craignure, and just a forty minute trip from Oban. The house has been tastefully refurbished and redecorated this winter, to the same standards as Mr. and Mrs. Leroy's other two hotels at Oban (page 222), and at Port of Menteith (page 217). Each of the six comfortable bedrooms are en suite with baths, and there is central heating throughout the hotel. The warm and cosy décor of both the lounge and bar is most welcoming, and during those colder days, open log fires are in full blaze. In overall charge, are Patrick and Margaret Freytag, who divide their time between Killiechronan House and The Manor House at Oban. Patrick, a very experienced chef, prepares the best of traditional Scottish cuisine, using fresh local produce. A special weekly rate is available, allowing consecutive nights to be spent at two, or all three of the Leroy hotels, but at least one night must be spent at Killiechronan. Dinner, room and breakfast from £46.00 per person.

GLENFORSA HOTEL
Salen, By Aros, Isle of Mull, Argyll PA72 6JW

Telephone: 01680 300377　　　　　　　　　*Fax: 01680 300535*

Salen 1, Craignure 10, Tobermory 12, Iona 60

F licence; 13 bedrooms (12 en suite); room service; baby listening; last orders for dinner 8.30 p.m.; bar meals; special diets; children welcome; dogs accepted; conferences max. 34; snooker/billiards and darts; sea bathing; shooting/fishing; sailing, boating, golf and riding nearby; squash courts 12 miles; open all year; Mastercard, Visa and Amex credit cards accepted.

The Glenforsa Hotel stands sheltered by trees, overlooking the Sound of Mull and the little air-strip. It is a chalet-style building with a traditional pine log interior. Not a luxury hotel, it is, however, comfortable and friendly. Resident owners, Jean and Paul Price, say that hospitality and service are the keynote of their operation, a statement endorsed by fellow travellers who recommended the place to me. In the kitchen, Jean makes full use of local produce, particularly sea foods, to prepare a variety of dishes, sometimes drawing on Gaelic traditions. A bottle from the carefully selected wine list, or a glass of real ale will complement your choice from the menu. After dinner, the observation lounge with its wide views, is a good spot to relax over coffee, or perhaps choose from the array of single malts. The rest of the hotel is on ground level with the cosy bedrooms tucked away in their own wing. Salen is conveniently situated for exploring this lovely island where time might have stopped, and wild life is abundant. Mull is reached by ferry from Oban or Lochaline, and the hotel is clearly signposted just south of Salen. Room and breakfast from £34.00 per person, per night, dinner, room and breakfast from £51.00 per person, and weekly half board rates from £347.00 per person including dinner.

ROSEDALE HOTEL
Portree, Isle Of Skye IV51 9DB

Telephone: 01478 613131   *Fax: 01478 612531*

Edinburgh 237, Invermoriston 90, Fort Augustus 97, Kyle of Lochalsh Ferry 34

F licence; 20 en suite bedrooms (7 ground floor) all with television, telephone, radio, tea/coffee making facilities, also 3 attractive twin bedded rooms with private bathrooms available in nearby Beaumont House; full central heating; boating; tennis and golf nearby; fishing by arrangement; good open air parking.

I was advised by friends in Uig to visit the Rosedale Hotel at Portree, and how glad I was to find this most attractive hotel, so well run by the proprietress, Mrs. Andrew and her son, Hugh. It is situated on the loch side facing the harbour and looking out across the Sound of Raasay to the Isle beyond. Mr. Andrew showed me round the hotel and I realised how much time and energy had been put into making this modernized, yet comfortably furnished and brightly decorated, hotel so acceptable. The Andrew family have done a wonderful job. The bedrooms are very well appointed and the public rooms, including the cocktail bar, are attractive and comfortable, creating an atmosphere of peace and quiet. I enjoyed my meals very much; the menus, without being extravagant, were good, admirably cooked and well presented. Whilst you are assured of a great welcome at any time, the Andrews do recommend an early visit when the weather is at its best and the Island less busy. Room and breakfast from £33.00 per person, inclusive of VAT. Other terms on application. Closed October to mid-May, but office open for enquiries and advance bookings.

UIG HOTEL
Uig, Portree, Isle Of Skye IV51 9YE

Telephone: 01470 542205. Guests 542367   *Fax: 01470 542308*

Edinburgh 252, Portree 15, Kyle of Lochalsh Ferry 49

F licence; 17 en suite bedrooms, direct dial telephone, colour TV; late meals to order; diets by arrangement; drying room; children welcome; sea, river bathing; boating; fishing; shooting by arrangement; pony trekking; major credit cards accepted.

The Uig Hotel is situated at the northern end of the lovely island of Skye looking down on the little bay and harbour of Uig. Grace Graham and her son David Taylor, the owners, must be justly proud of their attractive and elegantly furnished hotel with its warm and cheerful atmosphere. The furniture, pictures and colour schemes are very pleasant. There are 11 pretty bedrooms in the hotel and at the rear, offering lovely seaviews, the old steading has been converted into 6 attractive bedrooms, one with a sitting room and all with their own bathroom. Next door, Primrose Cottage has been converted into 3 very comfortable self-catering apartments. The restaurant provides a varied table d'hôte menu, and the dishes are plentiful and skilfully cooked. The excellent wine list is sure to suit all tastes. For lunch there are interesting snacks with very good coffee. The cocktail bar has an open fire and comfortable arm chairs, fronted by a sun lounge that has sweeping views over the bay. You will enjoy your stay and the scenery and peace of the surrounding country, which has strong associations with Bonnie Prince Charlie and Flora MacDonald. Uig is now served by the new roll on, roll off ferry to the Outer Hebrides, *The Hebridean Isles*. Room and breakfast from £30.00 per person inclusive of VAT. Other terms on application. Closed during the winter, but office open. See Bargain Break section for interesting ideas.

BARGAIN BREAKS

Readers are recommended to telephone the hotels to confirm rates and conditions prior to booking.

THE HIGHLANDS AND SCOTTISH ISLANDS

GRAMPIAN

THE MARCLIFFE AT PITFODELS, Aberdeen *page 232*
Available all year – dinner, room and breakfast on any Friday, Saturday or Sunday night from £59.50 per person, per night, sharing a twin/double room. Golf can be arranged.

DARROCH LEARG HOTEL, Ballater *page 233*
Packages available for stays of 3 days or more, and special rates during February, March, April, October, November and December.

MANSEFIELD HOUSE HOTEL, Elgin *page 234*
Weekend breaks are available for Friday, Saturday and Sunday nights – £70.00 per couple, per night for room and breakfast.

HIGHLAND

AULTBEA HOTEL, Aultbea *page 235*
Low Season Breaks available during the month of October, and from Easter– mid-May: £125.00 per person, to include dinner, room and breakfast for 3 nights. Winter breaks available from October–Easter: £65.00 per person, to include room and breakfast for 3 nights.

DALRACHNEY LODGE HOTEL, Carrbridge *page 236*
Spring, late Autumn and Winter 2 day or longer breaks – 20% off the tariff. Golf or fishing can be included. Central location, ideal for off season travellers of all persuasions. Please enquire for brochure and full details quoting Signpost.

CAPE WRATH HOTEL, Durness *page 237*
A 10% discount is available in April, May and October.

CULDUTHEL LODGE, Inverness *page 238*
From November 1994–March 1995; 3 days, dinner, bed and breakfast, £139.00 per person in a twin/double room.

THE HOLLY TREE HOTEL, Kentallen *page 239*
For Signpost guests, we offer a 15% discount on stays of 3 nights or more, at any time of year except June, July and August.

LOCHALSH HOTEL, Kyle of Lochalsh *page 240*
Lochalsh Breaks: 2 night break from £130.00 per person, which includes accommodation, Highland breakfast, table d'hôte dinner and VAT at the current rate.

INVER LODGE HOTEL, Lochinver *page 241*
Spring, Autumn and Winter breaks are available – tariffs on application.

EDDRACHILLES HOTEL, Scourie *page 242*
Reduced rates are available for stays of 3, 6 or 10 days.

SCOTTISH ISLANDS

KILLIECHRONAN HOUSE, Aros, Isle of Mull   *page 243*
£42.00 per person, per night for 2 nights in low season, and £62.00 per person per night for 2 nights in high season. Special weekly rates are available, allowing consecutive nights to be spent at either The Manor House at Oban or The Lake Hotel at Port of Menteith, and at least one night must be spent at Killiechronan House on the Isle of Mull.

GLENFORSA HOTEL, Salen, Isle of Mull   *page 244*
Bargain breaks available from October 15th–May 1st 1995 (excluding Christmas) – 2 nights, dinner, bed and breakfast £73.00 per person and 3 nights, dinner, bed and breakfast £94.00 per person.

ROSEDALE HOTEL, Portree, Isle of Skye   *page 245*
"Skye Explorer", 4 day holidays inclusive of return ferries, dinner, bed and breakfast and admissions, and 3 day special breaks – further details on application.

UIG HOTEL, Uig, Isle of Skye   *page 246*
Three day breaks – dinner, bed and breakfast, with or without pony trekking. Seven days, with pony trekking (2 whole, or 4 half days) from May–September, dinner, bed and breakfast. Prices on application. Bridge Weekends are on offer in April, and bird watching and wildlife holidays are also available.

GUERNSEY
SELECTED LOCAL ATTRACTIONS

Historic Houses, Gardens & Parks

Castle Cornet & Maritime Museum, Castle Cornet
Sausmarez Manor, St. Martins (venue for 'Le Viaer Marchi')
Specialist Gardens at Castle Cornet
Candie Gardens – St. Peter Port
Grande Marais Koi Farm, Vale
La Seigneurie, Island of Sark

Historical Sites & Museums

La Valette Underground Military Museum, St. Peter Port
German Occupation Museum, St. Peter Port
The Guernsey Aquarium, Havelet Bay
Guernsey Museum & Art Gallery, St. Peter Port
National Trust of Guernsey Folk Museum, Saumarez Park
Fort Grey Shipwreck Museum, St. Saviours

Walks & Nature Trails

The Saumarez Nature Trail, starting at Cobo Bay
Le Catioroc Nature Trail & L'Eree Shingle Bank
Portinfer; Port Soif Nature Trail; Grandes Rocques
Saumarez Park Walk, starting at Cobo Bay
St. Peter Port to St. Martin's Point Walk

Entertainment Venues

Guernsey Bird Gardens, St. Andrews
Le Friquet Butterfly Centre, Castel
'Oatlands', Guernsey's Craft Centre, St. Sampson's

GUERNSEY
DIARY OF EVENTS 1995

January 22–28	GUERNSEY OPEN INDOOR BOWLS TOURNAMENT
February 11–28	GUERNSEY EISTEDDFOD
April 25–27	GUERNSEY FESTIVAL OF FOOD AND WINE
*May 4–11	ROLLS ROYCE ENTHUSIAST CLUB RALLY
May 9	LIBERATION DAY
May 20–21	BRITISH BRIDGE LEAGUE SWISS TEAMS WEEKEND
June 18	HASH HOUSE HARRIERS HALF MARATHON
June 25–July 1	GUERNSEY SQUARE DANCE FESTIVAL
July 5	VIAER MARCHI (Traditional Evening)
July 14	ROUND TABLE HARBOUR CARNIVAL
July 22–30	ST. PETER PORT TOWN CARNIVAL
July 31–August 6	GUERNSEY INTERNATIONAL FOLK FESTIVAL
August 5	ROCQUAINE REGATTA
August 9–10	SOUTH AGRICULTURAL SHOW
August 16–17	WEST AGRICULTURAL SHOW
*September 9	KITE FLY '95
September 9–17	ENGLISH BRIDGE UNION CONGRESS
October 15–21	CHESS FESTIVAL

*dates to be confirmed

For further details contact:

States of Guernsey Department of Tourism and Recreation, PO Box 23, White Rock, St. Peter Port, Guernsey. Tel: 01481 726611.

HOTEL BELLA LUCE
Moulin Huet, St. Martins, Guernsey GY4 6EB

Telephone: 01481 38764   *Fax: 01481 39561*

St. Peter Port 2

F licence; 31 en suite bedrooms (3 ground floor), all with direct dial telephone and TV; room service; baby listening; last orders for dinner 9.45 p.m.; bar meals; special diets; children welcome; dogs accepted at managements discretion; conferences max. 20; outdoor heated swimming pool; sauna; solarium; open all year; major credit cards accepted.

The Hotel Bella Luce is a former 12th century manor house that is attractive both inside and out. There is an abundance of flowers, from the sweetpeas which line the swimming pool, to the wonderful hanging baskets on the walls. The pool, with its adjacent sauna/solarium room, is bounded on one side by a well manicured lawn. The Manager, Richard Cann, and his staff, take great pride in running this hotel, and do their utmost to ensure their guests happiness. All the public rooms are beautifully furnished, and are very comfortable. The lounge bar with its oak beamed ceiling, has a warm and friendly atmosphere, and is the ideal place in which to enjoy either a drink, or a dish chosen from the extensive bar lunch menu. The tastefully decorated bedrooms, three of which are on the ground floor, have most comforts and facilities that all good hotels provide nowadays. The freshly prepared food served in the restaurant is excellent, with a delicious choice of dishes from either the table d'hôte or à la carte menus. To accompany these, there is a comprehensive wine list to suit all palates. During my recent visit to the Bella Luce, my overall impression was one of total peace and tranquillity, where the only noise to be heard was that of the birds. The hotel is just two miles from the beautiful "capital" of Guernsey, St. Peter Port, and the magnificent cliffs and coastal scenery on this island, make breathtaking views. Room and breakfast from £42.00, dinner, room and breakfast from £54.00.

JERSEY
SELECTED LOCAL ATTRACTIONS

Historic Houses, Gardens & Parks

Samares Manor, St. Clement
St. Ouen's Manor Grounds, St. Ouen
Howard David Park, St. Helier
Fantastic Tropical Gardens, St. Peter's Valley
Jersey Lavender Farm, St. Brelade
La Mare Vineyards, St. Mary
Eric Young Orchid Foundation, Trinity
Jersey Flower Centre, St. Lawrence
Sunset Carnation Nurseries, St. Ouen's Bay

Historical Sites & Museums

Mont Orgueil Castle, Gorey
Elizabeth Castle, St. Aubin's Bay
La Hougue Bie, Grouville
Faldouet Dolmen, Gorey
Grosnez Castle & La Pinacle, Les Landes
The Hermitage, St. Helier
Battle of Flowers Museum, St. Ouen
Jersey Motor Museum, St. Peter
Hamptonne Country Life Museum, St. Lawrence
Island Fortree Occupation Museum, St. Helier
German Underground Hospital, St. Lawrence
St. Peter's Bunker Museum, St. Peter
The Pallot Heritage Steam Museum, Trinity
The Living Legend, St. Peter

Walks & Nature Trails

Town Walk, St. Helier
Jersey's Coastal Walks:
  i) Grosnez to Sorel
  ii) Sorel to Bouley Bay
  iii) Bouley Bay to St. Catherine's
Guided nature walks

Entertainment Venues

Jersey Zoo, Trinity
Jersey Butterfly Centre, St. Mary
Jersey Shire Horse Farm & Museum, St. Ouen
Fort Regent Leisure Centre, St. Helier
Jersey Pottery, Gorey Village

JERSEY
DIARY OF EVENTS 1995

April 19–23	JERSEY JAZZ FESTIVAL
April 28 to May 8	OFFICIAL E.B.U. JERSEY FESTIVAL OF BRIDGE 1995
May 4–10	LIBERATION OF JERSEY 50TH ANNIVERSARY
May 5–7	JERSEY INTERNATIONAL AIR RALLY
May 15–29	JERSEY ARTS & HERITAGE FESTIVAL
June 1–4	JERSEY GOOD FOOD FESTIVAL
June 19–24	JERSEY IRISH FESTIVAL WEEK
July 10–16	JERSEY FLORAL ISLAND FESTIVAL
July 31 to Aug. 6	CHINESE FESTIVAL WEEK
August 10	THE JERSEY BATTLE OF FLOWERS
September 14–18	THE 1995 JERSEY WORLD MUSIC FESTIVAL
October 10–12	ROYAL JERSEY PRO-AM GOLF TOURNAMENT
October 20–23	COUNTRY MUSIC FESTIVAL

HORSE RACING AT ST. OUEN RACECOURSE

*April 17th
*May 8th, 29th
*June 15th, 16th, 29th, 30th
*July 15th, 29th
*August 18th, 28th

*dates to be confirmed

For further information contact:
Jersey Tourism, Liberation Square, St. Helier, Jersey JE1 1BB. Channel Islands.
Tel: 01534 78000.

THE ATLANTIC HOTEL
La Moye, St. Brelade, Jersey JE3 8HE

Telephone: 01534 44101   *Fax: 01534 44102*

St. Helier 5, Airport 2

F licence; 50 en suite bedrooms including Garden Studio Rooms, and 2 luxury suites, all with telephone, colour TV and radio; late meals to 9.30 p.m.; lift; laundry service; conferences taken; diets available; children welcome; night service; sea bathing; golf nearby; health and leisure centre; tennis; indoor heated swimming pool; all major credit cards accepted.

With extensive refurbishments completed to the highest of standards, The Atlantic can now be recognised as a truly stylish and "international" hotel. Having been under local private ownership since 1970, great attention to detail in every aspect throughout, is paramount. From the imposing columned entrance, through to the reception hall and lounge areas, classic antique furniture, contemporary furnishings, and warm, inviting décor, all contribute towards a theme of understated luxury. Outstanding views across the gardens, the delightfully colourful, tropical outside pool area, and the coastline beyond, can be admired from both the lounge and the main restaurant. Innovative menus, a fine wine list, good presentation and attentive service in the elegant restaurant, are all supervised by the most professional of restaurant managers. The Palm Club provides a romanesque feature indoor pool, jacuzzi, solaria, sauna, gymnasium, and an outside tennis court is also available for the use of guests. The bedrooms benefit from sea or golf course views, and are extremely well appointed with good facilities and high standards of décor and comfort throughout. Conferences can be catered for, and the many attractions and facilities to be enjoyed at The Atlantic Hotel, make it an ideal venue for any stay, be it for business, pleasure, or sheer self indulgence! Without a doubt, The Atlantic is a first class hotel, perfectly located on the island of Jersey. Room and breakfast from £100.00.

LONGUEVILLE MANOR HOTEL
St. Saviour, Jersey JE2 7SA

Telephone: 01534 25501   *Fax: 01534 31613*

Airport 6, St. Helier 1½

F licence; 32 en suite bedrooms including 2 luxury suites (8 ground floor); late meals; diets; night service; dogs welcome; TV and radio; drying room; lift; own heated swimming pool and tennis court; large gardens; sea bathing ¾ mile; golf and squash ½ mile.

This privately owned 13th century manor house, run by the Lewis and Dufty families, is the perfect setting in which to be pampered. At the foot of one of Jersey's most beautiful valleys, the 15 acres of well kept garden provide most of the produce used in the kitchen, which is under the direction of the Chef de Cuisine Andrew Baird, previously of Hambleton Hall. There is an excellent wine list to complement the cuisine. Set in the gardens is a heated swimming pool where the day may be idled away with cocktails and lunch. The 30 bedrooms and two luxury suites, all individually decorated, have modern amenities. Only 1½ miles east of St. Helier and within easy reach of the beach and golf course, the Longueville Manor is perfectly situated for your visit to the island. The hotel is also the only one in the Channel Islands to have been granted membership of the Relais et Chateaux. Room and breakfast from £145.00 twin, including service.

253

BARGAIN BREAKS

Readers are recommended to telephone the hotels to confirm rates and conditions prior to booking.

CHANNEL ISLANDS

GUERNSEY

HOTEL BELLA LUCE, St. Martins *page 250*
Bargain Breaks available from 1st November 1994–1st April 1995. For any number of nights, on a bed and breakfast basis, the price is £24.00 per person, per night.

JERSEY

THE ATLANTIC HOTEL, St. Brelade *page 252*
Winter breaks (October and March). For a minimum stay of 3 nights in a Golf View Room, £60.00 per person, per day, to include room, breakfast and 5 course table d'hôte dinner. Subject to availability, all winter breaks will be automatically upgraded to Sea View at no extra charge.

LONGUEVILLE MANOR HOTEL, St. Saviour *page 253*
Winter weekend breaks from 1st October 1994–31st March 1995 (excluding 24th December 1994–2nd January 1995). A Saturday night must be included. Standard twin/double – £155.00, medium twin/double – £185.00, large twin/ double – £210.00 and a suite – £275.00. All prices are per person, for 2 nights and include accommodation, full English breakfast, dinner, 2 day car hire and service. Return flights available from £95.00 per person. Rates for single occupancy (available mid-week only) and longer stays on application.

Ten exclusive Westcountry Hotels.
Just a phone call away.

PRB Brend Hotels

SCOTLAND'S COMMENDED
A selection of distinctive
Country & Town House Hotels

Darroch Learg (Ballater)

Loch Torridon (Torridon)

Country Hotels and Town Houses
who like to make you feel welcome.
Superb scenery for touring, rural tranquillity
and historical houses to visit,
with the best of Scottish food freshly prepared
for when you return in the evening for dinner.
Most hotels have special short break holiday rates.

Ask for full details and a copy of our
colour brochure from our Central Reservation Office:

Tel: 01786 825550

SPORTING FACILITIES

Sporting facilities to be found at *Signpost* hotels are listed on the following pages. This section is arranged by regions within England, Wales, Scotland and the Islands and by counties within those regions.

KEY

A   Facilities available *at hotel*

b   Facilities available *within 5 miles* of hotel

c   Special arrangements can be made by the hotel

page	Hotel	golf	tennis	croquet	pitch & putt	boating	fishing	riding	billiards/snooker	swim/pool	sea/river bathing	sailing	squash	badminton	shooting	leis. centre	solarium	sauna	other
	DEVON (continued)																		
26	Tides Reach Hotel, Salcombe	b	b			a	a	b	a	a	a	a	a			a	a	a	Spa bath, steam bath, massage therapy, gym, wind surfing, water sports from own boat house.
27	Heron House Hotel, Nr. Salcombe	c	b					b				b			b	b			
28	The Saunton Sands Hotel, Saunton Sands	c	a			b	b	b	a	a	a	a	a				a		
29	The Royal Glen Hotel, Sidmouth	b	b			a	a	a	a	a	a		b		a		a		
30	The Victoria Hotel, Sidmouth									a	a	a		b		b	a	a	Spa bath, putting.
31	Gabriel Court Hotel, Stoke Gabriel	b	b	a		a	c	b		a	a	a	a	b			a	a	Archery by arrangement.
32	Homers Hotel, Torquay	b	b			a	a	b	a		a	a	a		c		a		Gymnasium.
33	Imperial Hotel, Torquay	c	a	a		a	c	c		a	a	a			c	a		a	
34	Livermead House Hotel, Torquay	b				b	c	c		a	a	b				b	a	a	Games room, surfing, clay pigeon shooting arranged.
35	Watersmeet Hotel, Mortehoe, Woolacombe	b					b	b		a	a						a		Short mat bowls, steam room, spa pool, own yacht.
36	Woolacombe Bay Hotel, Woolacombe	a	a			a	b	b	a	a	a	a	a		b	a	a	a	
	DORSET																		
37	Queen's Hotel, Eastcliff, Bournemouth					b			a	a		b				a		a	Games room, steam room, spa pool, trymnasium.
38	The Manor Hotel, Dorchester	b						b											
39	Salterns Hotel, Lilliput					a					a	a							
40	Kersbrook Hotel, Lyme Regis	b	a			b	b	b			a	b			b				Wind surfing.
41	The Haven Hotel, Sandbanks	b	a			b	c	b		a	b	b	a		c		a	a	Spa pool, gym.
42/43	Knoll House, Studland Bay	a				b	b			a	b	b				a	a	a	Health spa, games rooms, adventure playground, windsurfing.
44	Manor House Hotel, Studland Bay	b	a					a			b								
45	Springfield Country Hotel, Wareham	b	a			b			a	a		b	a			a	a	a	Spa and steam rooms.

260

page		golf	tennis	croquet	pitch & putt	boating	fishing	riding	billiards/snooker	swim/pool	sea/river bathing	sailing	squash	badminton	shooting	leis. centre	solarium	sauna	other
	SOMERSET																		
46	The Walnut Tree Inn, Bridgwater	b						b		A							A		
47	Alfoxton Park, Holford		A	A						A							A		
48	Combe House Hotel, Holford	b						c				b							
49	Swan Hotel, Wells												A			b			
	WILTSHIRE																		
50	Crudwell Court, Nr. Malmesbury	b	b	A			b	b		A			b				A		Jacuzzi.
51	Whatley Manor, Nr. Malmesbury	b	A	A				b	A	A			b	b	b	b	A	A	Gym, spa bath.
52	Blunsdon House, Nr. Swindon	A	A			c			A	A			A		b	A	A	A	
	BERKSHIRE																		
63	Swan Diplomat, Streatley-on-Thames	b	b	A			b	b		A					b	A	A	A	Spa bath, multi-gym, bike hire, beauty treatments.
	HAMPSHIRE																		
64	The Gordleton Mill Hotel, Lymington	b	b			b	b	b			b	b							
65	Passford House, Lymington	b	A			b		b			b	b			b				Multi-gym, table-tennis.
66	South Lawn Hotel, Milford-on-Sea	b	b			b	b	b			b	b			b				
67	The Chewton Glen Hotel, New Milton	A	A			b	b	b		A	b		b		b	A	A	A	Gymnasium, steam room.
68	Hotel du Vin & Bistro, Winchester	b	b					b					b	b					
	HERTFORDSHIRE																		
69	Stocks Hotel & Country Club, Aldbury	A	A					A	A	A	A				c	A	A	A	Gymnasium, hot air ballooning by arrangement.
71	St. Michael's Manor, St. Albans	b	b																
	KENT																		
72	Castlemere Hotel, Broadstairs					A	A												
	OXFORDSHIRE																		
73	The Spread Eagle Hotel, Thame	b					b	b					b	b	b				
74	Feathers Hotel, Woodstock	b	b				b	b						b					

page		golf	tennis	croquet	pitch & putt	boating	fishing	riding	billiards/ snooker	swim/ pool	sea/river bathing	sailing	squash	badminton	shooting	leis. centre	solarium	sauna	other
	SURREY																		
75	Chase Lodge, Kingston-upon-Thames	b	b					b		b			b			b			
	EAST SUSSEX																		
76	Flackley Ash Hotel, Peasmarsh	c	b							A						A	A	A	Spa pool, gymnasium.
77	Brickwall Hotel, Sedlescombe	c	c	A				b	A	A		b				A	A	A	Gymnasium.
78	Dale Hill Hotel & Golf Club, Ticehurst	A	c				c	c		A					c				
	WEST SUSSEX																		
79	The Chequers Hotel, Pulborough	b	b	A				c							c				
	DERBYSHIRE																		
86	Hassop Hall Hotel, Hassop, Nr. Bakewell	b	A				b	b											Clay pigeon shooting by arrangement.
87	Riber Hall, Matlock	b	A				c			b									Mountain bikes.
88	Makeney Hall Country House Hotel, Milford	b	b				b	b							b				
	LINCOLNSHIRE																		
89	Washingborough Hall Country House Hotel, Lincoln	b	b	A		b	b	b	A	A		b	b		b	b			Boules, water skiing centre nearby.
	NORFOLK																		
90	Blakeney Hotel, Blakeney	b	b			b	b	A		A	b	b	b						
91	South Walsham Hall, Nr. Norwich	b	A							A								A	Spa bath, mini-gym.
	NOTTINGHAMSHIRE																		
92	Langar Hall, Langar	b					A												
93	The Old England, Nr. Newark	b	A				b	b							b				
	SUFFOLK																		
94	The Smoke House, Mildenhall	b	A				b												
95	Ufford Park Hotel, Golf & Leisure, Woodbridge	A								A					b	A	A	A	Spa pool, gym, steam room.

page	Hotel	golf	tennis	croquet	pitch & putt	boating	fishing	riding	billiards/snooker	swim/pool	sea/river bathing	sailing	squash	badminton	shooting	leis. centre	solarium	sauna	other
	GLOUCESTERSHIRE																		
101	Bibury Court, Bibury						A	c							c				Ballooning and aerial Cotswold trips by arrangement.
102	On the Park Hotel, Cheltenham	b	b					b											
103	The Wild Duck Inn, Nr. Cirencester	b						b											
104	Tudor Farmhouse Hotel, Clearwell	b				b		c				b							Rock climbing and abseiling by arrangement.
105	The Manor House Hotel, Moreton-in-Marsh	b	A							A								A	Spa pool.
106	The Amberley Inn, Nr. Stroud	b		A				b											
107	Hare & Hounds, Nr. Tetbury								A				A						
	HEREFORD and WORCESTER																		
108	Dormy House Hotel, Broadway	b	b	A	A				A									A	Steam room, gym.
	SHROPSHIRE																		
110	The Redfern Hotel, Cleobury Mortimer	b					b	b							b				
111	The Feathers at Ludlow	c	A	A				c	A	b								A	
112	Hawkstone Park Hotel, Shrewsbury	A	A		A		b	b	A	A					c		A	A	Trimnasium.
	WARWICKSHIRE																		
113	Nailcote Hall, Berkswell	A	A	A	A		c	c		A					c	A	A	A	Pétanque, gymnasium, spa pool.
114	Nuthurst Grange, Hockley Heath		A	A															
115	Welcombe Hotel, Stratford-upon-Avon	A	A	A			c	c		A					c				
116	Billesley Manor, Nr. Stratford-upon-Avon		A																
	CHESHIRE																		
123	Rowton Hall Hotel, Chester		A				b	b		A						A		A	Steam room, gymnasium.
124	Sutton Hall, Nr. Macclesfield	b	b				b	b					b	b					

263

Hotel facilities table — CUMBRIA

page	Hotel	golf	tennis	croquet	pitch & putt	boating	fishing	riding	billiards/snooker	swim/pool	sea/river bathing	sailing	squash	badminton	shooting	leis. centre	solarium	sauna	other
125	Lowbyer Manor Country House Hotel, Alston	b	a	a		b	b	b				b			b				
126	Lovelady Shield Country House Hotel, Nr. Alston	b	b			b	b	b				b	b		b				
127	Kirkstone Foot Country House Hotel, Ambleside	b				b	b	b				b	b		a	b			
128	Nanny Brow Country House Hotel, Ambleside						a			b		b				b		b	
129	Rothay Manor Hotel, Ambleside		b			b	b				a	a				b			
130	Wateredge Hotel, Ambleside					a	a		a				b						
131	Appleby Manor Hotel, Appleby-in-Westmorland	b					b	b	a	a		b				a	a	a	Games room, jacuzzi.
132	The Pheasant Inn, Bassenthwaite Lake	b				b	b	b				b			b				
133	Overwater Hall, Nr. Bassenthwaite Lake	b				a	b	b			b	a							Games room.
134	Mary Mount Hotel, Borrowdale					a		b											
135	Hare & Hounds Country Inn, Bowland Bridge	b				b		b		b		a							
136	Tarn End House Hotel, Brampton	b					c	b				b		b	c				
137	Wheelgate Country House Hotel, Coniston		a				b	c	a		a			b					
138	Graythwaite Manor Hotel, Grange-over-Sands	b	b					a		b		a			b				Steam room, spa bath, beauty area.
139	Netherwood Hotel, Grange-over-Sands						b	b		a						a			
140	Aynsome Manor Hotel, Nr. Grange-over-Sands	b				b	b	b		b		b			b				
141	The Wordsworth Hotel, Grasmere	c	b			a	b	b		a		a	b		a	a	a	a	Mini-gym, jacuzzi.
142	Dale Head Hall Lakeside Hotel, Keswick	b				b	a	b				b	b		b	b			
143	Lyzzick Hall Hotel, Keswick	b	a			b	b	b		a		b					a		
144	Stakis Keswick Lodore Swiss Hotel, Keswick	b					c	c	a	a			a	a		a	a	a	
145	Underscar Manor, Nr. Keswick	b	a			b	b	a											
146	Scafell Hotel, Nr. Keswick						b	b			b								
147	The Barbon Inn, Nr. Kirkby Lonsdale	b				b	b	a				b			b				
148	The Mill, Mungrisdale, Penrith	b													a				Games room, clay pigeon shooting.
149	Swan Hotel, Newby Bridge					a	a	b			a								
150	Sharrow Bay Country House Hotel, Ullswater	b				a	a	b			a	a							Marina.

page	hotel	golf	tennis	croquet	pitch & putt	boating	fishing	riding	billiards/snooker	swim/pool	sea/river bathing	sailing	squash	badminton	shooting	leis. centre	solarium	sauna	other
	CUMBRIA (continued)																		
151	Fayrer Garden House Hotel, Windermere	b				b	c	b		b		b	b		c	b			Hot air ballooning by arrangement.
152	Linthwaite House Hotel, Windermere	b					A	b				b	b					b	Golf practice hole par 3.
153	The Mortal Man Hotel, Windermere	b	A			b	A	b		b	b	b	b	b	b	b	b	b	
154	Old Vicarage Country House Hotel, Witherslack						b	b					b						
	LANCASHIRE																		
155	The Georgian House Hotel, Bolton	A							A	A						A	A	A	
156	Mytton Fold Farm Hotel, Langho	b					A	b											
157	Chadwick Hotel, Lytham St. Annes	b	b			b	A	b		A		b	b			A	A	A	Games room, spa pool.
	GREATER MANCHESTER																		
158	The Victoria and Albert Hotel, Manchester	b						b	A	b						A	A	A	Gymnasium.
	COUNTY DURHAM																		
167	Ramside Hall Hotel, Durham	b																	
168	Royal County Hotel, Durham					b				A	b	b				A	A	A	Spa pool, gymnasium, steam room.
	HUMBERSIDE																		
169	The Waterfront Hotel, Hull	b	A				c								c				
	NORTHUMBERLAND																		
170	Waren House Hotel, Bamburgh	b	A	A		b		A			b	b							Local bird watching.
	YORKSHIRE																		
171	Appleton Hall Hotel, Appleton-le-Moors	b					c												
172	Rose and Crown Hotel, Bainbridge						A	b											
174	Devonshire Arms Country House Hotel, Bolton Abbey	b	c				A	c					c	c	A	A			

Table of hotel facilities (rows = hotels, columns = facilities).

page	hotel	golf	tennis	croquet	pitch & putt	boating	fishing	riding	billiards/snooker	swim/pool	sea/river bathing	sailing	squash	badminton	shooting	leis. centre	solarium	sauna	other
	YORKSHIRE (continued)																		
175	The Balmoral Hotel, Harrogate	b	c		b	b	b	b		b			b		b	b	A		
176	Grants Hotel, Harrogate	b	b			b	b	b		b					b	b	b	b	Affiliated to nearby Leisure Centre.
177	The White House Hotel, Harrogate	b																	
178	Stone House Hotel, Nr. Hawes	b	A			b	b	b							b				
179	Feversham Arms Hotel, Helmsley	b	A					b		A		b							Games room.
180	The Pheasant, Helmsley	b	b	A				b	A	A									
181	Ryedale Lodge, Nr. Helmsley	b					b								c				
182	George and Dragon Hotel, Kirkbymoorside	b	b				A	b							b				
183	Lastingham Grange Hotel, Lastingham	b				b		b				b							
185	East Ayton Lodge Country Hotel, Nr. Scarborough	b					b								b				
186	The Judges Lodging Hotel, York	b						c											
187	Aldwark Manor Golf Hotel, Nr. York	A			A		A								c				
	WALES																		
	CLWYD																		
193	Tyddyn Llan Country House Hotel and Restaurant, Llandrillo	c				b	A	c				b			c				
	GWYNEDD																		
194	Trefeddian Hotel, Aberdyfi, (Aberdovey)	A	A	b		b	b	b	A	A	b	b	b	b	c	b	b	b	Wind surfing, games room, pony trekking, local bird watching.
195	Bron Eifion Country House Hotel, Criccieth	b	b				b	b			b								
196	Bontddu Hall, Nr. Dolgellau	b						b			b								
197	The Empire Hotel, Llandudno					b				A	A		b			b	A	A	Spa pool.
	DYFED																		
198	Warpool Court, St. David's	b	A							A	A	b				A		A	

266

267

268

	golf	tennis	croquet	pitch & putt	boating	fishing	riding	billiards/snooker	swim/pool	sea/river bathing	sailing	squash	badminton	shooting	leis. centre	solarium	sauna	other	page
SCOTTISH ISLANDS																			
Killiechronan House, Isle of Mull	b				A	A	A			A	A			A				Stalking by arrangement.	243
Glenforsa Hotel, Isle of Mull	b	b			b	A	A	A		A	b			A					244
Rosedale Hotel, Isle of Skye	b				A	c	b			A				c					245
Uig Hotel, Isle of Skye					b	b	b			b									246
CHANNEL ISLANDS																			
GUERNSEY																			
Hotel Bella Luce, St. Martins									A										250
JERSEY																			
Atlantic Hotel, St. Brelade	b	A							A	b						A	A		252
Longueville Manor, St. Saviour	b	A							A	b		b			A	A	A		253

HOTELS WITH OWN TENNIS COURTS

HOTELS WITH OWN TENNIS COURTS (Contd.)

HOTELS WITH INDOOR SWIMMING POOLS AND LEISURE CENTRES

HOTELS WITH INDOOR SWIMMING POOLS AND LEISURE CENTRES (Contd.)

HOTELS WITH THEIR OWN 9 OR 18 HOLE GOLF COURSES

Leading Golf Courses

Blairgowrie

Gleneagles
Hotel

St. Andrews

Muirfield

Gullane

Pannal

Royal Lytham St. Annes

Moor Allerton

Shaw Hill

Royal Liverpool

Hollinwell

Royal St. Davids

Aberdovey

The Belfry

Little Aston

Woburn

Moor
Park

Frilford Heath

Sandy Lodge

CHANNEL
ISLANDS

St. Pierre Golf &
Country Club

Huntercombe

Wentworth

The Berkshire

Sunningdale

Royal
St. George's

Burnham &
Berrow

Walton Heath

Saunton

Liphook

La Moye

Sherborne

Bodmin Golf &
Country Club

St. Mellion

© GEOprojects (UK) Ltd.
© Crown Copyright

LEADING GOLF COURSES

Listed below are some leading golf courses which have a *Signpost* hotel within an approximate 20 mile radius.

LEADING GOLF COURSES

GOLF COURSE	HOTEL	PAGE NO.

Moor Allerton   Oakwood Hall Hotel   173
The Balmoral Hotel & Henry's Restaurant   175
Grants Hotel   176
The White House Hotel   177
Monk Fryston Hall   184

Moor Park   Stocks Hotel & Country Club   69
St. Michael's Manor   71

Muirfield   Cringletie House Hotel (40 miles)   205

Pannal   Oakwood Hall Hotel   173
Devonshire Arms Country House Hotel   174
The Balmoral Hotel & Henry's Restaurant   175
Grants Hotel   176
The White House Hotel   177
The Judges Lodging Hotel   186
Aldwark Manor Golf Hotel   187

Royal Liverpool   Rowton Hall Hotel   123

Royal Lytham St. Annes   Chadwick Hotel   157

Royal St. Davids   Bron Eifion Country House Hotel   195
Bontddu Hall Hotel   196

Royal St. Georges   The Castlemere Hotel   72

St. Andrews   Green Park Hotel (30 miles)   225

St. Mellion   Buckland-tout-Saints Hotel (23 miles)   22

St. Pierre   Tudor Farmhouse Hotel   104

Sandy Lodge   Stocks Hotel & Country Club   69

Saunton   Downrew House   16
The Saunton Sands Hotel   28
Watersmeet Hotel   35
Woolacombe Bay Hotel   36

Shaw Hill   Georgian House Hotel   155

Sherborne   The Manor Hotel   38

Sunningdale   Chase Lodge   75

Walton Heath   Chase Lodge   75

Wentworth   Chase Lodge   75

Woburn   Redcoats Farmhouse Hotel   70

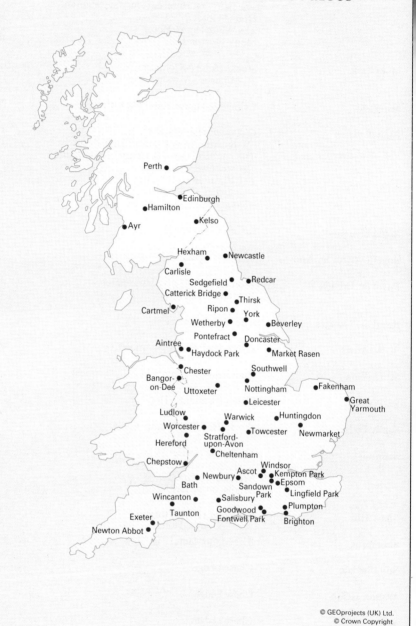

Racecourses

Perth
Edinburgh
Hamilton
Ayr
Kelso
Hexham
Newcastle
Carlisle
Sedgefield
Redcar
Catterick Bridge
Thirsk
Ripon
York
Cartmel
Wetherby
Beverley
Pontefract
Doncaster
Aintree
Market Rasen
Haydock Park
Chester
Southwell
Bangor-on-Dee
Fakenham
Uttoxeter
Nottingham
Leicester
Great Yarmouth
Ludlow
Warwick
Huntingdon
Worcester
Stratford-upon-Avon
Towcester
Newmarket
Hereford
Chepstow
Cheltenham
Windsor
Ascot
Kempton Park
Newbury
Epsom
Bath
Sandown Park
Lingfield Park
Wincanton
Salisbury
Plumpton
Exeter
Taunton
Goodwood
Fontwell Park
Brighton
Newton Abbot

© GEOprojects (UK) Ltd.
© Crown Copyright

RACECOURSES

Unless otherwise stated, the hotels listed below are within 20 miles of these racecourses.

RACECOURSE	PAGE NO.	HOTEL	MILES
AINTREE	123 ..	Rowton Hall Hotel	27
ASCOT	62 ..	The Howard Hotel	30
.. .. ..	63 ..	The Swan Diplomat	35
AYR	206 ..	Comlongon Castle Country House Hotel ..	65
.. .. ..	207 ..	Moffat House Hotel	60
.. .. ..	208 ..	Kirroughtree Hotel	48
.. .. ..	211 ..	Trigony House Hotel	46
BANGOR-ON-DEE ..	112 ..	Hawkstone Park Hotel	
..	123 ..	Rowton Hall Hotel	
BATH	51 ..	Whatley Manor	
.. .. ..	107 ..	Hare & Hounds	
BEVERLEY	169 ..	The Waterfront Hotel	
BRIGHTON	79 ..	Chequers Hotel	23
CARLISLE	136 ..	Tarn End House Hotel	
CARTMEL	135 ..	Hare & Hounds Country Inn	
.. ..	138 ..	Graythwaite Manor	
.. ..	139 ..	Netherwood Hotel	
.. ..	140 ..	Aynsome Manor Hotel	
.. ..	154 ..	Old Vicarage Country House Hotel	
CATTERICK BRIDGE	172 ..	Rose & Crown Hotel	30
	178 ..	Stone House Hotel	32
CHELTENHAM ..	101 ..	Bibury Court	
..	102 ..	On the Park Hotel & Restaurant	
..	103 ..	The Wild Duck Inn	22
..	108 ..	Dormy House Hotel	
CHEPSTOW	104 ..	Tudor Farmhouse Hotel	
CHESTER	123 ..	Rowton Hall Hotel	
DONCASTER	184 ..	Monk Fryston Hall	24
EDINBURGH	205 ..	Cringletie House Hotel	23
EPSOM	75 ..	Chase Lodge	
EXETER	29 ..	The Royal Glen Hotel	
.. ..	30 ..	The Victoria Hotel	
.. ..	20 ..	Combe House	
FAKENHAM	90 ..	The Blakeney Hotel	
FOLKESTONE ..	72 ..	The Castlemere Hotel	26
..	76 ..	Flackley Ash Hotel	27
FONTWELL PARK ..	79 ..	Chequers Hotel	
GOODWOOD ..	79 ..	Chequers Hotel	
HAMILTON	205 ..	Cringletie House Hotel	47
.. ..	221 ..	The Busby Hotel	

RACECOURSE	PAGE NO.	HOTEL	MILES
HAYDOCK PARK	123	Rowton Hall Hotel	35
	155	Georgian House Hotel	
HEREFORD	104	Tudor Farmhouse Hotel	26
	111	The Feathers at Ludlow	26
	199	Gliffaes Country House Hotel	28
HEXHAM	125	Lowbyer Manor Country House Hotel	
	136	Tarn End House Hotel	28
HUNTINGDON	70	Redcoats Farmhouse Hotel	29
KELSO	204	Sunlaws House Hotel	
KEMPTON PARK	75	Chase Lodge	
LEICESTER	92	Langar Hall	26
LINGFIELD PARK	75	Chase Lodge	25
LUDLOW	110	The Redfern Hotel	
	111	The Feathers at Ludlow	
MARKET RASEN	169	The Waterfront Hotel	34
NEWBURY	63	The Swan Diplomat	
NEWCASTLE	167	Ramside Hall Hotel	
	168	Royal County Hotel	
NEWMARKET	94	The Smoke House	
NEWTON ABBOT	31	Gabriel Court Hotel	
	32	Homers Hotel	
	33	Imperial Hotel	
	34	Livermead House Hotel	
NOTTINGHAM	88	Makeney Hall Country House Hotel	
	92	Langar Hall	
PERTH	219	Cromlix House	27
	225	Green Park Hotel	30
PLUMPTON	77	The Brickwall Hotel	30
	79	Chequers Hotel	23
PONTEFRACT	184	Monk Fryston Hall	
REDCAR	183	Lastingham Grange	24
RIPON	175	The Balmoral Hotel & Henry's Restaurant	
	176	Grants Hotel	
	177	The White House Hotel	
SALISBURY	37	Queen's Hotel	28
	41	The Haven Hotel	30
	67	The Chewton Glen Hotel	27
SANDOWN PARK	75	Chase Lodge	
SEDGEFIELD	167	Ramside Hall Hotel	
	168	Royal County Hotel	
SOUTHWELL	92	Langar Hall	
	93	Old England Hotel	
STRATFORD-UPON-AVON	108	Dormy House Hotel	
	113	Nailcote Hall	
	114	Nuthurst Grange	
	115	Welcombe Hotel & Golf Course	
	116	Billesley Manor	

RACECOURSES

HOTELS WITH CONFERENCE FACILITIES

These figures are approximate, and are based upon a theatre-style conference for non-residents, unless otherwise stated.

Conference Organisers are advised to telephone these hotels for the maximum number of residential delegates taken and any further information required.

Page	Hotel	Non-Res.	No. of bedrooms

ENGLAND

CORNWALL

Page	Hotel	Non-Res.	No. of bedrooms
2	Royal Duchy Hotel	40	50
4	Polurrian Hotel	100	39
7	Rose-in-Vale Country House Hotel	20	17
8	Carlyon Bay Hotel	125	72
9	Tregenna Castle	250	83
12	The Idle Rocks Hotel	20	17

DEVON

Page	Hotel	Non-Res.	No. of bedrooms
14	Blagdon Manor Country Hotel	14	7
15	Tytherleigh Cot Hotel	25	19
16	Downrew House	24	12
17	The Berry Head Hotel	100	12
18	The Hoops Inn	60	12
19	The Maypool Park Hotel	30	10
20	Combe House	30	15
21	The Cottage Hotel	50	25
22	Buckland-tout-Saints Hotel	16	12
24	The White Hart Hotel	90	20
27	Heron House Hotel	40	18
28	The Saunton Sands Hotel	200	92
30	The Victoria Hotel	100	61
32	Homers Hotel	50	14
33	Imperial Hotel	350	167
34	Livermead House Hotel	300	64
36	Woolacombe Bay Hotel	200	59

DORSET

Page	Hotel	Non-Res.	No. of bedrooms
37	Queen's Hotel	180	114
38	The Manor Hotel	60	13
39	Salterns Hotel	120	20
40	Kersbrook Hotel	20	14
41	The Haven Hotel	200	96

SOMERSET

Page	Hotel	Non-Res.	No. of bedrooms
46	The Walnut Tree Inn	70	28
49	Swan Hotel	100	38

WILTSHIRE

Page	Hotel	Non-Res.	No. of bedrooms
50	Crudwell Court Hotel & Restaurant	25	15
51	Whatley Manor	30	29
52	Blunsdon House Hotel	300	88

LONDON

Page	Hotel	Non-Res.	No. of bedrooms
62	The Howard Hotel	200	135

BERKSHIRE

Page	Hotel	Non-Res.	No. of bedrooms
63	The Swan Diplomat	90	46

HAMPSHIRE

Page	Hotel	Non-Res.	No. of bedrooms
64	The Gordleton Mill Hotel	30	7
68	Hotel du Vin & Bistro	30	13

HOTELS WITH CONFERENCE FACILITIES (Contd.)

Page	Hotel	Non-Res.	No. of bedrooms

HERTFORDSHIRE

Page	Hotel	Non-Res.	No. of bedrooms
69	Stocks Hotel & Country Club..	65	18
70	Redcoats Farmhouse Hotel	20	12
71	St. Michael's Manor	36	22

KENT

| 72 | The Castlemere Hotel.. | 30 | 41 |

OXFORDSHIRE

| 73 | The Spread Eagle Hotel.. | 250 | 33 |
| 74 | The Feathers Hotel | 25 | 17 |

SURREY

| 75 | Chase Lodge | 50 | 9 |

SUSSEX

76	Flackley Ash Hotel	80	32
78	Dale Hill Hotel & Golf Club..	50	32
79	Chequers Hotel..	20	11

DERBYSHIRE

86	Hassop Hall Hotel	70	13
87	Riber Hall..	12	11
88	Makeney Hall Country House Hotel	180	45

LINCOLNSHIRE

| 89 | Washingborough Hall Country House Hotel | 50 | 12 |

NORFOLK

| 90 | The Blakeney Hotel | 100 | 60 |
| 91 | South Walsham Hall | 40 | 17 |

NOTTINGHAMSHIRE

| 92 | Langar Hall | 20 | 10 |
| 93 | The Old England.. | 45 | 10 |

SUFFOLK

| 94 | The Smoke House | 150 | 105 |
| 95 | Ufford Park Hotel, Golf & Leisure.. | 150 | 37 |

GLOUCESTERSHIRE

101	Bibury Court	12	20
105	Manor House Hotel	70	39
107	Hare and Hounds..	150	30

WORCESTERSHIRE

| 108 | Dormy House Hotel | 74 | 49 |

SHROPSHIRE

109	The Old Vicarage Hotel	30	14
110	The Redfern Hotel	30	11
111	The Feathers at Ludlow	60	40
112	Hawkstone Park Hotel..	200	59

WARWICKSHIRE

113	Nailcote Hall	100	40
114	Nuthurst Grange..	80	15
115	Welcombe Hotel & Golf Course	100	76
116	Billesley Manor..	100	41

CHESHIRE

| 123 | Rowton Hall Hotel | 200 | 42 |
| 124 | Sutton Hall | 20 | 10 |

Page	Hotel	Non-Res.	No. of bedrooms

CUMBRIA

Page	Hotel	Non-Res.	No. of bedrooms
125	Lowbyer Manor Country House Hotel ..	20	12
126	Lovelady Shield Country House Hotel ..	12	12
129	Rothay Manor Hotel	20	18
131	Appleby Manor Country House Hotel ..	30	30
136	Tarn End House Hotel	30	7
138	Graythwaite Manor Hotel	30	22
139	Netherwood Hotel..	180	29
141	The Wordsworth Hotel	100	35
142	Dale Head Hall Lakeside Hotel ..	20	9
144	Stakis Keswick Lodore Swiss Hotel..	80	70
145	Underscar Manor	16	11
149	The Swan Hotel	20	36
150	Sharrow Bay Country House Hotel..	15 (residential)	28
151	Fayrer Garden House Hotel	24	14
152	Linthwaite House Hotel	20	18

LANCASHIRE

Page	Hotel	Non-Res.	No. of bedrooms
155	Georgian House Hotel	300	101
156	Mytton Fold Farm Hotel	300	27
157	Chadwick Hotel	50	72

GREATER MANCHESTER

Page	Hotel	Non-Res.	No. of bedrooms
158	The Victoria and Albert Hotel.. ..	350	132

COUNTY DURHAM

Page	Hotel	Non-Res.	No. of bedrooms
167	Ramside Hall Hotel	400	82
168	Royal County Hotel	140	150

HUMBERSIDE

Page	Hotel	Non-Res.	No. of bedrooms
169	The Waterfront Hotel	100	30

YORKSHIRE

Page	Hotel	Non-Res.	No. of bedrooms
172	Rose and Crown Hotel..	100	12
173	Oakwood Hall Hotel	50	20
174	Devonshire Arms Country House Hotel ..	150	40
175	The Balmoral Hotel & Henry's Restaurant	30	20
176	Grants Hotel	70	42
177	The White House Hotel	50	10
178	Stone House Hotel	36	18
179	Feversham Arms Hotel..	30	18
180	The Pheasant	12	14
181	Ryedale Lodge	20	7
182	George and Dragon Hotel	25	19
184	Monk Fryston Hall	50	28
185	East Ayton Lodge Country Hotel ..	100	17
186	The Judges Lodging Hotel	20	12
187	Aldwark Manor Golf Hotel	80	17

WALES

Page	Hotel	Non-Res.	No. of bedrooms
193	Tyddyn Llan Country House Hotel..	50	10
195	Bron Eifion Country House Hotel ..	30	19
197	The Empire Hotel..	40	51
199	Gliffaes Country House Hotel.. ..	25	22

HOTELS WITH CONFERENCE FACILITIES (Contd.)

Page   Hotel   Non-Res.   No. of bedrooms

SCOTLAND

SOUTHERN

Page	Hotel	Non-Res.	No. of bedrooms
204	Sunlaws House Hotel	20	22
207	Moffat House Hotel	20	20
208	Kirroughtree Hotel	30	17

CENTRAL

Page	Hotel	Non-Res.	No. of bedrooms
216	Culcreuch Castle	75	8
218	Ardeonaig Hotel	16	16
219	Cromlix House	40	14
221	The Busby Hotel	200	32
223	The Creggans Inn	85	19
224	Stonefield Castle Hotel	100	33
227	Dalmunzie House Hotel	20	18

HIGHLANDS

Page	Hotel	Non-Res.	No. of bedrooms
232	The Marcliffe at Pitfodels	400	42
233	Darroch Learg Hotel	20	20
234	Mansefield House Hotel	25	17
239	The Holly Tree Hotel	30	11
240	The Lochalsh Hotel	40	40

SCOTTISH ISLANDS

Page	Hotel	Non-Res.	No. of bedrooms
244	Glenforsa Hotel	34	13

CHANNEL ISLANDS

GUERNSEY

Page	Hotel	Non-Res.	No. of bedrooms
250	Hotel Bella Luce	20	31

JERSEY

Page	Hotel	Non-Res.	No. of bedrooms
252	The Atlantic Hotel	40	50

ENGLISH INDEX

THE WEST COUNTRY

Situation   *Hotel*   *Page*

LONDON AND THE SOUTH

SCOTTISH INDEX

ALPHABETICAL INDEX

Hotels in Britain and the Channel Islands, which are fully described in *Signpost* are entered below alphabetically according to location.

ALPHABETICAL INDEX

ALPHABETICAL INDEX

ALPHABETICAL INDEX

ALPHABETICAL INDEX

NOTES

<u>MAPS</u>

The following section contains road maps of Great Britain.

The names of principal towns are depicted in green.

THE LOCATIONS OF 'SIGNPOST' HOTELS ARE MARKED IN BLACK.

Only major roads are shown and we therefore recommend that you use a comprehensive road atlas when travelling ''off the beaten track''.

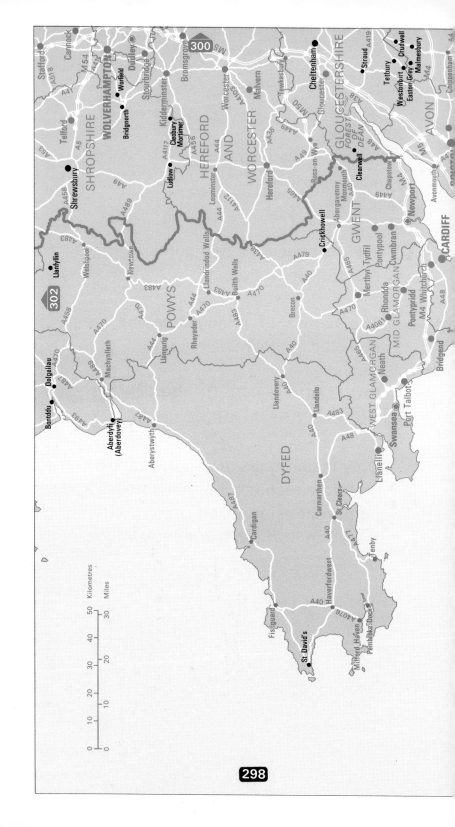

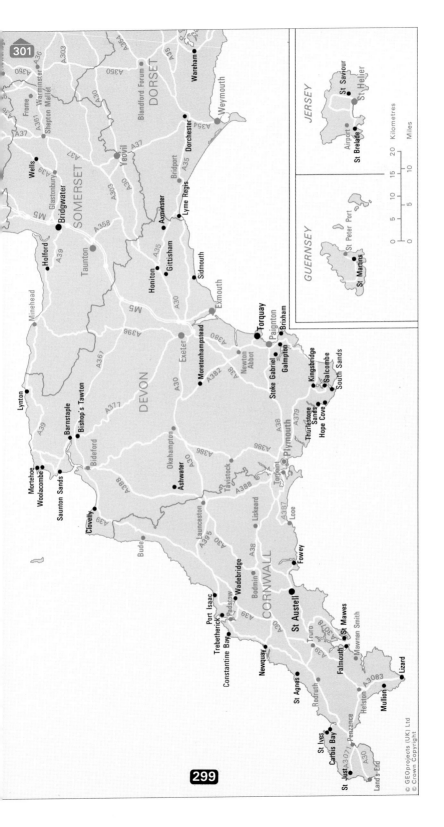

© GEOprojects (UK) Ltd
© Crown Copyright

JERSEY

St Saviour
St Helier
Airport
St Brelade

Kilometres
Miles
20
15
10
5
0

GUERNSEY

St Peter Port
St Martins

DORSET

Wareham
Weymouth
Blandford Forum
A350
A35
A303
A31
A37
A361
A350
Warminster
Shepton Mallet
Frome
Wells
Glastonbury
Bridgwater
A39
SOMERSET
Yeovil
A37
A30
A303
A358
Taunton
Holford
A39
Dorchester
A35
Bridport
Axminster
A35
Lyme Regis
Gittisham
Honiton
A30
Sidmouth
Exmouth
Minehead
A396
M5
A367
DEVON
Exeter
A380
Torquay
Paignton
Brixham
Moretonhampstead
A382
A38
Newton Abbot
Stoke Gabriel
Galmpton
Kingsbridge
Salcombe
South Sands
Lynton
A39
Barnstaple
Bishop's Tawton
A377
A30
Okehampton
A386
Ashwater
Tavistock
Plymouth
A386
A379
Thurlestone
Sands
Hope Cove
Mortehoe
Woolacombe
Saunton Sands
Clovelly
A39
Bideford
A388
Bude
Launceston
A395
A30
Liskeard
A38
A388
Torpoint
Loe
A387
Fowey
Wadebridge
Bodmin
CORNWALL
A30
Port Isaac
Trebetherick
Padstow
A39
St Austell
Newquay
St Agnes
Redruth
Truro
A39
Falmouth
St Mawes
Mawnan Smith
A3083
Lizard
Helston
Mullion
St Ives
Carbis Bay
A3071
Penzance
St Just
Land's End
A30
Constantine Bay

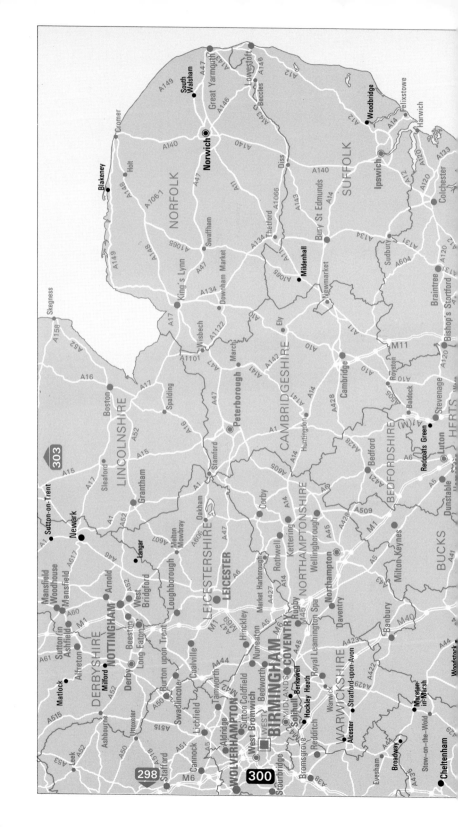

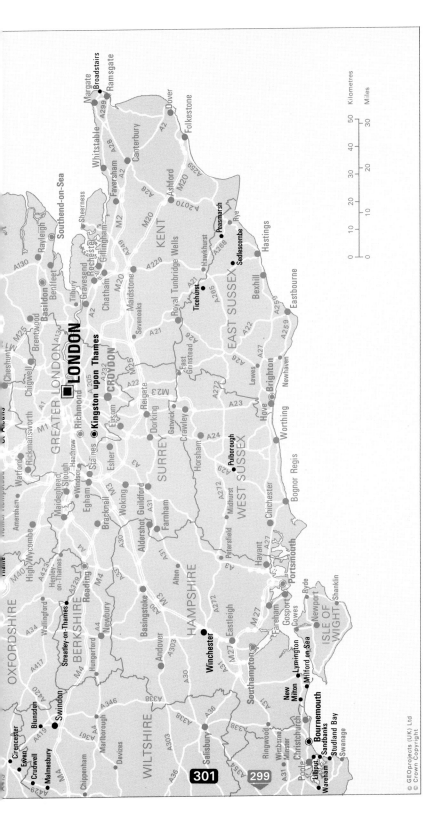

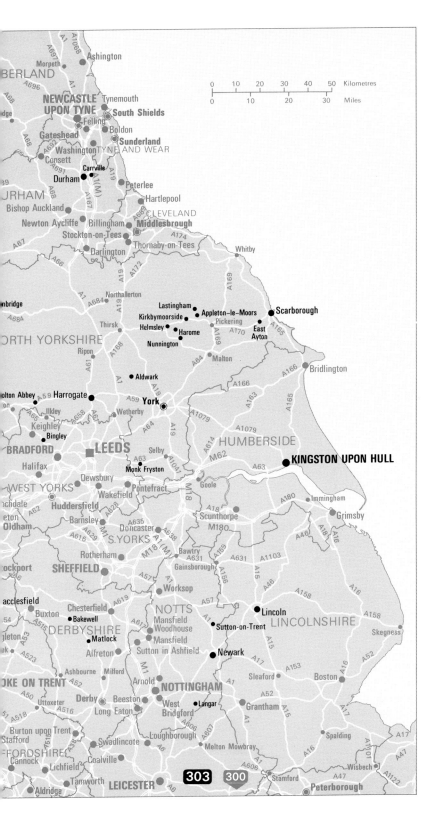

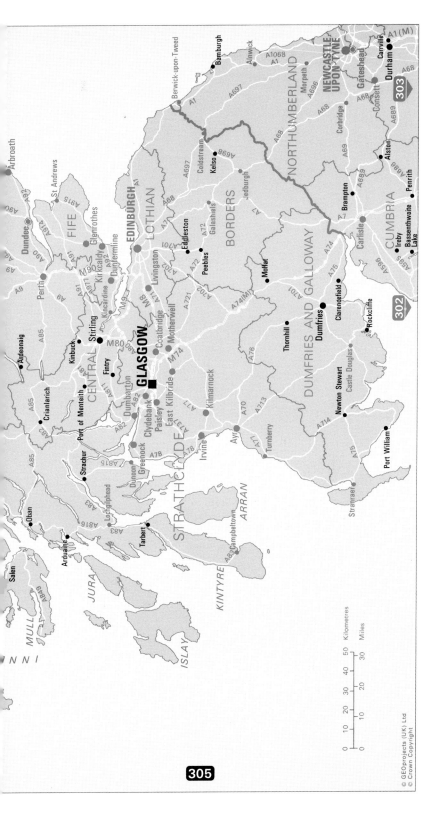

303

302

307

A WORD OF WARNING

The hotel tariffs we have quoted are likely to be increased and are, therefore, only included as a guide to indicate the level of hotels' charges.

TRADE DESCRIPTIONS ACT 1968

The facilities in italics are submitted each year to us by hotels but the comments on each hotel are the personal opinion of a member of the Signpost Team as he or she found it. Because of so many things, i.e. changes in management, chefs and so forth, we cannot guarantee that you will find any particular hotel as we did and naturally your particular tastes may differ from our own. We therefore cannot be responsible for such matters but we try to include in the book a wide range of hotels and we sincerely hope that you will not suffer disappointment when staying at any of them.

Fountain Court,
Steelhouse Lane,
Birmingham B4 6DT
0121-236 5979

© 1995 Signpost Ltd.